TRAITOR?

TRAITOR?

A JEW, A BOOK, A MIRACLE

AN AUTOBIOGRAPHY

DR. JACOB GARTENHAUS

International Board of Jewish Missions, Inc.
Post Office Box 3307
Chattanooga, Tennessee 37404

Library of Congress Cataloging in Publication Data

Gartenhaus, Jacob, 1896-
　Traitor? a Jew, a book, a miracle.

　1.　Gartenhaus, Jacob, 1896-　2.　Converts From Judaism—Biography.　3.　Missions to Jews.　I.　Title.
BV2623.G37A37　　　　269'.2'0924　[B]　　80-20036
ISBN 0-8407-5740-9
　　　　0-8407-5230-X　I.B.J.M. Casebound
　　　　0-8407-5753-0　I.B.J.M. Paperback

C O N T E N T S

INTRODUCTION

In the early part of this century Jacob Gartenhaus, with the strength and exuberance of youth, came to America seeking fame and fortune. In addition to an abundant native wit, he was well trained in the teachings of the ancient Jewish scholars, because his parents had planned on his becoming a rabbi, as his forefathers had been.

In his native Austria he had heard tales of instant riches in America, where money grows on trees. Jacob's "money tree" turned out to be a bottom rung position in one of the infamous sweat shops in New York's East Side. He rapidly climbed to the top, however, gaining money and friends along the way. His quest for fame and fortune accomplished, the worldly pleasures of New York were at his beck and call. But the Lord had a different, a higher road for Jacob to travel.

"The Lord works in mysterious ways, His wonders to perform." Nowhere is this more apparent than in the conversion story of this now world-famous missionary. The reader will find a treasure house within the pages of the early chapters, but the story does not end there. Persecution by family, colleagues, and friends immediately met the new Christian; and while this intolerance continued, pressures mounted from all quarters.

Gartenhaus began missionary work within a few minutes

after accepting the Lord Jesus as the Messiah of Israel. His enthusiasm cost him a severe beating, the first of many as he began his walk down the road his Lord had chosen for him. For more than sixty years Dr. Gartenhaus has been walking that path, going to "the Jew first, and also to the Greek." His service has been on two major fronts: winning the lost to the Saviour and fighting anti-Semitism wherever it is found. Legendary are his accomplishments in both areas. He has progressed from street witnessing to founding and presiding over a globe-spanning mission board. His correspondence against anti-Semitic groups and ideas is voluminous.

It has been my joy to know the man, Dr. Jacob Gartenhaus, and his ministry for more than thirty years. I knew him during the time of his rugged and exciting ministry with the Southern Baptist Convention, and I have known him in the years since he organized an independent mission to the Jewish people. I congratulate him on his success. I commend this man of God to you.

> Dr. Lee Roberson, Pastor,
> Highland Park Baptist Church
> and Chancellor, Tennessee
> Temple University,
> Chattanooga, Tennessee

F O R E W O R D

For the writing of an autobiography by a Christian Jew, we have both an historical and a scriptural precedent. In Philippians 3:4-6, Saul of Tarsus, who became, by the grace of God, Paul the apostle, ascribed unto himself the ultimate identification. Reviewing his excellent ancestral lineage, he declared boldly that he was ". . . an Hebrew of the Hebrews."And so is Jacob Gartenhaus! His very presence radiates that distinction among men which has been best expressed by the Lord God: ". . . Jacob have I loved"! Few men in Jewish history have made the impact upon both Jews and Gentiles that has been made by this outstanding Hebrew-Christian statesman. Far from being a "Meshummad," Jacob Gartenhaus has brought honor and dignity to a life and ministry that has touched millions of Gentile Christians and made them appreciate the "Jewishness" of their biblical faith.

Alluding once more to the pattern and precedent of the apostle Paul, I observe the same burning compassion, spiritual commitment, and religious zeal in the life of Jacob Gartenhaus that I see in Romans 10:1. Paul said, "Brethren, my heart's desire and prayer to God for Israel is, that they might be saved." For over sixty years, Jacob Gartenhaus has given himself unstintingly to the task of winning Jews to Christ! Few men in the ministry have been better prepared or more dedicated to the cause of Christ than has been this faithful servant. Some of us remember when he was "The whole department" of Jewish missions for the Southern Baptist Convention. The futility and frustration of laboring for almost thirty years on a very limited basis was finally relieved when the Lord led him to establish the International Board of Jewish Missions, Inc. As his faith and vision began to be blessed by the Lord, reports of Jews turning to Christ came in in unprecedented numbers.

Already, some seventy-six missionaries or "Ambassadors for Christ to the Jews" are serving worldwide under the auspices of this organization. An additional dimension to the missionary outreach of the International Board of Jewish Missions, Inc., is the extensive publication ministry of books and pamphlets authored by Dr. Gartenhaus. A magnificent and very functional headquarters building has been constructed in Chattanooga, Tennessee, adjacent to the campus of Tennessee Temple University. As part of the vision that God has given to this elder-statesman, Dr. Gartenhaus was responsible for the establishment of a "Messianic Center" in Chattanooga to which visitors come each year from all over the nation. Probably no Jew in America has done more to dispel anti-Semitism and to make friends for the Jew and for Israel than he has. Honors and recognition for his life and ministry have been innumerable.

Someone has said that ". . . behind every great man, standing in the shadows, there is a great woman." This is certainly true in the case of Dr. Gartenhaus. Over fifty-seven years ago, he met and married a Hebrew-Christian girl named Lillian Brown. To that union was born three daughters and a son. Like a tower of strength, Lillian has stood by her husband loyally in every aspect of his ministry. No biography of Dr. Gartenhaus would be complete without recognition of her contribution to this extensive ministry.

FOREWORD

Readers of this autobiography and the author's other publications will learn much about the Bible which they probably did not know before. Since the New Testament priority of ". . . to the Jew first" is generally ignored by most churches, the Jewish character of the early church is often a surprise to many Christians. The grand beginning of "The end of Days" is now transpiring in the state of Israel. The focus of the world is upon Israel and the Middle East. What happens in Jerusalem affects the entire civilized world! No one can view this struggle objectively without realizing that Jews everywhere are approaching the subject of Jesus as the Messiah with a new and more credible discernment. It is thrilling to see the discarding of almost 2,000 years of false teaching, preconceived notions, and religious bigotry. I like to think that Jacob Gartenhaus has been used by the Holy Spirit to help bring about that transition.

My own life and ministry have been greatly blessed and influenced by this spiritual giant for which I am profoundly grateful. He taught me the value of principle whenever he refused to compromise the Word of God. He challenged me to walk by faith whenever he launched a worldwide missionary outreach and produced "the substance of things hoped for, the evidence of things not seen." He gave me an example of ministry by his willingness to live sacrificially and by his determination to "finish his course." I am always stimulated intellectually by his writings and thrilled over his ability to express himself in a language that was not his by birth. Jacob Gartenhaus has been like a father to me; consequently, I love to walk by his side and hold his presence in highest esteem and admiration!

As Chairman of the Advisory Board, I can vouch for the fact that none of the love, warmth, or compassion so manifest when Jacob preaches is lost in the day by day operation of the Mission. I never cease to marvel at his strength,

FOREWORD

tenacity, and determination to carry on in this task of reaching the Jew for Jesus Christ. The capsule testimony of Dr. Jacob Gartenhaus is concise and to the point. He says, "I am an Austrian by birth, a Jew by accident, an American by choice, a Christian by the grace of God, and a Baptist by conviction!" Don't miss the blessing of reading the whole story. This man of God has been endowed with all of those gifts that push men to the pinnacle of success, and his gift for writing is definitely one of them.

Dr. Bob Gray, Pastor,
Trinity Baptist Church and
President, Trinity Baptist College,
Jacksonville, Florida

F O R E W O R D

William Hazlitt, poet and well-known essay writer, was ill and near death. He wrote to his publisher: "I have been nearly in the other world. My regret was to die and leave the world rough copy."

My constant fear has been that Dr. Gartenhaus would depart this world without leaving behind a full-length autobiography of a magnificent life. Where would one start to sum up the experience of a man whose entire Christian life has been devoted to his Master and to his people, Israel?

This conviction that Jesus was the Jewish Messiah was the dawn of a new era in his life, but one lit with a knowledge his community would not at first accept. To his father, a rabbi in Jerusalem, he was a disappointment; to his Jewish friends he was a nobody; to his acquaintances he seemed an idiot. Moses, while in Egypt, was once rejected by the elders of Israel, but he returned to deliver them from "the house of bondage." So with Dr. Gartenhaus: Once considered a "meshummad" (a traitor), he has since received many accolades from his own people as one of their foremost champions.

My own personal feeling for the man stems from the great influence that he has had on my life. While I was a federal prisoner, I received a letter of encouragement from him, my first exposure to a Jew who believed that

Jesus was the Jewish Messiah. After my own conversion and release from prison, he visited me. Our conversation in a hotel room lasted some three hours; the light of his genius shone into my soul like the sun's rays glittering in the puddles of the road. The passion of his soul for his Messiah and Israel set my own soul on fire.

At that time he was the first and only representative to the Jews of the Home Mission Board of the Southern Baptist Convention. Working tirelessly to arouse Southern Baptists to love and witness to Israel, he seldom took a day off to rest for over twenty-five years. His mighty influence reached beyond the confines of the Convention, far beyond and across the oceans. For some years he had begun to realize that he was called beyond the confines of American shores. Jesus had said, "The field is the world." Calls kept coming from Macedonia, "Come over and help us too." Dr. Gartenhaus found himself in the middle of a stream, where he must sink under the load or launch out into the deep.

We are told by the author of Hebrews that "by faith Abraham . . . went out, not knowing whither he went." By the same strong faith in the same God, Dr. Gartenhaus resigned as the head of the Jewish department of the Home Mission Board. However, he *knew* where he was going and what must be done as quickly as possible.

First, he gathered around him Christian men and women who shared his worldwide vision of reaching Israel. This resulted in an organization that raised funds through churches and individuals. As mighty oaks come from small acorns, so what started as a ripple became a mighty wave, an organization which is world-encircling indeed.

Second, he continued to be a goodwill ambassador, interpreting Israel to Christians to show the branches wherein their roots lay, and interpreting the Messiah Jesus to Israel to show the roots wherein their fulfillment lay. He did this, not only through personal contacts and messages from pulpits, but through his numerous books.

Whether pamphlet, booklet, or major work, he wrote everything as if the nerve of sensibility in him was tender to the point of pain, that he might awaken many people of his generation to deep feelings, feelings with which they previously had been unacquainted. In his books, he offered his readers his experience, though he never wrote anything that was trite. Behind every word was superb scholarship; yet, his language was plain, proper, clear, and thorough. He wrote as God Himself told us to speak and write, both as to matter and manner: "If any man speak, let him speak as the oracles of God." John Wesley would have appreciated the writings of Dr. Gartenhaus, for he once said, "I dare not write in a fine style than wear a fine coat." Let others write in a pedantic style, piling up adjectives and oratorical alliterations. Not so with Dr. Gartenhaus. Scholar that he is, his passion to get his message across keeps him from wearing "a fine coat."

Third, he stood firm against anti-Semites and anti-Semitism. Whenever and wherever this ugly reptile of prejudice raised its head, whether in speech or book or magazine article, he lifted his literary sword and did battle. Fully understanding that those who were at war with Jews on the personal or national level were not at peace with themselves, his written responses to anti-Semitism have appeared in national secular magazines, as well as in Jewish magazines.

Hegel, the German philosopher, wrote: "We ask men to study history, but the only thing that men learn from the study of history is that men learn nothing from the study of history." If anyone can read this autobiography of Dr. Gartenhaus without learning what God can do with a man completely given over to "this one thing I do," such a person is totally unteachable.

FOREWORD

Before the reader begins this book, I must of necessity add that by his side, through tears and trials as well as triumphs and trumpets, has stood the figure of one of God's finest works—Mrs. Lillian Gartenhaus. When at the Bema the names of the saints of God are read out of the Lamb's Book of Life, she surely will be very close to the top of the list.

May our God, who by His grace provided redemption through faith in the blood of Jesus, the Messiah, give this book the wide reading it deserves. May it rekindle the hearts of His children to love the fleshly brethren of our Lord, to pray for the peace of Jerusalem, and to invest their witness and means in an organization that was brought into existence not for its own benefit or profit, but as a Hebrew-Christian testimony to Israel. May this book lead the people of Israel to re-examine the life of Christ and to claim their very own as their Messiah.

Rare indeed are the books which contain the precious lifeblood of a master spirit. Such a book is this one.

Dr. Eddie Lieberman
Evangelist and Bible Expositor

AUTHOR'S PREFACE

For years I have been urged to publish the story of my life. My friends believed such a work would serve as an inspiration and encouragement to many; but for several reasons, including lack of time, I could not accede to their wishes. However, since my serious illness a few years ago when I was at the brink of death, they have become more and more insistent that I should write my autobiography.

I pray that the Lord may guide my hand to write only that which may be for His glory and the edification of others.

Jacob Gartenhaus, D.D., Litt.D., LL.D.

To my wife, Lillian,
faithful companion,
without whose encouragement
my ministry would never have been possible

C H A P T E R 1

BACKGROUND

Official documents state that I was born on January 15, 1896, in Bukowsko, a town somewhere in what was then the Austrian monarchy.

But that does not tell much. It would be more truthful to say that I was born somewhere "beyond," in some remote, nebulous place and age when everything was shrouded in mystery; when angels, demons, and departed souls walked the streets; when everyone swore to having seen and heard them or to having been helped or harmed by them. It was the age of the innocent child, when the authority of God and the divine right of the ruling class were not yet questioned, when established law and order were faithfully observed. There was still respect for human life and private property, and people feared hell and worked for heaven; but these laudable qualities were inextricably intertwined with superstition and petty bickerings which sometimes climaxed violently.

It was an age when light and darkness went hand in hand—usually in harmony and good faith. That age knew but little of "-isms" and schisms. As for the Jews, there was no question as to what Judaism was. Every Jew believed implicitly that what the rabbis taught was God-given, and they obeyed humbly, gladly, and without any reserve. It was during such an age and in such a place that I was born, seemingly aeons and aeons ago.

That age has now passed into oblivion, vanished like a tiny cloud in a stormy sky. The incursion of modern civilization, accompanied by modern communication and transportation, together with the modern implements of murder, have turned that age into a rubbish heap where future archaeologists may look for relics.

The town in which I saw the first light of this world was typical of many in Eastern Europe. It was divided into two sections, its center generally occupied by Jews, and the surrounding streets—which reached out into the fields—by Gentiles. But such a division was more than geographical; it was a racial, social, and cultural division—an impenetrable wall separating Jew from Gentile. During working hours of week days, some Jews mingled with Gentiles in buying and selling merchandise or labor, but most of the time each kept with his own. Kipling's words are apropos here: "East is East and West is West, and never the twain shall meet again."

There were no legal restrictions against the Jews in the pre-World War I Austrian monarchy. No ghetto walls of stone kept them segregated, but they locked themselves in self-imposed ghettos, confined and secluded from all outside contact for fear of spiritual contagion and contamination. The Jewish community was a kind of autonomy headed by an extensive hierarchy that could levy taxes and punish dissidents and law-breakers—usually by excommunication. This ladder of power included the chief rabbi, some judges, beadles, ritual slaughterers, scribes, copyists of the sacred books, readers of the Torah, leaders in prayer, circumcisers, and so forth. The Jews had their own schools. Their benevolent institutions provided care for the sick, the aged, and the orphans; burial; libraries (of sacred books); public ritual baths; and dowries for poor brides.

This was an exotic, anomalous, mythical people planted

as if by some magic power in the midst of a real, practically minded world. They spoke in a language foreign and unintelligible to the people surrounding them; they dressed in entirely different garb than their Gentile neighbors; they ate different food; they acted differently; and they let their beards and side locks grow freely. In short, the Jew in that bygone age was an altogether different creature from those surrounding him—different mentally, spiritually, and physically.

For hundreds of years Jews and Gentiles lived side by side in mutual suspicion which sometimes broke out in open hate and violence. Generally, however, everyone adhered to the laws of the land which demanded tolerance and peaceful relations among all subjects of the monarchy. Jew and Gentile were to a large extent interdependent, and at least in business and trade they had to rely on each other to deal honestly. Usually the Gentile was a man of the field, while the Jew was a town's man, a middle man. The Jew marketed and exported the Gentile's produce and in return supplied him with manufactured imported goods. The Jews were the artisans (tailors, cobblers, tinsmiths, gold and silversmiths, and carpenters), saloon keepers, and, even more typically, physicians, pharmacists, bankers, and civic clerks.

But on the Sabbath and holy days all work and business came to a stop, and there was no contact between Jew and Gentile.

CHAPTER 2

JEWISH LIFE
"Rise Ye to the Service of the Creator"

Jewish life as I lived it in my childhood is vastly different from the life of an average child in America. In the middle of the night my father, like most pious Jews, woke up and washed his hands (vessels for that purpose stood handy at the bed). He then recited a prayer thanking God for returning his pure soul to him (after its absence during sleep), lit a candle, and in its dim, flickering light seated himself on the floor (a sign of mourning). In this position he lamented the destruction of the Temple, the dispersion of Israel in exile, and, in particular, sorrowed for the Shechinah Glory, who, according to tradition, is with Her people in all their affliction, suffering with them in their tribulation. These lamentations were read from a special prayer book for midnight. After that, he sat up at the table and either recited some psalms or became engrossed in some Kabbalah book. Around four o'clock in the morning the beadle (shamash) of the synagogue made his rounds about town hammering on the door shutters and crying in a loud, plaintive tone: "Rise ye, rise ye to the service of the Creator." Then most homes were lit with faint candlelight, and my father began to arouse us children (males only) to bestir ourselves and hurry to the synagogue.

It was hard for me, as for the other Jewish boys, to get up, especially in winter when the room was cold, the water

22

for washing was icy, and the way to the synagogue dark, sloppy, and slushy. But this "supreme sacrifice" was well rewarded when we arrived at the warm synagogue, lit by candles and lanterns, where we could obtain a cup of hot tea for a small sum. The real pleasure came when we boys could sit at the long tables with the older scholarly men and indulge in the joys of some Talmudic debate, accompanied by fallacious reasoning (casuistry) in which both young and old partook.

At dawn, the first morning service began. Usually only artisans and traders took part in the first service. The boys, and those whose business was studying the Torah, remained at their tables along the walls and continued their study undisturbed by the service. When the scholars tired of study, they could join a later service. Prayer quorums of at least ten males (of over thirteen years of age) were easily formed, and thus one service took place after another, or even several at the same time, in different parts or annexes of the synagogue. Only after the morning service—late in the morning or at noon—could one eat anything. Breakfast was usually frugal, but like the other meals it was accompanied by ritual hand washing (before and after) and by particular benedictions.

My father devoted his life to the service of God, spending all his waking time in devotion and in the study of the Torah. He demanded that I, too, live similarly, which meant little food, little sleep, and no childhood pleasures. Had it not been for my mother (the proverbial Jewish mother, Yiddishe mamma), who secretly encouraged and comforted me, I would have broken out often in open rebellion.

Mothers in Israel

The mothers in Israel carried the burden of maintaining the family when their husbands shook off earthly responsibilities and lived only to prepare themselves for the life to come—"Olam-Haba," the equivalent to paradise. In such cases, as in my family, the woman took over the maintenance of the household. This was done ungrudgingly, submissively, and even with tender and loving care for the husband. The woman knew well that only for the sake of those who study the Torah could the sinful world be maintained. She herself was not allowed to study the Torah, and even the commandments she was supposed to keep were but few in comparison with those of the men folk. Woman was perceived as a pitiful, frail creature who had very little chance to get into the Garden of Eden in the world to come. Thus she thought herself fortunate to be able to relieve her husband of all care; he could then gather up many treasures in heaven which she would be able to share when the time came for the rich reward. My mother fulfilled this role by skillfully and prosperously managing her own fabric store.

Total Consecration

In those hazy, fanciful, dreamy days, the holy day was really HOLY *unto the Lord. No* work was done, no burden carried, no business transacted; there were no plays, no games, and no cooking (the food was prepared before the holy day set in). The holy day, then, was all worship. Even the meals, which were taken at home after the services at the synagogues, were themselves services. The food was ritually prepared, ceremoniously eaten, and accompanied by various benedictions, litanies, and sacred hymns as various rites and symbols were observed. If there was any important task to be done (as in an emergency sickness, fire, etc.), a Gentile was called in. Even the kindling of a light, or the extinguishing of one, had to be done by a non-Jew.

Many Jewish families kept Gentile servants, usually maid-servants, but I never heard of a Jew serving in a Gentile home. The whole atmosphere in the Gentile home, with its icons on the walls, was abomination to the Jew, as was the Gentile food.

C H A P T E R 3

MY OWN LITTLE WORLD

My childhood was similar to that of other Jewish boys in that far-off age, but even more intense and rigid because my father and forefathers were in many ways peculiar, even among the peculiar people. My father was entirely divorced from the humdrum life of this world; and although by title he was a rabbi, he refused to officiate as such because that office might divert his mind from total devotion to God and His Torah. Preferring the humble, reticent life, he expected each of us children also to live like a recluse, preparing for the next world. To attain this end he often used the rod when good words were of little avail. I learned very early to submit to his will and behave like a good Jewish boy, according to his interpretation of the term. I knew that a reward awaited (in the Garden of Eden) those who were good Jews, so I made every effort to earn it.

Early Instruction

I have some dim recollection of my first lesson in Hebrew: I was but three years old and an angel dropped a penny* on the page which served as my first lesson. I was allowed to use the penny at my discretion.

*The penny is dropped, as if from the sky, by the father or the teacher in order to encourage the tiny tot to go to cheder (a school for Jewish children where they are taught to read certain religious books in Hebrew).

MY OWN LITTLE WORLD

I can recall dimly the feast my parents arranged for the community when at five years of age I began to study the Bible in the original Hebrew. Adorned like a prince, I stood at the guest table holding an oration on the sacrifices which are ordained in the Book of Leviticus. The celebration of my bar mitzvah is even clearer in my memory, for I delivered a discourse on a difficult Talmudic subject before the distinguished guests. This time I was old enough to understand what I was talking about.

Long before I had become bar mitzvah, I felt fully responsible before God and Israel. Very early in my life I became God-conscious, for I had been inculcated with the various maxims of the rabbis that teach the omnipresence of God: "Know before whom you stand. . . . Know that the Eye sees, the Ear hears, and that all your deeds are being recorded in the book." It was generally believed that during sleep man's soul went up to heaven and there wrote down all it had done during waking hours. I was fully aware that one day I would have to give account for everything that I had done which was not in full harmony with God. To be in full harmony with God meant to observe not only the 613 laws of the Pentateuch as interpreted by the rabbis, but also the innumerable by-laws that rabbis, all through the ages, have added to that original number.

Thus I felt enormous responsibility towards the Almighty, my Creator, that I could neither shirk nor evade by any means. Was He not constantly near me, watching each and every action of mine, and was He not relentless in His wrath against sinners? Yet, heavy as the burden was, I usually carried it proudly and cheerfully. I counted it as a privilege that God had entrusted me with the keeping of His Law—thus enabling me to inherit the world to come if I continued my efforts to obey that Law. I felt important when in the morning service I recited the benediction, thanking God that He had not made me a Gentile. My parents, teachers, and the daily prayers repeatedly reminded me that I was "chosen"—that I belonged to God's favorite, privileged people. This sense of superiority led me to look with contempt upon those Jews who were not dedicating their lives solely to the study of the Law and who consequently could neither properly adhere to its precepts nor inherit the world to come in full measure.*

The "Goyim" (Gentiles)

From what I learned in books, from other people, and from my own experience, I knew that the "goyim" (Gentiles) were given to drunkenness, to sensuality, and to brawling, and that only the fear of the government deterred them from frequent crime. And no wonder: Were they not idol worshippers? Did they not bow to the statue of a dead man and his mother and other people whom they called "saints"?

In spite of the strong arm of the government, we all lived in fear and trembling lest one day the Gentiles would murder us. Blood-curdling stories of massacres reached us from other countries. We read no newspapers in those days; communication was very slow. Yet news of pogroms reached us speedily in diverse ways, usually in a distorted and exaggerated manner. Those alarming reports were usually accompanied by rumors that the local Gentiles were threatening to emulate their brethren of other places and kill us, too.

"That Man"

O, how I despised them! They persecuted us, because they blamed us for killing their God. How ridiculous, how

---

*Imagine what a shock I experienced in later years on learning that Jesus had no use for the self-righteous Pharisees, and, on the contrary, gave the promise of the kingdom of heaven to the humble and lowly.

wicked! Who told them to choose as their God that Jewish blasphemer—"that man"? That hateful Jesus had caused us trouble when he was alive and now was making still more trouble after his death. How I hated him! How I hated the "abomination" (the church) where they gathered on Sundays to worship him and the other idols—especially the cross, that symbol of unspeakable horrors committed against the Jewish people. Whenever there was the danger of seeing the cross* (and in our community it was often encountered on churches, roadside chapels, and most Catholic houses), I hastened away with fast-closed eyes, devoutly whispering, ". . . But thou shalt utterly detest it, and thou shalt utterly abhor it; for it *is* a cursed thing" (Deut. 7:26).

I think that most Jewish children at that time felt as I did when I heard the chanting which emanated from the church on Sundays and holidays. One church was an imposing building, standing aloft on a hill overlooking the Jewish quarter, and I always thought of it as a legendary monster ever ready to pounce on me and devour my body or my soul, by forcing me to sin. I had often heard that the Gentiles snatched Jewish boys and forced them to commit some grave sin. "Grave sin" meant kissing a cross (which they might force to the lips), uncovering the head, cutting off (or shortening) the side locks, or forcing a taste of pork (by stuffing it into the Jewish boy's mouth).**

Their religious processions on certain holidays always had a paralyzing affect on me. Once or twice I succumbed to temptation and peered out through a crack in our shuttered doors, and what I saw filled me with horror: They were carrying crosses, crucifixes, statues of the mother of God, and various other icons and pictures, while chanting those unholy, idolatrous prayers. I then wondered why

*Modern Jews explain this inimical attitude toward the cross because this sign was usually used to incite the mobs to attack the Jews.
**And, according to rumor, such things did happen.

God did not strike them down with His lightning from heaven—and me, too, for having defiled my soul by wantonly looking at such open rebellion against the one God.

Shuddering Hearts and Shuttered Doors

Jewish homes in those days had heavy shutters which were locked from the inside at night and on occasions when trouble was brewing—as on election day and conscription day, when the Gentiles got drunk and fought each other or smashed Jewish windows and attacked any Jew they could lay their hands upon. On such holidays the Catholic clergy sometimes took advantage of the large masses of worshippers and incited them to avenge the blood of their God by shedding the blood of Jews. We knew that the liberal Austrian government would not allow a repetition of such outbreaks of mob rule, but we felt more secure within fast-shut, strong doors. As a child I knew little of politics, but I heard much of those massacres, and I relived them in my mind whenever I heard the church bells ring. To my ears those bells sounded like: "We are not through with you yet. We are still going to make you pay for killing our God." O, those bells! They reminded all the Jews of auto-da-fés, of crusades, and of pogroms when thousands of Jews were slaughtered. How could those horrors be forgotten! Often I would think that I, too, would gladly die a martyr's death and thus sanctify God's Name. But I was so afraid of blood, so sensitive to pain. No, I wanted to live. Yet I could not understand how a Jew could live peacefully if the Almighty would not destroy the Gentiles or take us away from them to our own land.

Why Hast Thou Forsaken Us?

I pondered a great deal on such questions. I knew that the rabbis hinted that the Shechinah, too, is in exile from

Israel. I did not know exactly what the Shechinah was, but it was generally understood that it was God as He reveals Himself to man. I was confused: Is "Almighty" God so powerless that He cannot redeem Himself and His people from the power of Satan and the Gentiles? The oft-repeated prayers for the "unification of the Holy One, and His Shechinah" puzzled me. Nobody could explain what the prayer itself could only call a deep mystery.*

I meekly submitted to God's will and prayed for the coming of the Messiah, when all things secret would be revealed and settled and we Jews would be the masters and the Gentiles our slaves. In my childish imagination I thought of the Gentile as subhuman. For the child in those totally Jewish surroundings, "Jew" and "human" were synonymous. Indeed, when I saw non-Jews with my own eyes I could not imagine that they were human, because they did not dress like us "humans" nor speak like us; their men shaved their beards and side locks, were heavily built, walked erect, and had weather-beaten faces. They were, in short, altogether different from "us humans."

Jewish and Gentile Homes

Later, when I was about seven or eight years old and could walk some distance, my mother took me along when she went to the Gentile homes in the suburbs to hire workers (for wood-chopping, laundering) or to order agricultural produce (fowl, eggs, vegetables, fruit). It was then that I saw the inside of a Gentile home for the first time; it filled me with contempt and disgust. The furniture was primitive while ours was "modern," and I was horrified by

*This short prayer known as L'Shem Yichud, which preceded the performance of various precepts, is apparently of Kabbalist origin. The Kabbalists (Jewish mystics) were not afraid to teach that God appeared to man in a form that can be communicable to man's mind.

the absence of books and the presence of various icons and pictures on the walls of heathen gods (as I considered them). All around were swine, dogs, and cats—abominations all over!

What a difference from the Jewish home where there were no pictures except the mizrach.* There was no Jewish home without a collection of books. Our own was well-stocked with hundreds of books, all by saintly Jewish authors. And there were the closets containing the various ceremonial articles, the beautiful candlesticks for the Sabbath and the holy days and for the Chanukkah** lights. There were the various other paraphernalia, including the velvet Tephilin (phylacteries) bags,*** and the many other things which made my home a little paradise, a delight to my young and dreamy eyes.

Our Jewish home was also distinguished by the absence of "unclean" animals. I still remember the fright those Gentile dogs gave me. Their bark made me run, and my running made them pursue, and if no one came to my rescue soon enough they tore my clothes and even bit me with their ferocious teeth. I had early learned some effective charms to ward off dogs, such as repeating: "But against any of the children of Israel shall not a dog move his tongue." However, not every dog understood their meaning, or else many were too wicked to obey the sacred charms. Their bites along with a thousand other things proved to my young mind that we were God's own people, gentle, wise, and holy, and that they, the Gentiles, were of Satan.

*Mizrach means *East*. It was a large sheet of paper (framed) beautifully decorated and hung on the east wall—pointing towards Zion, in which direction the Jew faces while at prayer. This mizrach "picture" contained various passages from the Bible with the superscription in large letters: "I have set the Lord always before me . . ." (Ps. 16:8)—a steady reminder: "Be cautious: God is facing you."
  **Chanukkah—Feast of Dedication
  ***with the Tephilin inside

MY OWN LITTLE WORLD

That, in short, was the world of my childhood: A mixture of pleasant dreams, mature judgments, and philosophic speculations, intertwined with the prevalent attitudes, biases, and religious conceptions which in themselves were an admixture of sublime thought and gross superstition—a woeful combination of fact and fancy. Were it not for the grace of God, I might have grown up in that childish vanity, self-righteousness, prejudice, and superstition—separated from the *true* God and all mankind. When I was about ten the turning point came in my life. It began with a severe blow which breached a gap in my dream castle—a gap which grew wider until the whole castle toppled into a heap of rubble. This mishap led me gradually to the happiness which is real life—life eternal.

CHAPTER 4

AWAKENING—THE DAWN OF REALITY

In the vicinity of our house there was a shop where soda water was sold, and behind that shop was a storeroom where the soda water and various syrups were concocted. One Sabbath afternoon when all work was at rest, when the elderly folks either were taking naps or were at study, when the children were free from Cheder (and had a chance to sneak away from the surveillance of the elders and engage in non-holy secular activities), I yielded to the temptation of a friend to go and taste the wonderful syrups that were in that mysterious storeroom. He knew of a back window easily pried open, which was hidden behind thick shrubbery. So in we stole, and after tasting the delicious concoctions near at hand, my friend climbed up on an upper shelf where there was a strange-looking container. He handed it down to me, and I hurriedly uncorked the bottle, wishing to be the first to taste it. I was sure that, being out of reach, it must be very dear and therefore very good. I tasted it—and dropped down unconscious.

Hours later, when I regained consciousness (but with excruciating pain in my throat), I found out what had happened. That bottle contained a deadly poison, vitriolic acid. When I had dropped down as if dead, my horrified friend raised a hue and cry which aroused all the townspeople. I was carried home. The local doctor rushed in, and after rendering first aid, he pronounced that my only chance of survival was to get immediate treatment from a throat specialist who lived in the next town, about twenty miles away—a four-hours' ride by horse and buggy in those pre-automobile days. The whole town was agog: "Such a calamity!" "And this had to happen to that saintly Rabbi Moses' child." "And on a Sabbath day!"

Violation of Sabbath

After consultation of the chief law books, the town rabbi decided that in such a case of life and death the Sabbath might be violated permissibly by my trip to the next town. Almost all the town's folks stood by while I was packed into a wagon, my mother seated herself near me, and the driver made his last preparation for the journey. When the wagon started on its way all the bystanders broke out in loud lament and wails. They were not only bewailing my fate and that of my honored parent, but that the Sabbath had to be publicly violated, dishonored. That good, pious Jews such as my mother, the driver, and I had to infringe the holy laws of the Sabbath by riding was the first shocking experience in the town's annals.

Intercession

The next few days while I was away from my town being treated by the specialist, relatives and friends back home spent much time praying and saying psalms for my recovery. My grandmother, who lived with us, visited the cemetery invoking our departed relatives and other saintly people to intercede for me before the throne of mercy. Alms were generously distributed for that same purpose. In short, nothing that could be done was left undone. After several days I was brought home with certain instructions from the specialist which I was to observe strictly. For sev-

eral weeks my condition vacillated. Finally, our local physician told us that in order to avert the total closing up of my
throat and my choking to death, I should go for a lengthy
treatment under the care of a particular professor, an
internationally known authority on throat diseases, at the
national hospital at Vienna, the capital of Austria.

Among "Goyim" and Strangers

By the mode of travel in those days, Vienna was considered to be an immeasurable distance. It was an enormous
adventure to embark into that unknown world, where even
Jews reportedly looked and behaved like Gentiles. But
again, it was a matter of saving a Jewish life, and so, provided with various recommendations (to the hospital authorities and to some Jewish leaders), my father took me to
that city and placed me in the general hospital.

At first the doctors gave little encouragement for my
recovery; but under their splendid care, I soon began to
feel better. In the beginning I was bewildered by the
strange people around me—they were speaking a strange
tongue (German) and were very different from the people
I was used to. They surely did not look like Jews, nor like
the Gentiles I saw back home.

However, I was soon able to understand what was spoken around me; and since I had plenty of time and was
accustomed to reading books, in the absence of many Hebrew ones I quickly turned to the books which other young
patients lent me.* One of the nurses who discovered my
thirst for knowledge supplied me plentifully with attrac-
tively illustrated books and often tarried at my bedside to
explain any difficult passage I pointed out to her.

---

*The Jewish vernacular, "Yiddish," is an old German idiom and could
easily be compared with the modern German speech.

AWAKENING—THE DAWN OF REALITY

Change in Conception of "Goyim"

After the first few bewildering days in my new environment, I began to ponder all the new experiences. My first shocking surprise was the discovery that the world was not divided into two parts, Jews and Gentiles: The non-Jews, too, were divided into various nations with different kinds of culture and civilization. The Gentiles I knew back home were illiterate, rustic, coarse, noisy, bellicose, dirty, often drunk, weatherbeaten, and dressed in heavy homespun garb, while at the hospital everyone was gentle and refined in talk, in face, in dress, and in behavior. Everyone in my new world could read and write, so that, had they been dressed like Jews, they could have been mistaken for Jews.

Moreover, I found out that they, too, had books. All the children (most of whom looked like Jewish children except that they had no side locks) were reading books. The first books I saw were either fairy tales or romances in which there was a lot of fighting and shedding of blood, and I greatly wondered why such stuff should be printed and read. At my age (ten or eleven), Jewish children were reading quite serious books which either expounded the Bible and the Talmud or contained instructions about morals and ethics. We also had legendary tales, but they were *not* of physical prowess and exploits but of saints and their holy lives and charitable actions worthy of imitation. After a while I discovered other books of a more serious nature, dealing with geography, history, zoology, physics, and other such subjects, of which we Jewish children had not the slightest idea. Even then I felt that our books were of everlasting merit, while theirs were but of fleeting, temporal interest, contributing nothing to man's happiness nor to his preparation for the world to come.

My father stayed in Vienna for several weeks and came during visiting hours to comfort and cheer me. Each time he came, he reminded me that I was a Jew and should not deviate from the right path. He allowed me to go bareheaded and to hide my side locks behind my ears so as not to be a laughingstock to those strangers, but he warned me to eat only what I must have for my health, and by no means to touch pork or any other unclean food. I was careful to conceal the Gentile books whenever he came and kept handy and open one of the religious volumes he had given me.

After a few weeks the doctors told my father that I was out of danger but that I would have to remain for several months longer for daily treatment. He then felt that he could return home and leave me at the hospital. Strangely enough, I agreed—I, a little Jewish youngster, alone in a far-away city of total strangers. (Several weeks after my father left, my mother came and stayed for two months. My illness cost them a fortune, but they would gladly have given their lives to save me.) But somehow my heart told me that no harm would befall me among those good people. Still stranger was the fact that while some of the attendants were nuns who wore about their necks crosses or crucifixes, I was no longer horrified by their sight. Sometimes I sank into a reflective mood and asked myself what penance I would have to do when I returned home for the many sins I had committed while in the hospital. How would my eyes, which so often looked at the cross, be able to look at the holy scrolls?

C H A P T E R 5

CONTACT WITH CHRISTIAN RITUAL

One day I noticed great commotion in the hospital. Doctors, nurses, and visitors were happily discussing presents, organizing choirs and dramas, moving furniture, and so forth. My young friends told me that they were making arrangements for Christmas Eve. Perceiving that I did not quite grasp the meaning of that word and knowing that I came from a distant place and a foreign people, they tried to explain to me what they knew about Christmas.

Then I recalled that back home the Gentiles had a holiday in wintertime when they made merry and when their boys disguised themselves, going from house to house singing and collecting money. They even came to our house. My mother hastened to hand them some pennies so that they might depart before starting to sing their unholy carols, which were painful to our Jewish ears. I remembered that on that day which we called "Nitl"* we cheder children were huddled together listening to some elder boy read (from a hand-copied manuscript) the story of "that man," how he became the god of the Gentiles. Although we all knew that awesome tale from previous years (it was annually repeated), it filled our young hearts with consterna-

---

*Probably a corruption from the Latin "Natalia," the birth of Christ. The story we children were told on that day each year was an appalling distortion of the birth and life of Christ.

tion. Now in Vienna, I wondered how these good and intelligent people could celebrate such a holiday.

When Christmas Eve came and all the children in my ward went (or were wheeled) to the auditorium, I feigned illness and stayed behind. But, when in the course of the celebration, the cheerful singing reached my ears, I could not restrain myself any longer. I soon found myself peeping through the keyhole of the brightly lit, cheerful auditorium and attentively listening to the sounds. I ventured unobserved into the auditorium since I did not find the singing as raucous, as heathenish, as the Gentile singing back home seemed to be. It was almost as sweet to my ears as our Jewish singing. Then the sisters began distributing parcels which I saw piled around the Christmas tree. The names of the recipients were called, applause followed, and (woe is me!) I heard my name called. The nurse said I felt sick and could not attend, so she would deliver the present to me later on.

It was then that I spoke up and claimed my gift. When I opened the package I found in it, besides some candy, a beautiful little coin purse and a pen-knife—the things I had always longed to possess. I jumped up, embraced the sister who gave it to me, and pressed a fervent kiss on her cheek. And at that very moment I was struck by the thought that I had committed some cardinal, unpardonable sin. To a Jewish boy, it seemed ridiculous and sinful to kiss a woman, and here I had kissed a Gentile woman who believed in "that man"—the false god. I ran back to my ward and bed, covered my ears and eyes to shut out all the unholy world, and sank into reverie. All through the night I was plagued by thoughts of the torment in hell which awaited me in retribution for my sins. Here I was, a good Jewish boy, scion of great rabbis, defiling my eyes and my ears by looking at and listening to heathen practices. Even worse I had accepted an idolatrous offering! How could I ever atone for it?

CONTACT WITH CHRISTIAN RITUAL

It was a disturbing night. My young ward-mates thought I was sick and tried to cheer me by showing me the presents they had received and telling me how they usually celebrated Christmas at home. But only in the stillness of the following night did it occur to me that I had read somewhere in the Talmud something about a child who was captured by Gentiles and who, living among them, innocently learned their ways and practices. The rabbis were tolerant and ready to forgive the transgressions of such a child if, of course, he later returned to God and repented. I then resolved (as soon as I could leave my "captivity" among these Gentiles) to appease God and do penance for all my sins and errors.

C H A P T E R 6

HOME AGAIN: PERPLEXITY

A few days after that fateful Christmas, my father, notified that I was well enough to go home, came for me. How happy I was when I could again put on my Jewish clothes and expose my pretty side locks. How glorious to be again among Jews! Never in my life had I so devoutly recited the prayers as on that first day back home. For several days I was the proud hero of young and old. I had to answer thousands of questions about the life "over there" in the outside world.

As things quieted down, I began to think of the penance I should do in order to atone for my past sins. But the more I thought about it, the more perplexed I became. Uncertainty, anxiety, and scruples began to twitch at my heart. Questions began piling upon questions: Why were those people in Vienna so friendly, so helpful to me—an outlandish Jewish boy? Even here at home where the Gentiles were so crude, if they hated us, as I had always been taught to believe, why didn't they kill us? It would be so easy for them, being stronger and in such an overwhelming majority.

I knew many Jewish peddlers and tricksters who walked alone from village to village through fields and forest vending their goods, and nobody harmed them or robbed them. On the contrary, they were everywhere hospitably received; and if they did not partake of the Gentile food which was cordially offered to them, it was their own choice. And if some Gentiles hated the Jews, did not the Jews hate the Gentiles? Yes, I knew that at diverse times and in diverse places Jews had been outrageously treated, but why should I hold all non-Jews responsible for the misdeeds of the few? "They are idolaters," I told my querulous conscience. I remembered that the Talmud said that God was going about from nation to nation offering the people the Torah (Law), but all refused to accept it except for the Jews. Thus the Jews had become God's people, a holy people, while all the others were living under the curse of the original sin of Adam.* So how could we love or respect them? This answer was satisfactory only for a short time.

Under the Curse

One night—it was in the stillness of night that my brooding mind was most active—the alarming thought occurred to me that we Jews, too, live under the curse. I suddenly recalled the verse (Deut. 27:26) that he who does not keep *all the Law* is cursed, and when I began to count the 613 laws of the Bible, I found that most of them were not observed by our people. We observed thousands of laws and customs and tried our best, at great sacrifice, to please God. But here I found laws that God Himself, through Moses, commanded us to keep—and we *did not* keep them. These were the numerous laws of the sacrificial order, of purification, and others. Moreover, certain sacrifices were ordained to atone for our sins. What could atone in the absence of those sacrifices? Yes, we prayed several times daily that God might restore us to our land so that we

*That is the view expressed in the Talmud: Mankind was contaminated by the Serpent. The Jewish people, by accepting the Law, were washed clean of this deadly contamination. The Gentiles remained as before.

might reestablish the sacrifices, but why did He not hear our prayers? In the meantime, we neglected all those laws, and consequently we were under the curse.

Questions Outlawed

Jewish children were early taught not to inquire into matters of faith nor to ask questions about what is generally accepted as Judaism. So I had to grope and feel my way in the darkness of growing skepticism toward some rays of light. In a roundabout way I did, however, bring my quandaries and doubts before my elder brother, who was considered by all as a genius in Jewish lore. However, what I got from him was what I often heard from my father— religious problems are mysteries which may in time be revealed only to mature, pious, and learned Jews. Children have to believe implicitly and obey.

Messiah: The Comforter and Answer

The consensus, however, was that when the Messiah came and we were again able to serve God with sacrifices at the rebuilt Temple in Jerusalem, then we should all know God, and all mysteries would be revealed to us.

But why did Mashiach (Messiah) not come? For nineteen centuries we had been continuously praying for His coming: What more could we possibly do than we had already done to appease God, to make Him forgive us for our sins? Moreover, we all knew that our people were becoming less and less observant of the Holy Laws. In some lands they imitated the ways of life of their Gentile neighbors. We heard that in Western Europe, and especially in America, Jews became more and more assimilated—that is, they became less and less Jewish. What hope was there, then, that in the future we would be worthy for the coming of the Messiah, more than were our pious fathers who willingly died martyrs' deaths at the stake or endured excruciating torture?

At first, such questions occurred to me only at night when alone in bed, but soon they intruded into my daily life; they gave me no respite even at mealtime. My reflectiveness did not escape the attention of the people around me. My mother noticed it during meals; my friends, while talking to me, found me absentminded; and at prayer I was observed not responding properly with the worshippers (answering "Amen," rising when necessary, etc.). Before long the rumor spread that I might have been contaminated (spiritually harmed) when I lived among the Gentiles. After much consultation, my father decided to send me to a certain rabbi who was famed for his saintliness and his power to work miracles. He lived a great distance from our town, and it was a great expense for me to go and live with that rabbi; but my parents thought it a good investment, so off I went.

The Wonder Rabbi

My stay with the rabbi was filled with new experiences. People from far and wide came to seek his advice, to obtain his blessings, and to hear his discourses on and exposition of certain passages in the Talmud. I was in the midst of all these exciting activities. Somehow I found favor in the eyes of the rabbi and he appointed me as his personal attendant (a kind of royal page*). Thus, I was almost always at his side. It was a busy life for me, and I had to be constantly on the alert to fetch a book, to admit a visitor, to bring some food or drink, and so forth. When I lay down to sleep, I

*A post which was usually held by elderly men.

TRAITOR?

was so exhausted that I soon fell into deep and dreamless sleep and had no time for brooding over theological questions.

One day I heard the rabbi deliver a very scholarly discourse on the sacrifices, which he followed with a prayer for God to send us the Messiah so we could renew the prescribed sacrifices for the atonement of our sins. I was so agitated by his words that when I was alone with him, I asked him, "Rabbi, when will He come?" "Who?" he asked, surprised. "Mashiach," I answered. His surprise grew, but he replied thoughtfully, "Boy, our sages, blessed be their names, cautioned us not to speculate upon this question. He may come any day, even this very day." He turned his back to me, looking at a shelf of books as if to search for some volume. I knew this was a hint not to bother him any longer.

I did not bother him then, but the question continued to surface, growing even more provoking. Here was a great rabbi, generally considered a man of God, who was initiated in all divine mysteries, and he could not enlighten me on that question. Well, who could? For several weeks longer I grappled with these intrusive thoughts, trying by hard work, study, and prayer to suppress them, but they tenaciously persisted. I finally came to the conviction that I was not supposed to be better and wiser than everybody else, and I was not to worry about sin and the Messiah any more than any other Jew. Yet, on the other hand, I felt that I could no longer return to the simple life and implicit faith of my hometown.

Discovery of New Types of Jews

While away from home, I had learned that my town's standard of Judaism was only local. Here to the rabbi's court came Jews from all over the Diaspora. They spoke in

46

various dialects, wore various clothes, practiced various customs, even in prayer, and some even trimmed their beards and side locks. I saw that there were different kinds of Jews and different kinds of Judaism. I also heard that in various cities there was a so-called "Haskalah" (enlightenment) movement.

Jews not only were reading Gentile books, but also many Jewish authors were writing secular books—foolish love stories and idle poems—and, moreover, they were writing these useless books in the sacred tongue. I also heard that those writers were infidels and were ridiculing the faithful Jews who still tried to live in the mode of their forefathers.

What disturbed me most was the rumor that there had arisen a Zionist movement. Did not that mean that some people, tired of praying and hoping for the Messiah, had decided to take matters into their own hands? Jews in certain places had joined hands with Gentiles (and those of the lowest types) to overthrow existing law and order and establish socialism or anarchy. I saw the pillars of society and of our religion begin to shake, and I knew that I would not, could not, stem the tide of onrushing change. It was no use continuing to study for the rabbinate when my own faith was shaken.

But how could I so cruelly disappoint my parents who had sacrificed so much that I might study and be ordained and so perpetuate the lineage of our rabbinic family? How could I face my townspeople when I returned home disgraced? And what should I do for a living if I stopped studying? Who could extricate me from my complicated quandaries?

Trying to Escape My Conscience

Here again the Talmud came to my assistance: If one must commit a sin, it says somewhere, let him go to a place where he is unknown, so that at least he will not serve as an example. After much calculation, I decided to go to America. At the time that was an audacious, venturesome, and hazardous thought—almost revolutionary. We thought of America as a wild, anarchical country where gangsters and ferocious Indians were marauding, where gold was very cheap, as was life. Only a very few Gentiles had ever gone there from our province. These were fugitives from justice or men very deep in debt. Most of them returned after two or three years with some money saved up and gruesome stories about murder, robbery, and rape. As for Jews, only rarely did any of our town go to America, and then only to escape military conscription or some criminal accusation (true or false). We regarded such Jews as lost to Judaism because we heard that there was no possibility in America of eating kosher food, nor of keeping the Sabbath, nor of dressing like a Jew. I knew all that, but I also knew that an uncle of mine who had gone there some years before had made a fortune, and thus could afford to rest on Sabbath and to obtain kosher food. I was sure that he would welcome me as a near relative and help me find some suitable work where I could forget my religious queries and perplexities.

First, I had to return home to find out more about this uncle and to plan that adventurous, risky journey. When I arrived I told my parents that I did not feel well there at the rabbi's home, as I had to work hard with very little rest. Then after some days, when I thought the time opportune, I disclosed to them my intention of going to America.

Had I thrust a dagger into my heart, they could not have been more astonished and hurt. It took a few minutes before they could utter words. It was a shocking scene. There followed days of persuasions, threats, and enticements. I was told that a certain rich Jew wanted me for his daughter, his only child, his heiress, and I would be a most fortunate man if I married her. It was a very tempting thought, but I had made up my mind. One day I slipped out of town with only my bag of phylacteries and some money which I had saved secretly. On the way I met a peasant taking a load of produce to the next town, and he took me along in his wagon for a small sum. By the same peasant, I sent a letter back to my parents begging them to forgive my strange action, not to worry about me, and promising them that I would remain a good Jew and would write to them very often. I felt like a bird escaped from a cage, but alas! I had no fitting wings and knew not where to go next.

"And Jacob Was Left Alone" (Gen. 32:24)

For the first time in my sixteen years I felt alone, forsaken, and forlorn. Nobody around me cared whether I had a bed to sleep in, a piece of bread to satisfy my hunger, or whether I lived or died. A vague thought occurred to me that if I should return home and beg forgiveness from my parents, they surely would love me and care for my well-being as before. Nostalgia and remorse gripped me like a vise, and I imagined voices saying, "Go back! Go back!" Wherever I looked I seemed to see my mother's tear-drenched face beckoning "Come back!"

Several times that day while aimlessly roaming the streets of the strange town, I decided to return home. Had I found conveyance to take me back, I would not have hesitated any longer; I would have returned to security, shelter, loving parents, friends, and a promising future. But there was no vehicle going in that direction. That evening brought the train which, according to my original plan, was to take me to Krakau, one of the largest cities of the monarchy, near the border of Germany, from which I could depart for America.

In Krakau, a famous Jewish cultural center, lived a native of our town to whom I planned to apply for help and counsel. I arrived in the city after a sleepless, woeful night and found my way to the Jewish quarter and to one of its synagogues where my landsman (man of my town) worshipped. After morning service he took me home to his wife and children, and we had some frugal breakfast. On hearing my story, he said, peremptorily: "Your design to go to America will heap disgrace and sorrow on your parents whom I love and admire. If you change your mind and stay here in the local yeshivah [academy of rabbinic lore], I'll make it easy and worthwhile for you and your parents; but I would not help you in deserting them and going abroad." He gave me two days to think it over, and I did some hard thinking in those two days. The advantages of living in that beautiful, large city of culture were alluring, but I knew that I would not find an answer to my questions there. On the third day I took the train to the border town where I was to cross over to Germany.

CHAPTER 7

HOMELESS AND PENNILESS

Travel across national boundaries has always been a difficult matter, and for a Jew the process has been doubly difficult. I reached the border about midnight—without passport, of course.

"Where are you going? What are you going to do? Let's see your papers," the guards shouted at me.

I began my fabricated story: "I'm going to Berlin to consult a doctor about my throat. I had an accident when I was quite young and now need the help of a specialist."

"Why don't you go to Vienna, your Austrian capital?" I was asked.

"Because I have relatives in Berlin who will let me live with them while there. And so I. . . ."

I soon found myself on the cold station platform with about sixty other people, mostly young Jews, who like myself had good stories but no valid passports. Longingly, in despair, we stood and watched the lights of the train disappear across the border into Germany.

We were herded into a cold, dark jail. There was no room for us to lie down; it was either stand or sit. Some of us laughed bitterly; others cried. Some cursed everything that came to mind, including God.

I became acquainted with some of the Jewish boys, and together we shared our life stories and conspired how we might get across the border into Germany. With the coming of morning, I sought a quiet corner and began my usual morning devotions. I could not forego them even in prison; in fact, I felt all the more need to turn to the God of Abraham, Isaac, and Jacob and seek His aid in my desperation. I put on my phylacteries and began to pray, while a group of jeering Gentiles surrounded me, poking fun at me. When I did show signs of breaking off my prayers, some of the men actually showed pity and left me alone.

Later that morning each of us was called in for a police interrogation. I was put on a train for home, but at the next station I quietly sneaked off. During my night in jail I had learned a great deal of the fine art of border stealing. From a doctor who dealt in that business I bought a certificate directing me to a physician in Berlin who would treat my malady. I was informed of a man whose business it was to conduct people without passports across the border. But, not having the funds with which to hire him, I had to rely on myself. I soon learned of a route into Germany across a region of rugged mountains.

The winter of 1912-13 had already set in when I started. Snow was on the ground, and they warned me that in some places it would be waist-deep. But I would not be deterred any longer.

Night was the best time to travel undetected. My first one was a frosty nightmare, with tears of remorse and self-pity pouring out of my eyes as the path grew steeper and steeper and my baggage heavier and heavier. But I had to go on. I had been cautioned not to sit down in the snow for a rest, as I might fall asleep from exhaustion and never wake up again.

At what must have been about three A.M., I saw a light far ahead and hurried towards it. At the house a man, while refusing to take me in, directed me to an inn farther along the mountain trail. I reached the inn about two hours later. The place was hot and smelly, crowded with men who had dropped in for a drink before going to work. There was no place to sleep, so I rested for a while by the fire, had a cup of hot tea, and was again on my way.

After another hour of walking, I reached a city on the German side of the border where I was instructed how, with proper vigilance, I might reach Berlin. I boarded a train which took me to that city without any major incident.

Destitute in Berlin

As soon as I found a resting place, I wrote to my uncle in America and asked him to send me the fare for travel to the United States, explaining that as soon as I got work in that land of promise, I would refund to him every cent that he advanced me.* I sent the letter off with high hopes and began looking for work in the meantime.

I walked the streets of Berlin day after day, but each night I was no nearer a paying job than I had been in the morning. At first I lived high, hoping that I would soon have work and feeling there was no great need for economy. But as time went on I had to tighten my belt.

"Sorry. We're not hiring right now."

"Right at the moment we don't need any help."

What kept me from despair was the thought that my uncle would forward the fare to America and I could leave this city of frustrations. But no letter came from him. I later found out that he wrote to Mother of my intentions, and she advised him to send me nothing. Mother instead wrote me frequently, offering me every inducement to come home.

On my long walks in search of work I had become acquainted with a clannish group of men who perennially

---

*In those days—pre-World War I—American authorities did not demand passports or visas from immigrants coming from Germany, so all I needed was the fare.

looked for work in vain. They told me of the free soup kitchens where they were getting food and of the places where they could get a few nights' lodging without any charge.

For several days I kept the thought of eating non-kosher food at bay. How could I, a scion of rabbis and saints, think of ever placing unclean food into my mouth without choking to death and immediately going to hell? But the animal cravings within me made a more forcible demand than did the 613 commandments of my religion. The law of survival, of self-preservation, won out. If there was a place for me to sleep in a room with yellow men, black men, whites, Jews, or Gentiles, I could not think of refusing it simply because I was one of a people apart.

And when my strength was ebbing and hunger pangs excruciating, I could not question the source of the food that was offered me. It may have been touched by Gentile hands, but it restored my strength. It wasn't kosher, but it was edible* most of the time. Some of the food that I ate during that winter in Berlin was hardly food at all. I was sometimes given bread so hard and stale that I had to soak it in water before it could be chewed. Still, it was better than nothing at all.

Often during those crucial days I could not help questioning my actions. After all, I could have been well on my way to prominence and respect among my own people, enjoying comforts instead of enduring near-starvation. Instead I was propelled by the driving urge to get away from my doubts, questions, and perplexities—and away from myself.

---

*Once when I happened to see my image in a mirror I burst into laughter, as if I saw myself in a Purim disguise. I looked like a sheigetz (a Gentile boy). My side locks were gone, my new hat was no longer of the Jewish type, my long kaftan was gone, and even my face had become weatherbeaten like that of a peasant. I then argued that if I looked like a goy, I might as well act like one.

Day after day I was in the breadline of this or that free soup kitchen. But when it came to seeking shelter, I found there were tricks of the trade to be learned. Most of the shelters for homeless men allowed a man to stay only four nights; but I soon learned how to circumvent those regulations, and by certain tricks I could make the round of the various lodgings again and again. I became proud of my prowess as a gate-smasher.

"Haven't you been here before?" a desk clerk would ask me as I was walking past.

"Me? No!" I would insist even though I had previously stayed in that place two or three times. My brazenness, or perhaps my innocent, sorry looks usually worked well. In this way I eventually used up all the shelters in Berlin.

Sabbath-Guest at the Synagogue

Each Friday evening, taking advantage of an old Jewish custom, I attended a synagogue and sat near the door in the seat reserved for the stranger in town who had no relatives. After the service one of the worshippers would invite the stranger home with him for the Sabbath meal. I gladly accepted such invitations and ate enough to fill my stomach for two or three days.

But I never told these kind people my true name or story: I did not want to drag the good name of my family down with me. One Friday evening the beadle of the synagogue told me to come on a week day when a collection would be taken up and handed to me because I was such a picture of destitution and want. I could not refuse; I was all that I appeared to be.

Mother Calls Me Home

The Sunday I received the money there was another glad surprise. A letter from home informed me: "If you

55

must go to America, come home and we will help you on your way. Enclosed is money for fare, etc." I couldn't believe that I was actually reading these words, yet there they were and in Mother's handwriting.*

Nostalgia, the longing for love and friendship urged me to get home as soon as possible, but how? If I returned without the side curls, without my Jewish garb, looking like a goy, I would be the laughingstock of the town, a disgrace to my folks, and a burden to myself.

I decided to stop off in Krakau, where I could let my locks grow to a satisfactory length and provide myself with the traditional Jewish garments. I wrote Mother of my decision, asking her to be sure that Father was in agreement with her plan and would receive me in kindness. While the letters were going back and forth, I found a job delivering milk for a Jewish dairy. What a life! When after a few weeks the mirror told me that I looked somewhat presentable, I started homeward.

The train reached my home town at night, but before it screeched to a stop at the depot, I hopped off and hurried along back streets, looking both ways at every corner to be sure nobody saw me.

The street was pitch dark when I at last stood in front of my own home.

Return of the Prodigal

I knocked. Everyone came rushing to the door at once, and I was pulled into the living room. Father began to ply me with questions, but Mother and Grandmother only

---

*I later found out that the beadle in conversation with me got to know the name of my home town, and he wrote to the rabbi that a boy of his town lived in Berlin in great plight and something should be done about it. Of course, the rabbi guessed who that boy was; the result: my mother's letter.

stood by sobbing. I was a mere shadow of the healthy boy who had left them. There were deep lines in my face— mementos of my winter in Berlin. Mother hoped that at last I had learned my lesson and would settle down. But even the breadlines in Berlin and all of my other experiences in that city only spurred me on to greater adventures—to America.

A pall settled over our home as the days passed and we made preparations for my trip. Mother and Father brooded over their frustrated hopes. Their second son would not become a rabbi after all. Father still tried to win me back. He was more lenient now and treated me like a mature man, freely discussing with me theological subjects or legal points.

One day I asked him: "If the Jews are the chosen people of God [and I did not doubt that they were], and if God is all-powerful [and there was no doubt in my mind about this], why did He allow His chosen people to suffer at the hands of those who were not His chosen people?"

The answer was, "Sin."

"But," I asked further, "if seventy years of captivity in Babylon was enough time for the Jews to atone for their awful sin of idolatry, what enormous sin did they commit that should cause Jehovah to expel them from their land for nearly two thousand years?"

To that he had no answer. I was only reminded that I was sinning by even raising such a blasphemous question.

And so the doubts incessantly assailed me during those days, just as before my first escape from the town. My appreciation of my home town seemed to have changed in the short time that I had been away. The pious men in the synagogue awed me less.

When the time came that my parents were convinced they could detain me no longer, they provided me with the necessary funds and legal papers for emigration to America. But, as they stipulated, I was to go by way of

Vienna to say good-bye to my elder brother who lived there. They still cherished a last hope that he might succeed in bringing me back to my senses.

CHAPTER 8

WITH MY BROTHER IN VIENNA

My brother, who was now about twenty-one, was regarded as a celebrity and genius by the people not only of Bukowsko, our hometown, but by the people of Vienna as well, where he was teaching in a Hebrew school.

He met me at the station. We had been separated for years and were glad to be together again. I noticed that he did not dress as the more orthodox Jews of our hometown did, and when we reached his apartment, I noticed he had some books in German on his shelves. Both of us knew that no real Jew could have anything to do with books in a Gentile language, or any book that was not written by a pious Jew.

"You wonder about my books," my brother began. "There is quite a story behind some of these books. I'm sure it would interest you to hear it.

"Some time ago, Jacob," he began, "there was a man here in Vienna who created quite a stir. He came from England and stayed at a hotel. He was a *meshummad** and had 'sinful' literature with him, which he endeavored to distribute all

*A *meshummad* is a deserter, a renegade, one who has been reared in the Jewish faith (or Judaism), but who leaves it for some other faith. Jews tell their small children of the dreadful things that happen to those who become *meshummad* so that almost every Jew grows up with a deep aversion, hate, and fear of the very word.

around. The entire Jewish community here in Vienna was agitated by rumors that he had come to entice the Jews to worship idols. People only wondered why God didn't strike him dead if he had come to destroy the true faith in God and lead God's people astray.

"The rabbis cautioned their people that this meshummad had some occult power and that harm would come to anyone who got too close to him. Someone reported that in London millions of dollars were being raised to destroy the religion of the Jews. Thus, this mysterious stranger and his designs became the chief topic of discussion in the synagogues here.

"Such dreadful things were said about this meshummad," my brother continued, "that the curiosity of the young men was stimulated. They wanted to see what such a person looked like. They wondered, as did I, what the little books might be that he was giving away for free. But we did not dare to approach him, nor even to go near the hotel where he lived.

"However, I was determined to learn the truth about this man if the occasion would arise; and so one day, Jacob, when I was on my way home, all of a sudden that stranger came up to me. He held out a book to me; and, after glancing in all directions to make sure that I was unobserved, I seized it, squeezed it into my pocket, and at once turned back to my apartment.

"Back in my room I locked the door and opened the book to the first page. I saw that this book, which had created such curiosity and turmoil, was called The New Testament. But it was in our own Hebrew, and I was surprised to see the names of Abraham, Isaac, and Jacob in it. I was reading the first genealogy of Jesus Christ—'that man'!

"A falling leaf blew past my window, startled me, and filled me with terror; I thought someone might be spying on me, as perhaps someone happened to see me taking that book from the 'seducer.' But, before I had finished reading several of the pages, I wondered how this 'Book of Sin,' as the rabbis called it, could contain so many statements that soothed the mind and called upon each one of us to love all with whom we come in contact. My interest grew with each page.

The Impact of Truth

"In the Sermon on the Mount, I found words which, I had to admit, were far superior to any I had seen in Jewish books of learning. Would a Man so vile and filthy, so debased, so full of sin, so abominable, so contaminated in soul, so low in His thinking, and so mean in His outlook on life as the rabbis pictured Him, express such thoughts?

" 'Perhaps this Jesus is not as foul as we have been led to believe,' I said to myself. I wondered, 'Is this really Christianity?' And what surprised me most of all was that all through it, the words of Jesus were so like the words of our Bible. 'That man,' Jesus, always cited the books of Moses and the prophets in dealing with Jewish teachers as well as with the common people. Whenever He referred to the Tanach [Old Testament], I looked up the reference and discovered that it was really written *thus,* no error, no distortion, no falsification.

"I thought perhaps the man had not given me the true book of the Christians, but some other book to lead me on. But whatever this book was, I began to like it, to revere it.

"The Jesus of this book spoke of the God of our fathers and often referred to our Tanach. I was impressed, too, with the compassion that this Jesus showed not only to the poor and the helpless, but also to the despised, the ignorant, the outcasts, and even to sinners. He seemed to think only of those in need. He did not stay away from the upper ruling classes; yet He did not look up to them because they were rich. He was no respecter of persons.

TRAITOR?

"I read on into the Book of Acts. What kind of power did this Man possess that He imparted to others? Cowards became brave heroes. Men from ordinary walks of life became leaders and spiritual giants among men. On and on I read until I came to the conversion of Saul, a young, brilliant, well-educated Jew. Saul's argument about the law and its relation to life was not only clever, it was true, relevant, timely.

"I read the Song of Love, 1 Corinthians 13. It was the most beautiful thing I had ever read. Then and there Saul of Tarsus became the ideal of my life."

There was more to my brother's story. Throughout it all I sat dumbfounded. I could not believe that he would even touch a book so hated by our people, let alone come to love and admire it as he had. Yet, because he was a good teacher, able to inspire others with his own enthusiasm, I, too, was touched. Throughout the account of his reading of the New Testament, a warm glow seemed to pass from him to me.

Suddenly my brother said, as if it had just broken through his conscious thought, "But we're invited out to dinner and must be on our way."

Although my brother had told me something about our host to prepare me for the meeting, I nevertheless was surprised by a hitherto unimagined experience. I noted that the home was Jewish, to be sure, but there were unmistakable signs of a strange, foreign atmosphere: pictures that were not in keeping with an orthodox home and mottoes that did not come from the prophets or the rabbis.

"Shalom aleichem" (Peace be unto you), our host said when we arrived.

"Aleichem, shalom" (And unto you, peace), we replied in the best Jewish tradition. But it was all so different.

Had I not seen some of the goings-on among the Jews in Berlin, I don't believe I could have endured my visit to that home and the surprises I experienced in it. Our host did not put on the little skull cap as all orthodox Jewish men that I knew would have done. Instead, he laid his head-cover aside for the meal; and my very own brother did so, too. Nor did they observe the ceremonial washing of hands or say the prescribed Jewish prayers obligatory for meal-time. Then came my real shock.

The host bowed his head and addressed words directly to Jehovah. This was the first time in my life that I had heard Jehovah addressed in anything but the most formal prescribed and memorized prayer. Yet it was so genuine, so sincere, so appealing.

But can you imagine my astonishment when the man closed his prayer with, "In the name of our Lord and Re-deemer, Yeshua ha-Mashiach, Amen"?

The food, too, was different. It was not Jewish. In the Berlin breadlines, sheer want had forced me to eat any food handed to me. Now hunger was not urging, and I could not eat. I had to invent an excuse—a headache—for not partaking of the meal. And although I did not like the violations of tradition, I was deeply impressed in a strange way by this home. I did like, for example, the way the man treated his wife. He did not keep her in the background but made her feel a part of the home and just as free and easy in the family circle as he was. Little by little, I began to like many other things around me, until I felt that I loved that man. There seemed to be a wonderful goodness in him that made him superior to many other men of my acquaintance. As we parted that night, after a long visit, he gave me some little books and brochures to read at my leisure.

My Brother's Confession

When my brother and I were back in his room, he re-sumed his story: "All night long I read my little New Testament. And, when morning began to break, I was convinced—against my will—that the Messiah of the Old Testament is the Jesus of the New. More than that, I felt a relief, a release from a heavy burden in my soul. I knew that something similar to what had happened to Saul of Tarsus had happened to me. The rabbis had kept me, as every other Jew, in ignorance of the greatest and most wonderful Book of our people. I had found in it the answers to all my religious questions."

"So that is that"—the horrible thought pierced my heart—"my brother has become a meshummad!" For several minutes I sat speechless. Then I began to wonder just how this could be true.

It was the popular belief that when a Jew became a meshummad he was well-paid for it and became rich, but my brother had received no money. It was also said that only ignorant people could ever believe such ideas, but nobody had ever accused my brother of ignorance. I knew I was incapable of reasoning with my brother. Finally, I said, "I'm not going to argue with you or try to change you, but I'd rather die than believe in the blasphemous and treasonable words that you're talking about."

Another Example of Christian Love

It was time for my departure again. My bags were ready, and so was I. My brother gave me a letter of introduction to friends in Hamburg, where I was to board the ship to America. He had written in German—a very unorthodox thing to do. How could this brother of mine have a German friend in Hamburg?

The letter was very helpful, as it turned out, since when my brother's friend read it, he accepted me into his home and cared for me for two days while I was waiting for my boat to sail. Not even a close member of my own family could have been more kind, more helpful. And as we parted, my new friend handed me a package of books like those I was given in Vienna. I was so afraid of drowning with this kind of literature near at hand that I put them in the bottom of my trunk. I thought: Out of sight—out of mind.

But neither at the bottom of my trunk, nor at the back of my mind, could I put the memory of the beautiful homelife of that family in Vienna, nor the kindness of those total strangers in Hamburg, nor that Christmas in Vienna, nor the questions that had troubled me through the years. My troublesome doubts were growing like a snowball, getting larger and larger as they rolled on.

C H A P T E R 9

AMERICA

Life on the boat was miserable because I travelled as a steerage passenger. That quarter was quite congested (there were as many as fifty or more people huddled together, and we were in bunks, one on top of the other) with destitute immigrants from all over the globe. Some of them came from places where public and personal hygiene was little known. Some cared very little for the rights of others, and some who had always lived under oppression came to think that on the way to the "Land of the Free" they could take all liberties which in the old country they had been restrained from taking.

If my companionship down in the belly of the ship was as unsavory as the air down there, my stay on the deck (mind you, the lowest deck) was no better. Continuous bickering among passengers—often ending in fisticuffs—the sounds and scenes engendered by sea-sickness, and the continuous rebellion of my own stomach were enough to make life unbearable. Thanks to my hard life while in Berlin, I learned how to get along with these seemingly unbearable physical hardships.

But there was still another force I had to wrestle with: *fear.* I had heard terrible stories of the sinking of ships and of legendary sea-monsters. I had read of some in the Talmud, and I also had the awful story of Jonah in mind. So every time high waves began to beat on the sides of our boat (and they were most furious on the side where I was "down under"), I thought that the end had come. Moreover, it often occurred to me that, as in the case of Jonah, it was all my fault—because of my running away from the God of my fathers—that the ship was going to sink. In the course of time, I was consoled by passengers who had heard from the crew that high waves and the rolling of ships are quite natural in mid-ocean.

America–America!

Then came the great day when we sighted land and the Statue of Liberty. There was among us a young man who had been in America previously and was now returning from a visit back home. He was the center of attraction—a one-man information bureau. He told us the exact dimensions of the Statue of Liberty and what it symbolized. He knew everything about America, as there were none among us who could contradict him. Most of our questions now were about the gate of entrance into that land of liberty and money. He knew all about Ellis Island (in New York harbor), better known as the "Isle of Tears," where immigrants had to pass through a rigorous health examination which often resulted in refusal of admittance to the country. Although I was sure of my perfect health and of the political pull of my relatives who would come to redeem me, my apprehension and the suspense were nerve-racking.

My relatives, as expected, came and easily got me out of the clutches of the immigration officials, taking me to their home in Brooklyn. My first days in America were a succession of amazing and bewildering experiences and impressions. At times I paused to ask myself whether it was not all a dream or a nightmare. So many sights and sounds were new to me and so unnatural, so astonishing: the skyscrapers, the suspension bridges, and the din, clamor, and clatter of the various vehicles—horseless streetcars (and some hitched to horses), elevated trains overhead, and subways underneath, and the frequent clang-clang of ambulances, fire engines, and police vehicles, rushing to and from scenes of disaster and trouble. All this was terrifying to eyes and ears attuned to the standards of Europe.

Nor did I feel at ease in the home of my uncle. For the first time I lived among Jews whose language I did not understand. The young folks (my cousins) spoke English, of which I understood nothing. The older people tried to make themselves understood to me by speaking Yiddish, which was a jargon of old-country Yiddish mixed with a corrupted English. Either way, I felt like a "furriner," a "greenhorn." Yet, my relatives were proud of me and introduced me to friends and neighbors as a genius who might yet become a rabbi or a great leader.

What was most bewildering was the goyish behavior of my relatives. All were bareheaded, contrary to Jewish tradition. The men folk were bereft of beard and side locks; the women in décolleté and bare arms did not look like Jewish women at all. My relatives did not wash their hands ritually before sitting down to meals, nor did any of them recite the prescribed blessings over the food, nor were they careful about keeping the dietary laws—at least not according to the old-country standards. I felt altogether out of place. Again, were it not for the hardships I had passed through in Vienna and in Berlin, I would right then and there, on the first day at my uncle's home, have run away.

Within a few days I learned enough English to make excursions on my own into the various sections of Greater New York. I got to know the East Side, where thousands upon thousands of Jews pulled and pushed at each other. Many of the streets were congested with push-carts and vendors selling anything and everything. How these Jews could eke out a living from their push-carts was a mystery to me. Yet they, as well as the stand owners, not only succeeded in surviving but could afford to send their children to college and set them up as doctors and lawyers.

The Jews worked hard, either like slaves or like slave-drivers, but they did not complain. They knew that the work was for their own benefit; it would eventually make them independent and free. America had become their Promised Land, the land of milk and honey. They were very proud of the American-Jewish institutions, especially of certain social and cultural ones: large newspapers (in Yiddish), theaters, clubs, synagogues, etc. They were proud of their leaders who hobnobbed with famous men in politics. Some Jews occupied high government posts. It was rumored that even Theodore Roosevelt (one of the ex-presidents) was a Jew and that his name was an English version of Rosenfeld. Many were inclined to believe this rumor because it flattered their vanity.

Everyone was striving to become a full-fledged American by acquiring citizenship and some basic education; this, they felt, would enable them to aspire to higher levels of society or at least to pave the way for their children to become famous and prosperous. There was nothing in American law to prevent or hinder them from acquiring the good things of life. If there was any anti-Semitism at that time in America, the Jews living in Jewish centers had no occasion to sense it. In their endeavors to become Americanized they shed many of the old-country traits, habits, and customs. Thus, very little remained of what was called "Judaism." Even those who were nostalgic for life back home, for tradition, felt it their duty as Americans to let everyone else do as he pleased. "It is a free country" was the slogan often repeated and emphasized. For centuries the Jews had longed and prayed to be *free,* to speak as they liked; when in America they could enjoy this freedom, they considered it the greatest blessing attainable. Thus all sorts of "isms" arose, including various radical movements, especially among those who had escaped from czarist Russia, where oppressive laws and mob violence made Jewish life unbearable. As expressions of freedom, atheism and agnosticism were disseminated freely among the Jewish masses.

Later, I came to know that my Jewish brethren liberally tolerated all "isms," all ideas, however strange and contrary to their religious, national, or political feelings—except for one, and that was the preaching of the gospel. This, too, was an expression of their sense of freedom: They were free to suppress what for centuries they had been taught to hate and despise.

During my first days in America, I found my Jewish folks living as in a paradise of fools—happy-go-lucky, but heading towards self-effacement. And I, in spite of my gnawing doubts about Judaism, could not view with favor the prospect of the extinction of identity and culture within so many millions of my people.

But I asked myself: "Am I my brother's keeper? I came here to make money, like everybody else did—and so I shall do exactly that. No more troublesome brooding over imaginary things. No more concern about ideas and ideals."

Viewing the Melting Pot

I decided to throw myself into the cauldron of America—into the melting pot where millions of people of various nations and races and religions were coalescing into a single new society, where *of course* I could at will emerge at the top.

Many of the manifestations of democracy were at first repugnant to my old-country breeding. The equality of all men seemed vulgar to me and sometimes even sacrilegious.

The head of this great country was spoken of without due respect and title. Not "His Majesty," "Most High," "Most Excellent," but just "President," as if he were the mere president of a synagogue or some club. The ministers of the government were only "secretaries," and other functionaries of highest authority did not seem to inspire any awe and respect. A police officer, who in the old country evoked fear of the law and was implicitly obeyed, was here a mere "cop" whose word might be contested, and who sometimes was even bawled out and beaten. A doctor was only a "doc" whom anybody could familiarly pat on the back. The word lawyer suggested, at best, a clever man, and at worst, a shyster, a swindler, a liar. A rabbi, too, unless he achieved fame among the Gentiles, was considered an ordinary human being who could be hired and fired according to the whims of the congregation. In those days, when American Jewry was less organized and general ignorance and carelessness was more the rule than the exception, many of those who occupied the position of rabbi could hardly read Hebrew correctly, nor did they know much of Jewish law. Any greenhorn who was unfit for other work became a rabbi or a Hebrew teacher and got along fine as long as he could please everyone in the congregation.

This low regard for things sacred deterred me from taking up a rabbinic or teaching post in and around the synagogue.

Looking for Work

My uncle wanted me to live with him if I would study and graduate as a lawyer, which was then the favorite, easiest, and most remunerative profession. But I did not feel justified in taking advantage of his generosity. I thought of securing any kind of work until I could save a sum of money sufficient to study what would later be worthwhile.

With help-wanted ads in my hands, I visited various shops which needed unskilled labor, but I was always rejected for refusing to work on Saturday, which I still held sacred as the Jewish Sabbath Day.

It distressed me to see how my Jewish brethren desecrated the Sabbath just to get a little more mammon. It was the Sabbath that had kept the Jewish people alive all through the vicissitudes of their exile. And now with the Sabbath gone, how long could they survive? My heart ached all the more that Jews, who owned most of the shops and factories in New York, refused to employ me—a brother Jew—because I stipulated absence on Sabbath days. Ruefully I envisioned the doom of American Jewry. Once I found a shop which closed on Saturdays, but the owner who employed me could not or would not pay me a decent wage. It took me hours and days of mental anguish and struggle before I decided "to do as the Romans do"— to work on the days when all other people worked.

Everyone around me was striving to be a success, to become American—so why not I? I had no training for any skilled labor, but I did have plenty of training in intellectual reasoning and Talmudic casuistry, so why not exercise these talents to learn the intricacies of moneymaking or apply them to the learning of profitable trades? Sure enough, my early mental training helped me to learn the inside rules of thumb and apply certain secrets of trade. Soon after I went to work as an unskilled hand in a hat factory, I rose to the highest ranks and wages of that trade.

I could have become a success in every respect.

But God wanted it otherwise. He soon made me aware of the truth that a man profits nothing if he gains the whole world but loses his own soul.

CHAPTER 10

MY BROTHER AGAIN

During the time I was looking for work and later, when I began to climb the ladder of success, I received letters from my brother, discussing the need and the way of salvation. I considered them irrelevant and impractical for my material achievement in the new world and relegated them to the wastebasket.

I tried to put my brother and his letters out of my mind, but somehow thoughts or words would linger, causing me many a restless day and sleepless night. Why was he so insistent that I look up certain prophecies? Was there really something in it? Had the Messiah really come in the Person of this Jesus, as my brother said? How could anyone have deceived him, who was so familiar with the history and beliefs of our people? I knew that he was considered an authority on Jewish matters to whom other young rabbis would turn for elucidation when puzzled by a question.

Had he lost his mind? No. His way of writing gave every evidence to the contrary. Then what had happened? What strange power had taken hold of him?

One day a letter came from him that said, "I am coming to America." I was scarcely able to believe what I had read. My brother's training and work as a teacher in Vienna were fitting him to be a great rabbi in some large city of Europe. But in spite of the brightness of his future, he had already made one irreparable mistake by professing a love for the false Messiah, Jesus, a mistake which might soon become public.

What would our relatives say of his actions?

I wondered what would become of his ideals in America. There were many Jews in New York who had been rabbis in Europe but who became peddlers, clothing merchants, or labor union leaders here.

In previous letters, after I had become somewhat Americanized, I had tried to win my brother over to my new philosophy of eat, drink, and be merry. Obviously I had never made an impression upon him: His ideals were so firmly grounded that all of my inducements to divert him to the hedonistic life seemed to fall on deaf ears. Nevertheless, what I could not do, I thought surely America, with all its rushing effervescence, could. I would wait and see.

The day came when my brother arrived in America. Almost as soon as we were alone he told me he had left everything in order to win me to his faith. I could not help feeling sorry for him—coming five thousand miles only for my sake and in the face of my opposition.

My Stiff Resistance

I told him in no uncertain terms, hoping it would settle the matter forever, that I wanted *nothing* to do with his Jesus, that He could never be of any interest to me. America is a place for work and business, not for daydreaming and utopias, I told him.

My brother's eyes saddened as I clearly stated my position in aggressive terms. Instead of lashing out at me and calling me an ingrate—which would no doubt have made me feel much better—he placed his arms compassionately about me until I could hardly bear to resist and hurt him any more by my antagonism. Then he confided that he felt responsible for me, since he had put me off with angry rebukes when, in the old country, I had asked him questions. He said that he should have confessed to me that he was troubled with the same questions (as are most contemplative Jewish boys), but that the elders, the rabbis, had strictly prohibited indulgence in such problems. However, now that he was sure he had found the answer, he was bound to bring it to me. He had tried first to communicate his thoughts by letters, but when he saw that I did not pay any attention to them he had come to bring his ideas to me in person. Yet I did not yield, although I dared not contradict nor dispute his sincere words.

Of course, as soon as his conversion became known he was an outcast among our relatives, all of whom warned me to stay away from this evil, mentally deranged person with his talk of Christ, Christ, Christ! But the more I was warned to shun him, the more I wanted to be with him.

He took a room in New York and worked as a common laborer for a small wage. We often met secretly. Knowing my aversion to it, he never brought up the one subject nearest his heart. He did not have to, for I was learning that living the gospel is even more powerful than preaching it.

A Strange Sunday

My brother began urging me to visit the homes of his new friends. This I was reluctant to do, knowing what I would hear there, but one day when I finally consented to visit the family with whom he lived, my host said grace before the meal and closed it with the words, "For Jesus' sake." The mention of that hateful name aroused in me momentary nausea.

Yet I enjoyed myself in this home, because everyone and everything radiated cheer and happiness. I could not have been treated more kindly had I been the son of my hosts.

"Oh, well," I began to reason, "I'll eventually attain some happiness similar to what my brother and these people seem to have. But I will not have to obtain it from their false Messiah as they claim. After all, true happiness can be obtained in various ways."

Already my philosophy seemed to be paying off. By now, at age nineteen, I was a skillful designer of women's hats. I was receiving a good salary and frequent raises. I was in wonderful New York. What more did I need?

True, I often felt depressed when alone in my room; but if perplexing thoughts came to my mind, all I had to do was hurry out to some favorite spot or join in some adventure with friends. In New York, where so many Jews lived, a large Yiddish theater movement flourished. Most of the Yiddish plays were produced in the theaters on Second Avenue. There was always the more riotous and opulent Broadway when Second Avenue grew too tame. I could fend off all disturbing thoughts as long as I was on the go, so I cultivated a hectic pace of activities. I knew plenty of people who took me along to parties, to games, and to other entertainment.

C H A P T E R   1 1

MY MOST MEMORABLE "YOM KIPPUR"

The more I endeavored to subdue my conscience, the more it was aroused. The more I tried to extricate myself from the net which the "Great Fisherman of Souls" had cast around me, the more I felt caught. (See Hos. 11:4.) The happy-go-lucky pleasures which life offered became stale and tasteless: I was yearning for something higher, something nobler, which I could not yet define.

On the morning of the "Yom Kippur" (Day of Atonement) in 1915 every shop was closed, since almost everyone in our section of New York was Jewish. As a matter of course, every Jew is supposed to spend the day at the synagogue, which I was preparing to do when a little boy came into my room to tell me that someone outside had told him to call me. This was surprising, since I had made no plans with anyone to go out on this holiday. The surprise was even greater when I saw that it was my brother waiting for me out on the sidewalk. He didn't want to embarrass me by coming in—he knew that my relatives and neighbors hated to see me in his company.

After the preliminary exchange of greetings and news, I explained that I was on my way to the synagogue, and then asked if he would join me for the day. He said that he had no admission ticket, and I confessed that I didn't either. (Modern synagogues charge an entrance fee for the High Holidays, when most Jews feel it necessary to attend ser-

TRAITOR?

vices; these fees defray the upkeep of the synagogue as well as expenses entailed by hiring cantors.) As we walked in the direction of the synagogue, I suggested that we stand at the door, as many others would be doing, and catch some of the chants, since this particular synagogue had hired a famous tenor of the Metropolitan Opera to perform most of the morning service.

"Is it for such a purpose that American Jews attend synagogue on these 'Aweful Days'?" he asked mournfully.

"Well," I said sarcastically, "we live in a new age—in a new country. The old folks are drawn to the synagogue by old memories, but for us youngsters they have to find new bait to attract us. At any rate, we will be able to write home to the old folks that we attended 'shul' [synagogue in Yiddish], and let them think that even in America we cherish our heritage, keep the Law scrupulously, and are good Jews."

"You can deceive them," he replied, "but you can't deceive God."

"What do you care about God—you who deserted Judaism. . . ." I began a new diatribe, but was interrupted:

"And you?" he retorted, "Haven't you, like most American Jews, abandoned all that we were taught to consider as Judaism? You have cut off your side curls; now you shave your beard; you wear Gentile garments; you eat 'tref' [non-kosher food]; you desecrate the Sabbath by work and riding; and if that weren't enough, today—the most fearful holy day in the Jewish religion—you're on your way to hear an impious tenor sing some prayers!

"Is that all the Judaism you can boast of? Have you already forgotten how we used to celebrate Yom Kippur at home?" he mourned.

Yom Kippur at Home

"It was indeed a *fearful* day," he continued. "We all felt heavy-laden with sin, standing before the Almighty ready

78

to be sentenced to suffering or death. How we prayed; how we implored for pardon! How we used to picture Satan, the Accuser, trying to bring enough charges against us to assure our damnation, and how the good angels were trying to plead, to apologize, to exonerate, to gain our acquittal so that we would be inscribed in the Book of Life! This scene in heaven seemed so vivid before our eyes that we stood in fear and trembling lest the Accuser might win the case!"

I laughed, "Ah! Childish fantasy, hallucination—we have outgrown that stuff!"

"Well," he countered, "that scene, as portrayed by the rabbis, is indeed imagination, but the fear of *just retribution for sin was, and still is, quite justified.* The wages of sin *is* death, and we all *have sinned,* so we all *need forgiveness.* That was the original purpose of Yom Kippur—to be forgiven for our sins.

"I am sure you still remember the 'semi-fearful' days that preceded Yom Kippur. The whole month of Elul [preceding Tishre—of which Yom Kippur is the tenth day] was a month of repentance. Special night services, called Selichoth [Pardons], were performed. We made visits to the cemetery to invoke departed relatives and other saintly spirits of those buried there to intervene before the throne of mercy for us sinners. It was a month of much charity-giving. These half-fearful days became really fearful when the month of Tishre began.

"The first ten days were called 'the ten days of repentance.' The first two days were Rosh-Hashanah—the 'head of the year' [New Year]—and most of the days were spent in prayer at the synagogue. One ceremony of New Year was Tashlich, when all the congregation walked to some body of water and 'threw their sins into the water' while reciting certain special prayers for the occasion. During the remaining days to Yom Kippur, we were especially careful not to commit any sin and to perform many 'mitzvoth' [virtuous deeds].

TRAITOR?

Two Rites Preceding

"Then came the day before Yom Kippur which was high-lighted by two rites—'kapparoth' and 'malkoth.' The kapparoth came as a substitute for the sacrifices that were to be offered at the Temple—when it should exist again—as expiation of sin. This substitute sacrifice was a cock for the males of the family and a hen for the females. There are various laws and customs about the practice of this rite, but as a rule the fowl [victim] was to be lifted up above the head and turned around three times while the offerer recited an invocation that it should be the expiation and pardon for his sins.*

"Malkoth [stripes] was a rite required only of mature men. After he had cleansed himself in the public ritual mikveh [bath] and prayed the afternoon prayer, each man was to go to the synagogue and there recline in a specified position to receive a specified number of stripes with a strip of rawhide. During this performance he was to confess his sins, for which in olden times he would receive forty stripes less one.

"Now, these two rites are only man-made substitutes for the real substitutes instituted by divine order (as vicarious atonement) and thus, of course, are not valid for the forgiveness of sins."

"Ridiculous!" I declared. "What does God care whether I cover my head with a skull cap, whether I shave my beard, or kiss the mezuzah, or whether I eat this or that food, or when I eat it, or how I eat it? You know—the more I think of what I learned in the Talmud and in the various so-called religious books, the more I realize that religion—or call it Judaism if you will—is a sham, a deception!"

"That's just where you err," he interjected. "You con-

*This rite lately has fallen into disuse, and now is practiced only by the very pious Jews.

sider the rabbinic books—their tenets and precepts—as Judaism, as religion, and this simply is not true. True Judaism is based on the Bible."

"But the rabbis based their laws and customs on the Bible, didn't they?"

Tenets Not Biblical

"Yes," he answered, "some of them. But a great part of their laws and tenets are contrary to the Bible. They have ignored or abrogated many biblical laws, and distorted and changed many others beyond recognition—in fact, most of the rabbinic laws are their own inventions and have nothing to do with what God commanded in the Bible. In short, the rabbis have brazenly violated God's injunction against adding to or subtracting from His given Law."

When he saw my utter astonishment, he extemporaneously cited many examples from the Torah to substantiate his assertions. I admitted that now, looking back to my early years at home when I wasted hundreds of hours studying Talmudic discussion with hair-splitting sophistry about some trifle, I had changed my opinion about the greatness and infallibility of the rabbis.

"But," I asked him, "you would not accuse them of purposely or wantonly distorting, altering, or even just ignoring God's Word?"

"No, I do not accuse them of all that," he replied, "but I do say that they were human, and probably well-meaning. Yet, they—like all humans—were subject to the frailties of the flesh: ignorance, prejudice, misjudgment, and last but not least, selfishness. Taking all this into consideration, we may excuse them and sometimes even justify their teachings. But, surely, we cannot blindly follow them. These were their own ideas—good or bad—but certainly not of God as are those of the Bible."

"The Jews," I countered, "always have believed that both the written Law (Bible) and the oral Law (Talmud) were given by God on Sinai, and thus they are of equal validity, of equal holiness. Now you differentiate between the two. What makes you so sure that the Bible is of God and the Talmud is of man?"

"First," he replied, "because the prophets who authored the Bible spoke in the name of God—'Thus saith the Lord'—while the rabbis never dared to make such a claim. Secondly, we know that what the prophets said was God's Word because what they predicted was fulfilled. You can't say that about what the rabbis said. Thirdly, all Jews, including the rabbis, believe and declare the Bible to be the Word of God, while there always have been various sects (the Sadducees, the Karaites, and others) that rejected the rabbis' teaching because it was not of God and often contradicted the Word of God. Lastly, the rabbis themselves contradicted each other. Very often one group of rabbis declared a certain precept to be good or lawful or binding—while another group declared just the opposite. They both could not be right.

"For example: There is a volume among the books of the Talmud called 'Egg' which asks whether an egg laid on a holiday may be eaten. One famous school of rabbis decreed, 'No!' Another famous school said, 'Yes! It may be eaten.' Such *vital* problems—supported by hair-splitting discussions—are the main topics of the Talmudic books.

"Now, which of the two opposing parties—if either—was speaking in the name of God? Final decisions were made by majority vote, or by other rabbis, or in course of time, by customs. At any rate, they were not of God."

"That's just what I was saying," I offered. "All this puerile talk of heaven and hell, sin and atonement, fasting and praying, and those fantasies of God sitting in judgment, with Satan and the angels busying themselves about the fate of a little creature like me, or you, is just humbug."

While thus talking and walking, we reached a vacant bench in a quiet corner of Central Park and sat down.

Arguments That Changed My Life

To my previous statement he replied, "Again, you mix fact with fiction, truth with falsehood. Let's leave the rabbis with their legends and return to the Word of God. While Rosh Hashanah, or New Year, which the rabbis connect with Yom Kippur as the fearful days or 'days of penitence,' is purely a rabbinic invention—Yom Kippur *is* a biblical holy day which has been much distorted by the rabbis."

"Does that mean that we ought to go to synagogues for a whole day, as well as the previous night, and shout all those prayers, litanies, and hymns as the Jews in our old home used to do?" I queried.

"Nothing of the sort. All those prayers were initiated at a much later date, and most of them were composed in the Middle Ages. As far as going to synagogue is concerned, there were no synagogues in biblical times, and the people certainly were never told to worship there."

"But what are we to do on Yom Kippur?" I insisted.

He turned in his Bible to Numbers 29:7–11 and read:

And ye shall have on the tenth *day* of this seventh month an holy convocation; and ye shall afflict your souls: ye shall not do any work *therein*: But ye shall offer a burnt offering unto the LORD *for* a sweet savour; one young bullock, one ram, *and* seven lambs of the first year; they shall be unto you without blemish: And their meat offering *shall be* of flour mingled with oil, three tenth deals to a bullock, *and* two tenth deals to one ram. A several tenth deal for one lamb, throughout the seven lambs: One kid of the goats *for* a sin offering; beside the sin offering of atonement, and the continual burnt offering, and the meat offering of it, and their drink offerings.

Then he read Leviticus 17:11 and other passages. Closing the book, he said, "So you see what God ordained the Jews to do on this day."

But Jews Have No Temple!

Astounded, I retorted, "But all it says is what sacrifices the priests have to offer and how to offer them! You know well enough that we now are in exile, and we have no Temple and no altar and thus cannot offer any sacrifices! That is why we pray God to bring us back to our Promised Land, and there we shall reinstitute the various sacrifices as ordained of God!"

"Of course, I know all that," he replied. "Now, you also know that American Jews, as well as most Western Jews, don't want to go back to the Promised Land nor do they have any desire to reinstitute the bloody sacrifices. They think that they do enough for Judaism when they give to charity and attend a synagogue once in a while to hear a good chazan, or if they occasionally eat typical Jewish food.

"But let us consider observant Judaism as it still is practiced in many countries, as it is in our native town—as you and I practiced it when we lived there. We really hoped and prayed for the coming of Messiah, for a return to our land of Israel—and we wholeheartedly intended to reestablish the ancient sacrificial service.

"In fact, we were doing everything which the rabbis told us to do in order to appease God and induce Him to forgive our sins and reconcile us with Him. For nineteen hundred years we confessed our sins and prayed for forgiveness, and He, the *merciful God,* remained relentless. Why?"

Why I Left Home

"Why?" I agreed. "That is what I was asking years ago, and as an answer I received only rebuke for asking questions that should not be asked. That is why I left our home and with it all its theological perplexities and all of the silly practices and beliefs that are called the Jewish religion."

"That is what we call throwing out the child with the bath water," he protested. "The silly practices, as you call them, are of men—while the Jewish religion is of God. The Jewish religion, which emanates from, and really is, the spirit of the Bible gives the answer to the question, 'Why?' "

Eagerly, I asked, "So let's have it: Why?"

"I already have read it to you," he explained. "God was forgiving the sins of Israel upon certain specified sacrifices. No sacrifices—no forgiveness. It is strange, even incomprehensible, why it should be so, but the Bible—God's Word—says plainly that it is so."

"Are we not in some vicious circle? We cannot sacrifice before we are redeemed and have rebuilt the Temple; we cannot do that because we cannot be atoned without sacrifices and thus cannot be redeemed to return to our ancient land and ancient practices. So, it's no use praying, no use trying to be good according to the Law," I concluded.

"But," he continued, "if a man becomes dangerously ill and people around him say it's no use trying, no use wasting good money on him, because there's no remedy in such a case—do you think that those who love that man will give up hope and idly sit down to watch him die? No, of course not. They will try this and that, call in another doctor, call for a consultation of various other doctors in the hope that somehow a remedy will be found to save the patient's life. Perhaps one of the doctors will find the true diagnosis and thereby the true cure.

"And so it is with our Jewish people; we are a very serious patient, a seemingly incurable people. But we *are* curable—only we first have to make the proper diagnosis.

"Let us look at the Jewish prayer and confession of sin. During the Day of Atonement we repeat several times a long list of sins and crimes which any one of us may or may not have committed. Many of these sins can be expiated only through capital punishment, and we pray for a general pardon for all of them.

"In our daily prayers, we again and again pray that God will bring us back to our land so that we again can offer the ordained sacrifices as expiation of our sins. On New Moon and the other holidays, we confess that 'for *our* sins *we were exiled* from our country,' and implore God to return us so that we again can offer sacrifices.

"Now, why do we say, 'for our sins *we* were exiled'? Is it not a fact that not *we* but our *forefathers,* about nineteen hundred years ago, were exiled? And how may *we* say that they, at that time, were exiled for *our* sins today? There can be but one answer, and that is that we all through exile have identified with the sins of our forefathers and have not repented of them. Thus we keep on sinning the very same sin. We logically and truly can say that 'for *our* sins— our common sins—we have been exiled,' and for the same sins we still are kept in exile.

"Now, what is this sin—or sins? What is that sin of our ancestors that we continue committing, at least by acquiescence and conformity, and which God does not pardon— for which we do not even ask pardon? Do you know? Does the average Jew, who so fervently and passionately prays for forgiveness, know?"

Jewish Partners in Sin

"Well," I said, "let's hear it."

"It may shock you, but I am sure that this is the only reply: It is the rejection of Jesus. He came to save the people. He did no harm to anybody, and yet the highest Jewish court of justice condemned Him to death and delivered Him to the Romans for execution.

"Now, no matter who those judges were who condemned Him, and no matter who were in that rabble that shouted,

'Crucify Him!'—the fact remains that the Jewish people as a whole, with a few exceptions, assented or acquiesced to that judgment and have never really regretted nor repented of it, so that we are partners in that sin. Thus we *justly* can say, 'For *our* sins were *we* exiled,' and are kept in exile."

Shocked, I exclaimed, "Do you mean to say that we are guilty of Jesus' death? Do you mean to say that those who call us 'Christ-killers' are right and that their killing us for that sin is justified?"

He calmly replied, "Again, you are mixing things together that ought not to be mixed. If you, or I, or any Jew were arraigned before a proper court of law for killing Christ, the case at once would be dismissed—because no witness could be produced to prove that we actually took any part in that killing. It is no business of any hoodlum, or pogromist, or inquisitor, or anybody else, whether Jews have or have not killed Christ. This is a matter between Jews and their God. He alone, the Judge of all flesh, may judge whether you or I or anybody is guilty of that or any other sin.

Guilty or Innocent?

"Now, you well know that our people—you and I included—have shared the opinion with our ancestors that Jesus was an imposter, a renegade, a blasphemer, and the like, and therefore deserved to be condemned to death. In other words, we all are participants in that trial, conviction, and execution."

"That's right," I agreed. "But the tribunal had the full right and the duty to judge Him, and whatever they did was according to the Law."

"Yes," he explained, "while there was a trial, although with false witnesses, and while the whole procedure was according to Jewish law, with the exception of the mode of execution, we also know that the rulers and judges of that time were corrupt and selfish, seeking only their own wealth and job security.

"However, let the dead take care of the dead. We Jews, everyone of us, must reconsider that trial: Jesus claimed to be innocent of the accusation of sedition against Rome imputed to Him. The many people who knew Him and followed Him could have testified to His innocence, but the rulers had their way, and the people, as a whole, agreed— and retribution was quick in coming. Our rulers accused Him not of blasphemy, but of sedition before Pilate. The Temple, the altar, the Holy City were destroyed, and those rulers as well as the common people who were not killed were dispersed far and wide. So now we justly pray, 'And because of our sins were we exiled from our land. . . .'"

I interrupted, "But how could we know that what He claimed to be was right and that He was not guilty of blasphemy?"

"Whatever Jesus was teaching, or claiming to be, He based on the Bible, or, to be specific, on what we today call the Old Testament. Just as thousands of people have found His assertions to be in accordance with the Bible, so could everyone else, including the rulers and you and me, search the Scriptures and verify His words and claims."

"Do you mean to say," I asked, "that our Torah [Bible] spoke of 'that man'?"

"All the life and death of this divinely incarnate Son was predicted by the ancient prophets. He died on the cross as the Lamb of God to expiate the sins of the world. The participants in His crucifixion, both Jews and Gentiles [Romans], were blind instruments executing God's will. They knew not what they were doing. Christ said this on the cross and implored His Father's forgiveness for their ignorance. His apostles, Peter and Paul, declared the same thing. There is not a hint in the Bible that indicates that anyone—a single Jew or the nation as a whole—should be punished for that foreordained guilt. Certainly there is not in the Bible the slightest indication or suggestion that anyone or any group has any right to avenge that guilt.

Paul Loved the Jews

"A true Christian is entitled to that name only if he imitates Christ and emulates the apostles, all of whom preached love and forgiveness. Christ emphasized that He came not to judge (John 3), and He exhorted His followers to love even the enemy. Peter and Paul, for example, after the declaration of Christ with His last breath of life, 'It is finished!,' never demonstrated any resentment or hostility concerning that guilt. They had only love, understanding, and pardon for the Jews. Paul, the apostle to the Gentiles, so loved the Jews that he was ready to be anathematized for their sakes."

He stopped for a while. It seemed that this talk from heart and soul was quite an exertion for him. But I took advantage of him and stated: "Whether there are good Christians or bad ones, I don't care. I agree that it might be a great advantage for the Jew to become a Christian—a goy—and assimilate with the goyim, be like them, and enjoy life with them and not keep apart—as Jews usually do to their great disadvantage. But to say that Christ and His teachings are all based on the Jewish Tanach [Old Testament] and that this is the real, true Judaism is farfetched and unfeasible—a thought repugnant to every Jew."

After a brief rest he replied: "Alas! Various tragic events during the centuries have widened the gap between the Jewish people and their true Messiah. Thus false Christianity—as is nominal Christianity—and false Judaism—as is nominal Judaism—are not and cannot be reconciled, can never be blended together. But true Christianity and true

Judaism are one and the same thing. Incontrovertible proof for this statement you can easily and plainly find in the Bible—the most holy Jewish book.

Jesus Is Our Messiah

"Our Bible portrayed a vivid and clear picture of the Messiah to come, and every detail fitted what Jesus was, did, and claimed to be."

"Well, well," I argued, "I never noticed that, and I thought I knew the Bible by heart."

"First," he answered, "all you know of the Bible is the Pentateuch and the few portions from the prophets which are being read on Sabbath days at the synagogue. Secondly, usually you do not notice things if you aren't looking for them. You can live in America for years and never see the beautiful sights that abound here. You know very well, as I said, that although all the books of the Bible are considered sacred and are found in every synagogue and in many Jewish homes, yet only the five books of Moses and the Psaltry are in use. On occasion certain portions of other books are read in synagogue, but the prophets, as a whole—Isaiah, Jeremiah, and so forth—are shunned.

"It once happened that I opened the Book of Isaiah and casually began to leaf through it. Suddenly I was attracted by its grandeur and loftiness and made up my mind to read on. I was so engrossed in it that I did not notice I was being watched. Well, I was severely rebuked for reading such books. Nevertheless, I was so fascinated by the glory of the prophetic words that I had to read on and on, and I reread them again and again. But I had to do it secretly, sneaking away once in a while to the privacy of the attic—freezing in the winter and sweating in the summer.

"Those were my happiest hours, alone with the immortal words of the holy prophets. In such hours I wanted to run out and proclaim to all my friends—all students of the Talmud—the glory that is in these books.

"Yet, I refrained and kept my peace because those books were considered taboo. Now I never have heard a good reason why these sacred books have been so rigidly avoided but, adding things up, I think that the main reason is that our people consider the Talmud all-sufficient for the Jew. Any other book, sacred or otherwise, that would divert one's mind from the Talmudic books is to be shunned. Moreover, they think that the words of the prophets are too profound to be understood by simple beings and, therefore, one should first fill his belly with all that the rabbis have written.

New Thoughts to Me

"In our youth there was still another reason: The Has-kalah (enlightenment) movement and later the Zionist movement made great use of the prophets—to the detri-ment of the Talmud—and urged everyone to study them. In reaction to these movements, which were considered heretical, our pious people thought it better to keep away from the prophets. And last, but not least, missionaries made much use of the prophets, quoting copiously to sub-stantiate their arguments about the Messiahship of Jesus."

"Well," I answered, "I have never thought of that. I'll have to look up these things."

"Yes, that is what you should do—search the Scrip-tures—and I'll give you again a long list of passages about the Messiah from Moses and the other prophets which were all fulfilled in 'that man,' as our people derisively call Him."

"It is strange," I protested. "How can you say that He fulfilled the Law when He broke all laws and instructed the people to disregard the laws of the Bible? Look, all His followers eat pork, desecrate the Sabbath, and. . . ."

"Yes, I know," he interrupted, "and I know also, as you do, that many Jews eat pork, desecrate the Sabbath, and break most laws of the Bible. The only difference is that the Jews do it contrary to God's will, and the Christians do it in full harmony with the Divine Will."

"How is that?"

"Let me first tell you that, contrary to the Jewish fairy tales about Him, Jesus did not break any law. He even instructed His followers to keep all the laws and to submit to the rulings of those who sit in the 'Seat of Moses.' "

"Oh, yes," I replied thoughtfully. "I remember glancing through that book you gave me in Vienna, the New Testament. Yes, He really said so, but why, after His death, did His disciples allow the Christians, His followers, to eat forbidden food? They even abrogated circumcision—the sign of the covenant between the Jews and God."

Plan of Salvation

"But if you had read that book *thoughtfully* and not just given it a cursory glance here and there, you would have understood what the New Covenant really is. I implore you now to make a thorough study of it. However, let me introduce you to this study through an illustration which will give you a comprehensive picture of what is called the plan of salvation. Imagine that a man gets sick; the physician prescribes for him some medicine, a special diet, and some exercise which the patient is to follow in order to get well again—or at least in order that his condition not worsen. But the patient often disregards the orders, and in consequence there are relapses, and the malady becomes more aggravating. Again the patient obeys the orders and gets better; and then he ignores them and relapses recur. This cycle is repeated over and over in the man's life.

"Then the physician announces: 'I see that the regimen I

prescribed for you has been too hard for you to keep. Now because I like you, and I would not like to see you die, I'll give you a new remedy. It can't be obtained anywhere else, and it can't be reproduced. I have only one drop of it, but it's enough for the whole world. One has only to expose himself to its radiation in order to get well. I am willing to entrust you with this secret remedy on the condition that you proclaim its wonderful power to all the world and let all who are sick be healed by it free of charge.'

"I may add that that patient then throws away the remedy, partly because he does not trust his doctor and partly because he already is accustomed to his malady and its recurrent relapses. Some neighbors pick it up and make good use of it, though the physician continues to wait for his patient to get it back and administer it in the proper manner.

Profound Mysteries

"Now, I don't pretend to understand God's ways. No creature can understand the Creator's purposes. There are profound mysteries, which we mortals will never comprehend. All that we are permitted to know of them is what God has revealed to us through His prophets, as recorded in the Bible. The Bible tells us that God created the world. He also created man. It tells us of many other things that He did, but we are not told why He did these things. We cannot understand why He, the All-wise, the Almighty, should have done or spoken such and such a thing. Perhaps in the world to come, when our souls are united with Him, we shall comprehend what our mortal senses cannot now comprehend.

"But as for now, we only have dry facts: In Eden, man disobeyed God, and thus brought upon himself the curse of death. Instead of destroying man—His handiwork—He worked out a plan of salvation, or reconciliation. To this end He chose one family out of all mankind, the Jewish people, to serve as a paragon—that is, a model of perfection. In diverse manners, He revealed His wish to them in order to transform them into a holy people, so that they could become a kingdom of priests and thus bring His Word to all nations of the earth. He prescribed to them various ways to keep themselves clean from all sin, which emanated from the first, the original sin. Knowing the frailties of man and his propensity to sin, He instituted the bloody sacrifices to cover up sin.

"Such vicarious atonement would remind man of his guilt and of the fact that he deserved death and thereby encourage him to sin no more. But all this training was of little avail—the Jewish people did not try to become a blessing to all nations, nor did they even try to be worthy of such a task. Therefore, they reverted to the original sin.

"But God loved His handiwork, and in order to save mankind He Himself made for them the supreme sacrifice by offering up His Son in the image of Jesus."

I quickly retorted, "Now, this already is idolatry, pagan ideas, and no Jew is going to accept such."

"I told you that we can understand but little of God's ways, but all that I have told you is in the Bible—in the Jewish Bible."

A Question Answered

After he showed me the various passages in support of his assertions, I reminded him that he had not yet answered my question about why a Jew who becomes a Christian does not keep God's commandments.

"I was getting to that," he replied. "Every Jew is enjoined to keep all the laws of the Bible. If he breaks even *one* law, he is under the curse: 'Cursed *be* he that confirmeth not *all* the words of this law to do them. And all the people shall say, Amen' (Deut. 27:26). As I said, Jesus reiterated this obligation of keeping all the laws. But since He has made the supreme sacrifice, and thereby wiped out the original sin entirely, there is no longer any reason to keep those rules and regulations which, even if observed strictly, are only palliatives to cover up the symptoms of the disease—that is, sin—but not to cure it thoroughly.

"Now when a man, whether Jew or Gentile, accepts and claims His sacrifice, then he no longer is under the curse of sin. And with a cleansed and purified heart and mind, he innocently can decide how best to live and be a blessing to his fellow man. He does not have to learn from the ancient stone tablets that he is not to kill, or steal, and so forth, because all these laws are impregnated in his heart. As far as ritual, diet, and the like are concerned, he may choose what he sees to be good for him and his fellow man. His reborn, purified heart will dictate to him what to do and what to leave undone."

"That," I replied sarcastically, "would be a pretty bad world to live in—where every man is given a free hand to do what he pleases. In fact, that's anarchy!"

"I spoke only about rites—things between *God* and *man.* As to civic law and order, this has to be maintained in accordance with common consent. I said that a follower of Christ will do all in his power to help his fellow men. If any of his actions are harmful to man, then he is no Christian and has to be forced by common law to do right."

I still was not satisfied. "That sounds very nice, but it is not Jewish. We have been taught that the Law is immutable, eternal."

Using the Scriptures

"That's true, in so far as the spirit of Law is concerned. Have not the rabbis of old changed or abrogated most of the ancient laws, such as the law of an eye for an eye, the Sabbatical law, laws of purification, and so forth? Haven't they said that when Messiah comes, all laws will be abrogated? But let's leave the rabbis to themselves. Let's see what the prophets have to say about the Law."

Again he opened the Bible and pointed out various passages to substantiate his arguments. He emphasized especially Jeremiah 31:30–33, which reads:

> But every one shall die for his own iniquity: every man that eateth the sour grape, his teeth shall be set on edge. Behold, the days come, saith the LORD, that I will make a new covenant with the house of Israel, and with the house of Judah: Not according to the covenant that I made with their fathers in the day *that* I took them by the hand to bring them out of the land of Egypt; which my covenant they brake, although I was an husband unto them, saith the LORD: But this *shall be* the covenant that I will make with the house of Israel; After those days, saith the LORD, I will put my law in their inward parts, and write it in their hearts; and will be their God, and they shall be my people.

"In short," I asserted, "you would like all the Jewish people to become Christian, and that, you well know, is impossible."

He retorted, "It depends on what you mean by Christian, as I have already said before. If this word means to you 'goyim' as our people usually interpret it, then of course it is impossible, as well as undesirable. If, on the other hand, it carries its original meaning of 'followers of Christ' or 'believers in Christ,' why it not only is quite possible, but according to prophecy—which always has proven to be true—it is bound to happen so. The Jews always have believed in the Messiah—translated 'Christ' in Greek—but they have had confused ideas about Him. Some thought that the Messiah was to inaugurate an age of peace and prosperity for the Jews only; some included also the righteous of all nations. Some pictured Him as a mighty Conqueror who would defeat all Israel's foes and make the Jews rulers of the world.

Two Messiahs?

"Some said that he would bring a time of material bliss, when man would obtain all the pleasures of life without the need of laboring for them because the earth would produce food and clothing without any effort of man. Some confused the coming of the Messiah with the world to come, when the righteous Jews will dwell in the Garden of Eden and there feast on the meat of Leviathan, and of the wild boar, and imbibe of wine which is preserved since the six days of creation. Some of the rabbis, becoming aware of the suffering and death of the Messiah (as depicted, for example, in Isaiah 53), invented two Messiahs: one Messiah, Son of Joseph, who was destined to defeat and death, and the second Messiah, Son of David, who would be the triumphant King of glory.

"Only a few rabbis wrote of the Messiah as bringing spiritual bliss, or salvation, not only for the Jewish people but for all mankind. These confusing and conflicting conceptions have been the main reasons that deterred our people from accepting Jesus as the Messiah. If only we could make them see the Messiah as the prophets depicted and described Him, they easily could recognize Him in Jesus, whom they rejected."

I protested, "Do you think for a minute that Jews could ever accept or acknowledge all those foreign doctrines of the Trinity, of the Messiah being one of three, and so forth?"

"Why not?" he asked. "These are not foreign doctrines. They are purely Jewish."

"How can you say such a thing when you know very well that the unity of God—monotheism—is the very essence, the soul of Judaism?"

God Is One, Not Three

"Yes," he countered, "and this also is the very essence of Christianity. But, according to the Bible, God—who *is* One—has three manifestations. Perhaps we don't express it properly, but we have no better words in human language than God the Father, who is unfathomable by the human mind; God the Son, the form or image in which He appeared to man; and God the Holy Spirit, the means by which He spoke to man in vision or in dream. Thus there are not three gods in Christianity; there is only one God in three manifestations.

"It was only long after certain Christians transformed these simple Jewish beliefs into doctrines that Jewish rabbis began teaching that God is an absolute unity. Now it is only a case of rabbis versus the Bible. You know that the Bible uses the word 'Elohim'—God—always in the plural. As to the divinity of the Messiah, why, not only the Bible but even many of the greatest rabbis have taught it. The Kabbalists, who adhered to the mystic interpretation of the Bible, have emphasized the divine nature of the Messiah. The writing of these rabbis are kept as sacred as all the Torah."

"The day is almost gone," I said, "and we have not eaten anything. After all, we have fasted like good Jews. At any rate, this has been my greatest Yom Kippur. I am shaken with new impressions; I'll have to take time to digest them. It is all so new, all so strange. Let me go home, lie down, and think things over."

"You are right. I pointed you to the Way—to Him who said, 'I am the way'—and now it is up to you to walk in it. Satan probably will lay many impediments to block your progress, but if you pray God to guide you, you will arrive at the destination safe and sound. However, remember, as soon as you find the real Day of Atonement, tell others of your discovery that they, too, may be pardoned." This was a momentous day for me, a day on which I learned the meaning of sin. I discovered that no man is without it, that sin needs atonement, and that there is no remission of sin without the shedding of blood (Lev. 17:11 and Heb. 10:4).

Before we parted, my brother handed me a long list of Old Testament passages that refer to Christ, telling in detail of His life and work almost as they really happened hundreds of years later. The list contained the same passages he had pointed out to me earlier in letters which I had torn up.

Searching for Truth

I don't remember whether I tasted any food after the long day of fasting and argumentative discourses, but I do remember that I lay awake all that night trying to consolidate my thoughts and impressions. At first everything seemed so incongruous and illogical, so fantastic and alien, that the thought struck me, perhaps it was not my brother with whom I had spent the day—perhaps it was Satan in disguise who had come to lead me astray and to deprive me of my right mind.

At dawn, I fell asleep. When I awoke about two hours later I felt refreshed and calm. I hurried to my shop with the intention of suppressing my new thoughts during work and resuming them after arriving back home. But my foreman noticed that I was working absentmindedly and, thinking I was ill, suggested that I might as well go on home and rest. I took his advice, admitting that I really did feel strange, and went home.

I spent the remainder of that day and most of the following night recapitulating things. All my past life unfolded before my mind's eye: The implicit faith of my childhood days; the precocious problems that began early to trouble my mind; the change in religious conceptions, consequent to my experiences in Vienna; my growing skepticism and agnosticism; then the happy-go-lucky life of the Epicurean—Eat and drink, for tomorrow we die; and now that astounding change, a total subordination to a God in whom I didn't yet believe. I was beginning, nevertheless, to feel that I was being permeated by Him. And strangely, I was not embarrassed or perturbed at all. On the contrary, I began to feel more and more happy, although the experience still needed elucidation and enlightenment.

Many of the following nights were spent in comparing the Old Testament prophecies with their New Testament fulfillments, until I found that the two are inseparable, mutually dependent on each other. When I realized this truth—that day became my Day of Atonement.

C H A P T E R   1 2

NEW REVELATIONS!

My study was now guided by the list of Old Testament prophecies which my brother handed to me before we parted on that memorable Yom Kippur. Alongside each Old Testament prophecy was its corresponding New Testament fulfillment. He urged me to study them diligently, attentively, and prayerfully. In this way, he assured me, I would be guided by the Holy Spirit, and the truth would gradually be revealed to me. Again and again he urged me to pray earnestly to God with the Psalmist that His Word should be a lamp unto my feet. "Thy word *is* a lamp unto my feet, and a light unto my path" (Ps. 119:105). And I did my best to follow his advice.

What a revelation this proved to be! What an eye-opener! To think that such things really existed in our own Bible and I had been so ignorant of them. I soon discovered that the Old Testament contained a clear biography of the Messiah. It predicted the tribe and family from which He would come, the manner, time, and place of His birth, His rejection by the rulers, and finally His vicarious atonement.

When I compared these prophecies with the New Testament records, I found the striking similarity between them astounding. Later I learned that St. Augustine had already expressed this thought beautifully:

TRAITOR?

The New is in the Old contained;
The Old is by the New explained.

A New Impetus

At about that time my attention was drawn by headlines
in the Jewish newspapers to a mass meeting which was to be
held in New York by converted Jews. This really was
news—strange, exciting, yet revolting news. The editors
and commentators expressed their indignation in most vi-
tuperative language. The general contention was: "The
audacity of those meshummadim [converts], apostates,
traitors all, despicable turncoats, incurable idiots to come
out into the open, inviting the Jewish public to come and
hear their vile propaganda, to come and fall into their
snares!"

After I wallowed through a mass of abusive verbiage, I
gathered that a number of Jews who were converted to
Christianity were convening in New York to organize into a
Hebrew Christian Alliance, and on that occasion they had
invited (by advertisements and hand bills) the Jewish
people in New York to come and hear the reasons for their
belief in Jesus the Messiah.

While some commentators counseled their readers to ignore the meeting, others argued that those creatures
should be taught a lesson, should be made to feel what "we
Jews" think of them.

I was among the readers who decided *not* to ignore that
meeting. Neither did I decide to go and teach them a lesson. Rather I made up my mind to learn a lesson, if there
was a lesson to be learned. At the appointed hour I found
myself in a stream of people flowing towards the church
where the meeting was to be held. From all sides, I saw
people converging, and while some in the crowd were poking fun at the expense of the converts, most were whisper-

ing or shouting threats of exterminating the "pestiferous vermin." Some illustrated their intentions by showing sticks, stones, and knives which they had brought with them for bringing home their "lessons."

As I surveyed the scene, I was reminded of the Crucifixion about which I had read and shuddered. With much effort I gained entrance into the church, densely crowded with milling, elbowing people.

As speaker after speaker stood up, each was hissed at so loudly that not a word was audible. In vain did those followers of the Nazarene plead for tolerance, for the right to be allowed to speak; one after another they were forced to take their seats.

When things began to look very serious, the police intervened, and their presence quieted the outrageous disturbance.

I shall never forget the admiration I felt as the men stood up to speak again; their patience and sincerity in the face of such grave danger profoundly impressed me. When the rumbling subsided a little, one of the speakers addressed the crowd. His melodious voice soothed the people, who gradually became quieter. He seemed to hold them in a trance as he related Israel's sorrowings and sufferings amongst intolerant nations. Pleading with his hearers— victims themselves of intolerance—not to treat their own brethren with the same prejudice, he urged them to become the staunchest defenders of tolerance. His plea was enough to melt a heart of stone. It melted mine.

But some instigators in the large throng must have interpreted this touching address as the subtlety of the seducer. There were shouts: "Let us not be ensnared by these apostates!"

The crowd, thus infuriated, burst out again in wild pandemonium. The few policemen present found it difficult to control the maddened mob and consulted with the pastor as to whether to call for reinforcements. The pastor feared not only the destruction of church property, but bloodshed and scandal, which would, by wide repercussion, lead to general resentment against Jewish intolerance. He suggested that the meeting be ended. While the Hebrew Christians were escorted to a side door, the police gradually dispersed the crowds, who vowed vengeance when and if the opportunity arose.

This Hebrew-Christian conference was, to outward appearances, a complete failure, because the infuriated mob frustrated all attempts of the speakers to tell the people just who they were and what they represented. But to me personally, it was a great blessing, a revelation. For the first time in my life, I had come in contact with Jewish missionaries.

Is a Meshummad Human?

Anti-Semites, who hate everything Jewish, picture the Jew as a disgusting, repellent figure whose anatomy is out of proportion in keeping with his deformed mind. In like manner, I, like many other Jews, intensely and implacably had hated and despised the Jew who became a Christian. This meeting dispelled many of my ingrained prejudices. I saw a nobility of deportment displayed by these Christian Jews, their calmness in facing a jeering, cursing, hate-filled mob. It was a graphic lesson in comparative religion, and it vividly brought back to my mind's eye that greatest and holiest of tragic events in human history: on the one side, the mob shouting, "Crucify Him!"; on the other side, "Father, forgive them. . . ." That meeting was to me an affirmation of historic and divine truth, and I was thoroughly shaken up. People like those in the pulpit, whom I had hated all my life, I now began to respect and almost venerate for their calmness in that pandemonium. I clearly saw the difference in character between the followers of the gentle Jesus and their adversaries who, by the impetus of misguided leaders, had been induced to act as if they were the kin of Satan, the arch-fiend.

A Church Is Not an Abomination

I learned still another lesson a day or two later. It occurred to me that the building where that meeting had been held was a church. In my early childhood I had learned to fear, hate, and despise the church. My conception of a church was typical of most Jewish children: a house full of idols and other such abominations where Gentiles gathered on Sundays and holidays to worship "other gods," especially "that man" and His mother, whom they called "Mother of God." In that house, I was sure, the Gentiles, instigated by their priests, schemed and plotted the destruction of the Jewish people and the holy Torah. Whenever we children had to pass by such a place we accelerated our pace, and in fear and trembling recited: "Thou shalt utterly detest it, and thou shalt utterly abhor it; for it *is* a cursed thing" (Deut. 7:26). And, if no Gentile was in sight, we accompanied our words by spitting in utter disgust.

The Spirit Is Willing, but the Flesh Is Weak

I was now grown-up and considered myself liberal-minded and unbiased—quite an American. I had even read and re-read the New Testament, spending all night reading it, and had become saturated with Christian thought, which I even had begun to appreciate. And yet, ingrained old ideas and fantasies still lingered, and the idea of "church" still filled me with aversion.

But I had been in a church, and nothing had happened.

I tried to pacify my conscience by thinking that it was not a real church, at least not at that time, since it had been stripped of all graven images and other signs and symbols. No ungodly service had been held, and moreover, it had been full of Jews, so it was just a meeting hall.

Yet a still small voice began whispering in my mind's ear: May it not be that you are as mistaken about church as you were about Jesus, about the New Testament, and about converts? Before long I yielded to the voice, and ventured into a church.

I had learned at the meeting that there were mission halls in various sections of New York and Brooklyn, and I secured their addresses from the leaflets which were scattered among the crowd. One could go to the mission places to read the daily newspapers, magazines, tracts, and the Bible, and discuss religious problems and Bible passages.

"Shall I visit such a place?" I thought. At once I dismissed the idea with an emphatic "No!"

I still remembered the warnings of the Talmud regarding the great spiritual hazards lurking in such places and how they (usually, Christians) ensnared people unawares. Longstanding fears are not easily obliterated.

Within a Mission Hall

Nevertheless, the Lord one day led me into a mission, and I came out unscathed.

I was out walking when a sudden downpour of rain accompanied by thunder and lightning forced me to look for shelter. Scanning my surroundings, my eyes fell on a brightly lighted shop window where a large sign invited the passerby to come in. There was no time for hesitation. I followed others and entered. I at once discovered the place was a mission hall, but it was too late to retreat. Cozy, warm, and pleasant inside with fine comfortable chairs, it had a wide selection of reading material. Someone was playing the piano, and the workers were all pleasant and ready to help. When the storm outside abated, I reluctantly left. I felt calm, peaceful, and relaxed.

CHAPTER 13

A DIVE INTO THE DEEP

Like the swimmer's first plunge into deep water, I had finally done it, and now the missions held no terror for me. I was exhilarated and soothed, returning again and again to this mission and visiting others. I knew enough English to understand most of the tracts, some of which I could take home to study. Most of my free time, by day and at night, was occupied in reading them and in discussing with the missionaries questions which then arose. With their guidance I re-read the Bible. A thousand and one questions formulated themselves: Many things were still obscure and enigmatic, and I yearned to understand everything although, as I later learned, mortal man is incapable of that feat.

So frequent were my visits to the mission places that the Jews in the neighborhood began thinking of me as a missionary myself. Strange to say, I even began to appreciate this. Somehow I felt some spiritual bond with those devoted workers. I also felt that I owed them a debt for their help to me in solving my problems. As payment (partial at least) of my obligation, I often helped them perform various chores, distribute tracts and leaflets to passersby, and receive people who came in. Later, after my conversion, I intensified my participation in the work of the missions.

Often on the way home from such a place I thought to

myself: "You fool, you idiot, is this the success you came to America to achieve? A nice career you got yourself—a servant, an errand boy for people you have always hated, whiling away your time in places you have always abhorred. What if your relatives and friends and fellow-workers at the shop find out about your new 'hobby'? They would call it a very dangerous obsession." I sometimes decided to sever my connections with the mission, but I was always too weak to abide by my decision. I was drawn there by an overpowering need, and I generally yielded.

My First Prayer Meeting

It was the last of December. We were let off early for the New Year's holiday, so I went to see my brother. After the usual exchange of news, he suggested that instead of throwing myself into the whirlpool of confusion that is customary in New York during New Year's, we should spend the evening in a more profitable way at some place of worship, a mission. Since the words "church," "that man," and "mission" no longer filled me with terror and aversion, I agreed.

Later that New Year's Eve I found myself in a cheerful, well-lit, warm hall full of people whose faces expressed a similar cheerfulness, spiritual light, and warmth. From all sides came the sounds of "Praise the Lord," "Praise the Lord," and when I looked around, I saw that these people had good reason for praising the Lord. Their faces mirrored the inner happiness in their hearts—a happiness that comes only from the Lord.

This was a band of Christians who had met for prayer and thanksgiving. For an hour I sat as one hypnotized, listening spellbound to the inspiring testimonies coming from those who had been redeemed by His precious blood. How it thrilled my soul to hear them contrast their miserable pasts with their joyous and wonderful present and their still more glorious future! Prayer and more testimonies followed, and singing of hymns in happy unison; during it all the Spirit of God was speaking to my soul: "You can be one of these happy people if you will only yield to Me."

Satan immediately reminded me of the many trials I would have to endure in His name at the hands of relatives and Jewish friends. There would be ostracism and even persecution. My brother was aware of the struggle going on within me, just like the struggle of Jacob of old. Quietly he said to me, "Won't you pray to God?"

That is all he said. The next thing I knew, my eyes filled with tears and I was on my knees. Others, too, got down on their knees to pray for me.

I felt great happiness in the knowledge that these people—strangers—were so interested in my well-being. I felt such gratitude that I thought for a moment of hugging and kissing each one of them. But here again Satan, the arch-fiend, interfered, whispering into my mind's ear: "It would be madness to succumb to childish sentiments." So I sneaked out, calling myself "coward" and "fool" alternately.

My Most Memorable Church Service

Several days after that New Year's Eve, my soul was torn by anguish, vacillating between the broad path which leads to destruction and the narrow path which leads to life (Matt. 7:13, 14)—between the natural instincts and inclinations of the flesh and the Lord.

It was a bright Sunday morning. After a sleepless night, I went out for a while, hoping to divert my mind by mingling with the crowds on the sidewalks. The Lord in His infinite mercy led my feet into a church. The sound of sweet music first attracted my ear, and a compelling voice inside whispered, "Go in!"

I went in, and when the worshippers silently prayed, it was the same compelling voice that whispered, "You, too, pray. Your time has come. Don't delay, don't defer any longer! Ask and it shall be given unto you." I could resist no longer.

I went down on my knees, and as I did so I felt that my spirit was flying upwards, up to the throne of grace.

I do not remember the prayer I uttered, but I do know that I asked God to make the truth known to me. If this Jesus were the One, I wanted God to reveal Him to me, and I vowed to live for Him and if necessary to die for Him. I closed the prayer in the name of Yeshua ha'Mashiach.

I Have Found Him

Right there a change took place, and I cried out, "I have found Him! I have found the Messiah!" A great peace and joy flooded my soul.

I felt that I just had to give vent to my feelings, to cry out to all the world of my great salvation. So I rushed out to the street, stopped the first two men I saw, who happened to be Jews, and said, "The Messiah has come!" Then raising my voice emphatically, I shouted in Yiddish, the language I knew best, "Unser Mashiach is gekommen" (*Our* Messiah has come!), repeating my words more and more joyfully.

C H A P T E R 1 4

BEATEN AND BRUISED

Within a few minutes others came around, and soon there were fifty or more people there wondering at my strange words. Every newcomer asked, "Who is this fellow?," pointing at me.

"I don't know," said one man. "I have just come here, but he talks like a missionary or is just crazy: Some screw must have gotten loose in his brain."

When I found myself surrounded by an increasing crowd, I calmed down a little, trying to explain my discovery. That only infuriated my audience, and they changed from a curious crowd into a hostile mob. They began to beat and kick me. Only when they saw blood on my face and head after I had been kicked down did they fear that they had killed me and hastily dispersed. I went back into the church where someone led me to the washroom. I washed the blood off and straightened up my appearance.

Changes

The metamorphosis of my life must have been manifest in my face and in my actions, because the folks around me began asking for explanations. One wanted to know if I had won the sweepstakes, another if I had hooked a wealthy bride, and so forth. When I revealed to them my recent discovery, they thought at first that I was joking; but during the following days as I used every opportunity to talk about my new faith, they began wondering about my mental stability. My foreman (a friend of my uncle in whose apartment I lived) reported to my uncle what had been going on in the shop. They discussed whether I should have a mental examination.

After my uncle and other relatives had discussed the matter with me and had become convinced that I would neither submit to medical treatment nor give up my "foolish and morbid ideas," he ordered me out of his apartment and cautioned me never to see him again. My friends with whom I previously had spent my leisure time and to whom I was now preaching my new ideas about sin and atonement, about Jesus, and about a clean life, left me one by one as a hopeless case; some of them became implacable enemies.

As for my work in the shop: Although I was now producing more than ever before, nobody seemed to like my presence there. Many attempted to pick quarrels with me, but when they found me calm, indulgent, and unwilling to retaliate, they told me in plain words to clear out and not come back to the shop again, as none of them could stand the sight of a meshummad. When I did return to work the following day, a group of the workers was waiting for me. Jeering and mocking, they began to shove and toss me one to another until I fell down. Then after some severe kicks I was raised up, and the real beating commenced. Not before they saw me bleeding (nose, hands, face) did they leave me with the renewed warning not to come to the factory any more. When I came to myself, I went up to the shop again. I must have been a sight. The manager asked me what had happened: Why were my clothes dirty and torn and my face bloody? When I told him what had happened, he commiserated and said the workers should not have re-sorted to violence.

"It's a free country and one may believe what he pleases," said my boss, "but I cannot let our work be ruined by quarrels and fights. I am sorry; you'll have to go. You've been a good worker, but they threaten to strike if you stay here."

Now I was homeless *and* without work. After staying a few days in my brother's crowded little room, until my wounds healed, I rented a small room for myself. With my savings I could afford to take a vacation and devote some days to study and planning for my future. I also was freer to attend meetings at church and at missions where I was known as a friend.

One day I heard the inner voice urging me to dedicate my life to the service of the Saviour. I volunteered for mission work and began distributing tracts and testifying at open-air meetings. There was much to discourage a beginner in this sort of work: Hardly a day passed without severe trials. All sorts of missiles were thrown (rocks, rotten eggs); sometimes heavy fists beat on me; and almost always there were malicious, acrimonious epithets hurled, often accompanied with generous mouthfuls of spit.

Servant Not Worthier Than Master

Once I complained of this treatment in my brother's hearing, and he made it clear to me: "What did you expect by serving the Master, who Himself was nailed to the cross for no reason except for telling the people what is good for them? Do you consider yourself more worthy than He? And yet He prayed: 'Father, forgive them; for they know not what they do.' Just put yourself in their place; were you not as eager as they to stone, to crucify, the meshummad whom they consider as traitor to His persecuted people? Did not Saul persecute the believers before he saw the light? So you, too, must forgive them, if you want God to forgive you. Yet I don't blame you; few of the great prophets were willing to bear God's message to the people. They all tried to be excused, to send somebody else, but God constrained them to go and give the people His Word, whether they would hear or not. You heard the call, and you can't escape or evade it. Remember Jonah when he was disobedient to God. Remember it is a great privilege to suffer for His name's sake."

Still Wavering

His words were like balm to my wounded spirit, but I made another attempt to calm my exuberant zeal and began looking for work in the only trade in which I was an expert. Several managers turned me down outright. I finally found one who told me frankly that he had heard that I was a good worker, but he had also heard of the cause for my discharge, and he added that the success of his factory lay in the harmony and teamwork of the employees. He was afraid that I might sow discord. He would hire me, however, if I promised never to mention the name of "that man" and never to discuss religion—at least not on, or near, his premises. He further added that, as far as he knew, only poor, destitute, helpless Jews turned to the missionaries for help (and even sold their souls to them). "But you," he said, "such a splendid designer with initiative and imagination, could within a short time become a most successful manufacturer. You must leave religion to the rabbis and the priests."

This was a tempting invitation to deny my Master. After the manager finished and was waiting for my decision, I heard within me the silent voice quoting: "And he humbled thee, and suffered thee to hunger, and fed thee with manna, which thou knewest not, neither did thy fathers know; that he might make thee know that man doth not live by bread only, but by every *word* that proceedeth out of the mouth of the LORD doth man live" (Deut. 8:3). Also, "Behold I set before you this day a blessing and a curse" (Deut. 11:26). It was a temptation, but I could not accept the manager's offer.

Nearer to God

I came to my room weary and worn and fell down on my bed, crying out to God to lend me strength and courage to be steadfast in faith and not to lead me into temptation. I got up refreshed and reassured of God's grace and hurried out to the mission halls, where I renewed my offer to be of help. Just as I had formerly despised these mission centers, I now found them sanctuaries. I attended every meeting, and more often than not I was there before the missionary, standing out in the cold and snow waiting for him to open the doors. As soon as a meeting was over at one center, I immediately rushed to a meeting at another. This was my life—to be in contact with these godly people, to join them in prayer and praise. What wonderful days these were for me! What an inspiration and encouragement when I needed it so much!

CHAPTER 15

FURTHER STEPS IN MISSION WORK AND STUDY

I volunteered regularly to stand at the entrance of the mission halls calling the people in as they passed by, even though it often meant being cursed, spit upon, and kicked or slapped in the face. Some of the assailants claimed to belong to a Jewish group organized to harass and counteract missionaries and mission work. Their primary business was to find out the names, addresses, and occupations of the individuals who frequented these missions with the purpose of boycotting them. In the case of a minor, the parents or guardians were informed of his whereabouts. Frequently they came up to me threatening, warning me, "If your life means anything to you, keep away from this place; one day when we find you here again we'll kill you." But now with the Lord on my side this threat had no deterrent affect on me.

A few days later I found out they really meant what they said. As I approached the mission entrance two of this group lay in wait for me, and with an almost indescribable fury rushed upon me. Before they could finish, my screams brought people to my aid.

One of the duties I took upon myself was to make personal house-to-house, store-to-store visits, distributing literature and circulars announcing the mission services. Even though I was beaten and otherwise abused on every such assignment, I always went to those hazardous places, because in them were the very people most in need of the gospel. I knew that the Lord is always with His own, and with this assurance I had nothing to fear.

Dwelling with Brethren Together
(Ps. 133:1)

One of my greatest joys those days was to sit through the testimonial meeting which was held once a week. Words cannot describe the exultation and ecstasy of my soul when we raised our voices in glory to Him:

> "Blessed assurance, Jesus is mine,
>   O what a foretaste of glory divine!
> Heir of salvation, purchase of God,
>   Born of His Spirit, washed in His blood."
>   (Fanny J. Crosby)

and

> "Take my life and let it be
>   Consecrated, Lord, to Thee;
> Take my hands and let them move
>   At the impulse of Thy love."
>   (Frances R. Havergal)

I felt like I was actually sitting in His presence and speaking with Him face to face. What a fellowship was ours at such spiritual feasts! This was true communion with the Master and with fellowmen. I longed for the Jewish people and Gentile Christians I knew to be present at such a meeting. Surely the brotherhood we felt would have convinced the former of the sincerity of the missionaries; for the latter it would have been the best proof of the power of the gospel to save the Jew. What blessed days they were for us brethren to dwell together in unity.

It was during this period that I felt a call to definite service, and as my new friends and I prayed for guidance I felt led by the Spirit to go to Chicago, where I could attend the Moody Bible Institute and become better grounded in the faith. At the same time I could avail myself of the wonderful opportunity for service among the more than three-hundred-thousand Jews of that city. I shall never forget the loneliness of those first days in Chicago. How I missed my friends in New York! Because of my limited knowledge of the English language, I could not take part in many of the student activities; in fact, I had to have someone interpret for me most of the time. But it did not take me long to feel perfectly at home in this splendid institution. The fine Christian teachers and students took a special interest in this lonely Hebrew, and every courtesy was extended to me. It was a joy to mingle with so warm and excellent a group.

Practical Work at the Chicago Hebrew Mission

I soon found my way to the Chicago Hebrew Mission—a mission whose board included men like Dr. William E. Blackstone, author of the book *Jesus Is Coming;* Dr. Charles Blanchard, president of Wheaton College; as well as other men of God, devout students of His Word who recognized the great part Israel had played and was yet to play in the evangelization of the world. Some of the most capable Hebrew-Christian missionaries of that time were connected with that mission. After a long interview with the godly superintendent, Mrs. T. C. Rounds, we knelt in prayer. The result was that I was asked to join the mission staff as an assistant missionary. My task was to help in the mission hall, in open air meetings, and in "house-to-house" visitation during four afternoons and evenings a week. For my services I was to receive the sum of three dollars a week, provided God's people sent it (and very often they did not send it), and the privilege of eating supper at the mission house every Thursday. Out of this small sum I had to pay my own car fare and expenses. Even so I would not have exchanged those days for a life of ease in any palace.

The pitiful sum of three dollars a week did not go far; it was less than half of what I needed for keeping body and soul together; and so it was necessary to find additional employment. Sometimes I shoveled snow or scrubbed floors in the school building, for which I received twenty-five cents an hour. In this way I put in twelve hours a week. I also worked every Saturday at Marshall Field's, hanging up the dresses which customers had thrust aside. In order to keep up with my studies it was necessary to burn the midnight oil, especially since in addition to my regular studies I had to take a special course in English. A dictionary was constantly before me while I prepared my lessons. Often I did not retire until the early hours of morning.

A Surprise Visit

All during this time I had not heard from any of my relatives, and I longed to see or at least hear from them. But they, it seemed, were through with me. Imagine my great surprise when one day I received a telephone call from a cousin saying that she had just arrived in the city and wanted to see me. Of course, I knew immediately that the reason for her coming was to persuade me to give up my faith. After a minute's reflection, I boldly invited her to the mission. To my utter surprise she at once accepted the invitation.

During the next several days every possible courtesy was

extended her, and she became as one of the family. For the first time this young American Jewess came in direct contact with Christianity in its practical applications so that she could see the difference between genuinely saved persons and so-called Christians. Here she learned of the simple life of the missionaries, their sincere love for Israel, and the sacrifices which they gladly and willingly made. All of this, I was quick to see, made a profound impression on her. Such a life, she told me, was only fit for those who are willing to renounce the world. But she also admitted that their joy was infinitely greater than that of most people. It was a revelation to her, and she could not quite comprehend it all. This emissary who had come to use her influence in winning her cousin back to the fold, who had been greatly confident of her success, was almost in danger of being herself persuaded. Like Balaam, she came to curse and found herself blessing (Num. 23:8).

Before leaving she remarked, "I'm afraid if I stay here too long I'll become one of you."

Mother Rounds, whom she had learned to admire, would not let her leave before taking her to the throne of grace. What a touching scene it was: we on our knees, Mother Rounds leading in prayer, and this worldly girl standing by with head bowed. We shall never know how this affected her, but it must be said that there was no bitterness and no disrespect. As a parting gift she left a sum of money which she said was to be used for a party in the mission house. A few years later when I visited her city for a speaking engagement, her young daughter, seven years of age, hearing that I would speak in a Baptist church, slipped from her classroom to come and meet me, unknown to her parents. It was then I learned that she had been attending a Christian Sunday school. No, the blessed seed sown in faith is not wasted; it always produces fruit.

THE CHICAGO HEBREW MISSION

Those days in Chicago were days of unceasing labor for Christ in the face of grave difficulties and hazards. Great courage and undying faith were especially necessary for the Jew at that time who undertook to proclaim the message to his own people. In order to accomplish our task, the mission hall and the methods we used were made as appealing as possible to Jewish people. The building was located in a business section in the heart of the ghetto.* Outside hung a sign, "Free Reading Room." There was a large window display of Bibles, Testaments, Gospels, and tracts written in the Hebrew, Yiddish, and English languages, while in the center was a large sign with the word "Welcome" in English and in Yiddish, in large letters. This window was partially concealed by a curtain which rendered it less conspicuous, a protection to those who desired to enter the hall but feared to be seen by those passing by.

The hall became a rendezvous for many who wished to take advantage of its warmth during the chilly winter days and nights and of its cool comfort on hot summer days. Of course, suitable literature was placed all about the room, and everyone who came in could casually pick up a tract whose cover or title appealed to him. Discussions on vari-

*Ghetto—the term applied to that part of any city or locality chiefly or entirely inhabited by Jews.

ous subjects were always underway. At the time of my services there, World War I was already at its fiercest, and of course this stimulated many conversations. Sometimes the arguments became so heated and loud that the participants had to be called to order several times before calm could be restored.

When I was sure of my audience, I explained that there will always be wars and, as a result, misery and suffering; always the strong will seek to subdue the weak until Christ, the Prince of Peace, comes back to this earth and establishes universal peace. Then there will be no need for peace treaties or pacts, which are generally repudiated or annulled anyway. But, I added, every person can have that peace now through faith in Him. This provided food for thought and soon another discussion would follow, and I would lead up to man's sinfulness and shortcomings and his need for the salvation which is offered by Christ.

People of every sort frequented the mission, notable among them being those who made no pretense whatsoever of any religion, claiming to be disciples of Karl Marx. We were especially glad for such people to visit the reading room with its profusion of Christian literature to arouse their curiosity. There was always an occasion for discussion, which I directed into the channels of salvation.

Every evening special services were held, and when I announced this to the visitors, usually they would slip out one by one so that often by the opening of the meeting, I would be left with only the two or three workers as an audience. But the meeting went on as if the whole world were attending it. Usually one of us would stand just outside the building inviting people to come in, and normally we would succeed in persuading a few to enter. Often the speaker was rudely interrupted during the course of his message, nor was that all. Frequently in the midst of such meetings a stone would break through the windows.

But discouraging as the work often was, it was not without its recompense, for many of the very ones who used violence in opposing our efforts were the ones whom the Lord chose to lay His hand upon, leading them to see the error of their ways. Some of them rose in testimonial meetings at later dates and confessed all of their past bitterness and the persecution of which they had been guilty. It was encouraging to hear them confess and then listen to their present remarkable experience in Jesus the Messiah. In such cases, usually someone present would viciously interrupt them, accusing them of insincerity, declaring that they had been bribed. Such scenes were enacted again and again.

Visit of University Students

One Sunday afternoon when I was sitting in the hall with a group of inquirers gathered about me, our discussion was interrupted by the entrance of three young Jews. Walking up to where I sat, one of the men, who acted as spokesman for the others, asked to see the man in charge.

"I am he," I replied, wondering what would happen next.

Thereupon, they introduced themselves as students of the University of Chicago and at once began to ask questions.

"If you will show us the name Jesus and His identity in our Bible, we will believe in Him," said one.

This I answered by relating a personal experience. "Several years ago in Austria," I began, "when still a lad, I decided to journey to this new land. Communication was made with my uncle here and arrangements were made for my departure. Going to a new land where I knew no one, not even my uncle who had left the old country before I was born, I was confronted with the question, how should I recognize this uncle when I arrived in America?

"Then my mother suggested that I carry with me a picture of this uncle which she had kept for a number of years and which she greatly cherished. Of course, he would have changed in appearance after all those years, she said, but we all decided it would serve as an identification.

"And so with the promise that I would return the picture soon after landing at my destination, I departed for America.

"As soon as I got off the boat I brought out the treasured picture and began to compare it with every likely man who came to meet the newcomers. Once or twice I was almost sure I had found my uncle, but no—with one there was a difference in the shape of the nose, with another the forehead was different, with another the chin was different. Then my attention fixed on a man coming my way. I glanced at the picture for comparison and let out a joyous shout. Yes, there was no doubt about it, this was my uncle. I identified him by the picture. I had found him at last!

"In like manner, in my search for the Messiah, I turned to the one Book which I knew could give me authentic information. It was the same Book in which you would like to see Jesus. I learned from the Book that He was to be born in Bethlehem, of the seed of Abraham, the house of David, and the tribe of Judah. I learned that He was to be a prophet like unto Moses, that He was to suffer for His people.

"I began to wonder who this wonderful person might be. Was it Jeremiah, as a certain commentator alleges? No, for while some of the pictures portrayed of the Messiah resembled him, yet the complete painting could not be that of Jeremiah. Nor was it any of the other prophets, nor the nation of Israel, as some commentators on Isaiah 53 would have it. And then I began to study the life of Jesus of Nazareth. Surely nowhere else could I find such a perfect resemblance to the description of the predicted Messiah. Jesus was the Messiah; there wasn't a doubt in the world.

This was He of whom Moses in the law and all the prophets did speak. If this Jesus were not the Messiah, no other could ever claim to be He, for the prophecies relating to Him were long past due."

I finished. Without a word the men picked up their hats and walked out, submerged deep in thought.

Walking in Twos—Circumspection

One of the most interesting and perhaps most hazardous phases of our work was distribution of literature on the streets and in house-to-house visitation. Almost always we went in twos because we could accomplish more by taking both sides of the street at once, and we always kept our eyes on each other in case of physical attack, which very frequently occurred. Often, no sooner had we started out than I would glance across the street at my companion and find him in trouble, or vice-versa. Of course, I would rush to his rescue immediately, or he would come to mine. Often the commotion thus created necessitated a call to the police. By the time they arrived on the scene we usually had already been beaten up and knocked about.

We employed all kinds of tactics to get our message across. Sometimes we would hand a man a tract and walk on. Soon he would be pursuing us, shouting threats and curses. This, of course, brought others together, which afforded us an opportunity to hold improvised open-air meetings. Or again, we would drop a tract on the street, move to the corner, and watch to see what became of it. On one occasion, for instance, we saw a pious Jew with a long beard pick it up and immediately begin reading it. After scanning it for a few moments he looked around to see if he was observed. Then hiding the tract in his bosom pocket, he went on his way, probably to read it again unobserved at home or to discuss it at the synagogue.

Whenever I came across one who gave evidence of interest I would offer him a New Testament. Oftentimes when we returned to a home where we had left a New Testament, we would find it lying in the same position as we last saw it with a thick layer of dust as its covering. More often, it became one of the children's favorite playthings, if it was not first destroyed. To avoid this, I decided to ask a minimum charge for it. For example, I would walk into a store, hold up a nicely bound copy of the New Testament and ask the man to guess its worth. Sometimes he said fifty cents, seventy-five, or even as much as one dollar.

"Now look here," I would say, "you may have it for ten cents."

That was a bargain, and nearly always my listener took advantage of it. Of course, many wanted to know what the book contained and that afforded me an opportunity to read a portion of it. People are more likely to esteem things which cost them some money than those they obtain free of charge.

Manhandled by Gangsters

Some of our experiences were quite rough. On one occasion in a gospel auto* during an open-air meeting in the west side of the city known as "Gangster Land," I had just opened the meeting when I was roughly seized and pulled from the auto by an angry mob. I was singled out because I was the only Jewish man in a group of Gentile Christians. In the chaos which followed, raucous, hoarse cries pierced the air: "Let's kill this apostate, this renegade. Let's do away with this Christ worshipper."

They beat on me with their fists, sticks, and stones—and anything else on which they could lay their hands. There I

*an open touring car

lay, helpless victim of their cruelty. Were it not for the police patrol, summoned by one of my helpers, arriving just in the nick of time, I would not have survived that encounter.

We Were a "Stiff-necked" People

But if such treatment was accorded us with the intention of scaring us away, it accomplished quite the contrary, for we were all the more determined not to let Satan defeat us. The following week saw us back in the same part of the city. No sooner did we open the meeting with a favorite hymn ("We're Marching to Zion"), than one after another of the passersby stopped. From all appearances we were going to have a great meeting. But suddenly a man angrily protested against our being there and ordered us to leave. His indignation infected and incited the others, who then began to shower us with decayed vegetables, rotten eggs, and other more substantial missiles. We were forced to retreat amidst warning shouts of, "If you value your life, don't come back here!"

Realizing as before that to give in to this boisterous crowd once would mean not only an end to all of our open-air meetings but the closing of the premises and the silencing of our testimony, we returned to that very same district the following week. As our auto approached the place, we noticed that a multitude of people had already gathered there. At first the idea occurred to us that another meeting was in progress, for that neighborhood was the gathering site for propagandists of the various "isms" in American Jewry—Zionism, Communism, and the like. We stopped the auto and began to sing, and to our surprise we saw the entire crowd coming our way. The crowd increased, and my heart began to beat faster and faster as it closed in upon us; there seemed no escape.

Taken in 1921, the year I was appointed a
pioneer Baptist Jewish missionary.

In June, 1922, I married Lillian Brown at the College Street Presbyterian
Church in Toronto, Canada. The ceremony was held during a Hebrew-
Christian conference in that city.

Here I am a proud young father; on the right my wife is seen with our daughter.

Here is my late uncle, Rabbi Samuel Gartenhaus, who was a rabbi in New York. He is shown here in a synagogue in Israel.

I had an opportunity to witness to a rabbi in Poland in 1925. I traveled by coach and horse and buggy, going from city to city.

Taken in Paris, France, when as a younger man I carried the message of Christ there.

I have crossed the ocean more than thirty times in my missionary ministry. Here I am on one of Holland's oldest Holland-American liners.

My wife and I surrounded by Japanese Christians.

On platform in Japan with (L. to R.) the Israeli Ambassador, his interpreter, Rabbi Solomon, myself, and Rev. Nakamura, my interpreter.

I spoke at meetings in Southampton, England, in 1960.

In my earlier years I held many street meetings both in this country and overseas. One such meeting was held in Sao Paulo, Brazil, in a Jewish district, November 17, 1963.

On the right is my only brother, Zev, who won me to Christ. Zev lived in Tel Aviv until his death at eighty-seven in 1979.

Here are my phylacteries, traditionally worn on the forehead and arm by Jewish men during morning prayers. They are small leather square boxes containing slips inscribed with scriptural passages.

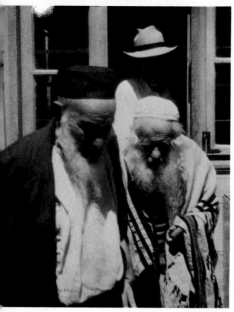

My father, Rabbi Moses Gartenhaus (center) emerges from the synagogue in Jerusalem. He was ninety years of age at the time and has since gone to be with the Lord.

In 1971 we dedicated our world headquarters building of IBJM (The International Board of Jewish Missions) in Chattanooga, Tennessee. Standing with me is my wife, Lillian.

Our IBJM staff photo taken in 1978. The world headquarters building is seen in the background.

Dr. Robert G. Lee (left) was the Advisory Board Chairman of IBJM from its beginning until his death at age ninety-one.

Dr. and Mrs. Lee Roberson with my wife and me at the Messianic Center on the occasion of my eighty-third birthday.

We trusted ourselves to Jesus' care and prayed that His mighty arm would save us from the designs of the enemy. In my usual way, I stood up to announce a hymn, keeping my eyes steadily upon the immense throng, among whom a great deal of whispering was going on. When the song was finished and the crucial moment had come, I said, "My dear brethren of Israel, hear what I have to say."

But this was as far as I got, for just then my eye caught a glimpse of what I think was the most ferocious-looking bulldog I have ever seen. I could hear my heart beating clear up in my throat. The dog was urged upon me and came dashing towards the auto, leaping up into it. But to my surprise he refused to open his mouth. Again and again his master's voice was heard, "Sic him, sic him," but he would not move. The mob began to wonder, asking the owner of the dog what ailed him, but he only shook his head, saying, "Don't ask me; I don't know. I have had this dog for some time, and he always obeyed me until now. I don't know what has happened today."

Mutterings of surprise ran through the crowd, for they were aware that something unusual had taken place. Soon they saw the police coming towards them, and greatly disappointed they began to disperse. A few remained to listen to the gospel message; others meekly accepted literature and went away. One youngster was heard to question an older man as they walked away: "Wasn't that a 'ness' [miracle]?"

I was reminded of the words of Daniel 6:23, and they deeply impressed themselves upon me: "Then was the king exceeding glad for him, and commanded that they should take Daniel up out of the den. So Daniel was taken up out of the den, and no manner of hurt was found upon him, because he believed in his God." Yes, the God of Daniel was still alive, and just as He had protected the prophet of old from the angry beasts, so He protected those of us who went forth to make His name known.

TRAITOR?

Letter to Editor

There were many such meetings which were obstructed by violent attacks upon our workers. Since there was danger that the threats and attempts to kill the "apostates," the "traitors," might end in disaster not only for the persons killed but for all Jewry (the Hebrew adage is that "All Israel is responsible for each other," and unfortunately the Gentile world usually condemns all Israel for the sins and crimes committed by some individual Jew or Jews), I brought this fact to the attention of the Jewish public in Chicago through a letter to the editor of the local Jewish press. I pleaded for tolerance of other people's ideas, even of those with which one does not agree.

The editor, who printed my letter in full, only half-heartedly reprimanded manifestations of intolerance in free America. At the same time he blamed us, asserting that "missionary preaching in Jewish neighborhoods is too provocative."

C H A P T E R 1 7

SOUTHERN BAPTIST THEOLOGICAL SEMINARY

As the time for my graduation from the Moody Bible Institute drew near, I was as yet undecided about my future vocation. Two avenues of approach were open to me: First, remain at the mission in Chicago; or, second, pursue my studies further in another school. After much prayer and thought, I decided upon the latter.

Some time previous in Chicago it had been my privilege to hear that great scholar, Dr. A. T. Robertson of the Southern Baptist Theological Seminary, who profoundly impressed me. This admiration led me to make plans to enter his school. Arrangements were soon made, and the fall of 1919 found me in the city of Louisville, Kentucky, ready to start my studies at the seminary.

After I settled into school, I went into the town "to seek my brethren." I had not been strolling long before I noticed a store and from its sign I could readily see that the proprietor was Jewish. In I went and as a preliminary introduction offered him one of my tracts. He took it, thanked me, and at once began to scrutinize it. I wondered what his reaction would be. After a few minutes of silent reading, he closed the tract, tore it into two pieces, and returned it to me. I tried to reason with him, but to no avail; after bidding him good-bye I walked out.

I was no more successful when I entered another Jewish

131

store and handed a tract to the storekeeper. No sooner did this man learn of my mission than he too tore the tract I gave him into tiny bits and threw it in my face. I met with the same results when I entered a third and a fourth store. I was becoming more and more discouraged and decided to turn back to the seminary. But as I drew near yet another store I noticed a man standing in the doorway. Not wishing to miss such an opportunity I began to slow my pace, and as I drew near to him opened my mouth to say something. He advised me to keep on walking. Evidently he had received some kind of warning from the others, not an unusual thing when a missionary appears in the community.

Loneliness

My first days in Louisville were days of loneliness and discouragement. My feelings were akin to those of Elijah (1 Kings 19:4) under the juniper tree. Were my efforts worthwhile? I mused. Would they accomplish anything? Surely my first experiences with my own brothers were not promising of success. After one of my discouraging attempts I walked slowly, with a heavy heart, back to my room.

The first thing I noticed when I opened the door was my Bible lying on the table. Like a drowning man clinging to a straw, I opened it, and my eyes rested upon these words: "There shall be showers of blessing." I read on and on until I came to that passage in Ezekiel 36:24–28, where the Lord says that He will gather His people Israel, take the stony heart from them, cleanse them from their evil ways, and give them a new heart, breathing His Spirit upon them. And then that remarkable chapter 37 of Ezekiel. It was like water to a fainting person. Immediately all my doubts and discouragements were dispelled; I revived. I felt that I possessed the courage to face lions, to go on in His blessed service in spite of the difficulties and impediments. Results? Of course there would be results. I had God's word for it. My duty was to give the gospel—the rest was up to the Lord. He is good to those who obey His voice, for later I was destined to witness some wonderful results from my ministry in Louisville.

What of my first defeats? Was not the Lord Himself rejected by His own people? His disciples, His apostles, too, were rejected, and yet they did not abandon their ministry, so why should I? Why not try and try again as long as He provided me with the strength to do so? I could only answer, "Thy will be done!"

Appeal to Students

I appealed to the students for volunteers to accompany me on visitation work and at open-air meetings, and some of them eagerly responded. Two or three times a week our faithful little band went out into different sections, pleading with the sons and daughters of Abraham to acknowledge their true Messiah. Needless to say, we met much opposition. Every possible device was used to frustrate us, but we were not deterred, for we were more than repaid for our efforts by the new seekers after truth who requested personal interviews. It was this that increased the interest and zeal of the students.

Encounter with President of Synagogue

One day in the company of another student I started out to do some visiting, carrying with me my large brief case filled with Bibles, Testaments, Gospels, and tracts. As we entered one of the stores we found the merchant in unusually good spirits, and he seemed anxious to have a word with me. However, I noted that he was exceedingly wary as he led us to the rear of the store where he started our conversation. We had been talking for about fifteen minutes when the door at the front opened and in walked a man. Later I found out he was president of one of the synagogues.

The proprietor turned quickly to me and in a subdued and frightened voice said, "For goodness sake, don't tell this man who you are, or you'll get yourself into trouble." I sensed that he was more concerned for himself than for me. He feared that he would be severely reproved for having secret conversations with missionaries. I was introduced as Mr. Gartenhaus of Chicago. At that moment, the proprietor was called to the front of the store, leaving the three of us alone.

"What business firm are you representing?" the man asked me. Before I could answer he noticed in my open case a New Testament.

I told him I was a student at the school located at Fifth and Broadway and was deeply interested in making this Book known to my own people. It was to be deeply deplored, I continued, that such a book which had revolutionized the whole civilized world, which breathed the spirit of the prophets and had been translated into hundreds of languages, should be closed to our people. To my astonishment, the man requested a copy and offered to pay for it, adding that he would prefer that the proprietor of this store not know about the transaction.

Furthermore, he then invited me to his home for the next Sabbath meal. Of course I accepted, though I was very dubious and wondered what such hospitality might hold in store for me.

When I reached the seminary I related this incident to some of the students, and as a precautionary measure I

gave them the name and address of the man and instructed
them to come and call for me if I was not back by eleven
o'clock.

I was cordially welcomed when I came to my new friend's
home. He introduced me to the other members of the family, who had evidently been told who I was. So sociable and
pleasant were they that I began to wonder if the man was
setting a trap for me or if he was just trying to win me back
to Judaism. After a sumptuous meal, we removed to the
parlor where in the presence of the whole family I had the
privilege of relating my experience in Christ, how I was led
through my many questions to study the prophecies more
closely, and how at last I found in Jesus of Nazareth He of
whom the prophets spoke.

How they listened! It was evident from the pertinent
questions he asked that this man had already devoured
several pages of the New Testament which I had presented
to him.

I glanced at my watch. It was 10:30 P.M., and suddenly I
remembered my instructions to the students. I did not
want to wait until they called for me. Reluctantly I rose to
go, and reluctantly they let me go.

I met the man again on several occasions after this, and
always he had a hearty handshake and friendly greeting
for me. That he was deeply stirred I had no doubt, and I
have often liked to think that in his heart of hearts he has
acknowledged the true Messiah.

Eager Volunteers

Interest in Israel's salvation was growing among those
fine seminary students who volunteered to go with me regularly in this work. We met all kinds of people; there were
those who conversed with us for a length of time, asking
questions, agreeing with us in some things, disagreeing in

others. There were those who confessed that they were not in a position to discuss the subject because of their lack of knowledge. Appallingly, many of them barely knew the names of the major prophets, much less their teachings, and when we quoted from the Old Testament sometimes they would accuse us of having quoted from the "Christian Bible." What truth there is in Zechariah's lament: "My people perish for lack of knowledge."

Tackling the Rabbi

On many occasions when the subject of Christ was introduced, a Jew would say, "If what you believe is the only true faith, why don't our learned men believe it?" Then he would suggest that I visit the rabbi and talk with him about it. Why shouldn't I go to such a rabbi who exercised so great an influence over his people? Gathering up all my courage one day, I telephoned a leading rabbi in Louisville and expressed a desire to see him.

"Where are you?" he asked.

"At the Southern Baptist Seminary," was my reply.

He seemed rather puzzled that a man with a name like mine should be in a Baptist school and quickly informed me that he was quite busy. He was about to hang up when I told him that one of the professors wanted to know whether I had made his (the rabbi's) acquaintance.

It was known to all that this rabbi posed as a very liberal, broad-minded person, and to refuse this request of mine in which one of the city's religious leaders was involved would not have helped his reputation any. The rabbi changed his tone. "If you can come to my office right now, I shall be glad to see you, but I have another important appointment in a very little while."

Without a moment's hesitation I ran to my room, picked up my hat and some suitable literature, and in a few minutes was on my way to his residence. As soon as I opened the door and introduced myself, even before offering me a seat, the man asked, "Are you a Christian or a Jew?"

"Both," I replied.

"No," he said, shaking his head vigorously, "you are either one or the other."

Then he began enlarging on that nonsensical argument that the Jews are not a nation but a religion; therefore, if a Jew changes his religion he ceases to be a Jew.

My reply to this was that not only the Bible but most other Jewish authorities have considered the Jews a nation. "What about the thousands of Jews who do not adhere to the teachings of Judaism—what are they?" I asked. I knew that this rabbi, as many others, regarded them as Jews, particularly those who had risen to great prominence and distinction. Take, for example, Felix Mendelssohn or Benjamin Disraeli or Heinrich Heine: What Jew would not claim them as his own brothers according to race!

By now the man was greatly interested.

"What have you found in Christianity that Judaism did not offer you?" he asked.

"Christianity has given me a personal, living Messiah who is the fulfillment of all our hopes and aspirations. Through faith in Him I have found a peace which passeth all understanding, a peace made possible by the assurance of forgiveness of sin through His vicarious atonement. The prophecies contained in our Scriptures concerning the advent of a Messiah are minutely fulfilled in Jesus of Nazareth; if He is not the Messiah then there never will be one."

The rabbi referred to Christianity as a religion entirely separate from and in opposition to Judaism, which was God's final revelation, and then he said, "Cursed is the man who addeth thereto and taketh therefrom" (see Deuteronomy 12:32).

I reminded him that most of the rabbinic laws were

added to the teachings of Moses and many of the Mosaic laws were practically abolished or changed. Furthermore, God, through His prophet, prophesied a new Law which I quoted to him from memory:

> Behold, the days come, saith the Lord, that I will make a new covenant with the house of Israel, and with the house of Judah: Not according to the covenant that I made with their fathers in the day *that* I took them by the hand to bring them out of the land of Egypt; which my covenant they brake, although I was an husband unto them, saith the Lord: But this *shall be* the covenant that I will make with the house of Israel; After those days, saith the Lord, I will put my law in their inward parts, and write it in their hearts; and will be their God, and they shall be my people. And they shall teach no more every man his neighbour, and every man his brother, saying, Know the Lord: for they shall all know me, from the least of them unto the greatest of them, saith the Lord: for I will forgive their iniquity, and I will remember their sin no more (Jer. 31:31–34).

"But," the rabbi put in, "that is not in our Bible." Although I had heard this argument from many Jews previously, I was shocked to hear a rabbi manifesting such ignorance.

I asked for his copy of the Old Testament and requested him to look up the passage for himself. He was greatly surprised to find it, and in a rather defeated voice he said, "It is some time since I have read this passage, and it slipped my mind just now."

Then, perhaps in an effort not to let me get the best of him, he began to insist that this had no reference to Christianity. And so it was that instead of five minutes I spent two hours in his study. During that time I showed him that most of what is now called "Judaism" consists of additions to and subtractions from the laws of Moses. What became of his other "important appointment" I shall never know. I missed my dinner at the seminary, but such a visit was well worth many dinners. It raised my worth among Jews; a meshummad who can spend two hours with a famous rabbi in religious discussion must be a somebody!

An Understanding Rabbi

Having thus broken the ice, I planned a visit to another outstanding rabbi, a man well thought of and famous for his learning. This time I was accompanied by an elderly Hebrew Christian who was assisting me in a series of meetings. After certain maneuvers, we had been invited to the rabbi's home, and from the very first he showed us every courtesy. He was particularly anxious to know how we were won over to our belief and listened with intense interest as we related our Christian experiences. When we told the price we had to pay—persecution, ostracism, etc.—he said, "Yes, I am sure it must require almost superhuman courage to openly confess faith in Jesus of Nazareth." He went on to admire such courage and declared that he for one did not hold to the popular opinion among his people that Jews accept Christ solely for mercenary or other ulterior reasons.

Just before we left, he surprised us by saying, "If someone should ask you what your mission in the city is, a good text to give them is the story of Joseph who was sent by his father to seek his brethren."

First Mass Meeting

It was during my student days that simultaneous evangelistic meetings of the Long Run Association were held under the able leadership of Dr. W. W. Hamilton, in charge of evangelization for the Home Mission Board of the Southern Baptist Convention. When I met Dr. Hamilton I laid before him the burden of the salvation of the twenty thousand Jews in the city of Louisville who were far more neglected than if they had been on an island ten thousand miles away. This godly man saw the great need. Besides assuring me that he would urge the evangelists to remember the Jews in their efforts to win souls, he concurred with me in a plan for a mass meeting with churches of the city cooperating.

This was a pioneer undertaking, and many of the older citizens of Louisville were doubtful and offered little or no encouragement. "The Jews will not come," they declared, "and apart from this, Louisville is no place for a religious meeting, particularly on a Sunday afternoon."

My heart was set on this. I felt that the Lord would bless our efforts. I argued with the doubters: "How do you know that the Jews will not come, when such a meeting has never been held before? Moreover, suppose we are able to reach only a few; that is no reason for us not to go forward in this plan. We have an obligation to these people, and it is about time that we were doing something for them. As to results, well, we must leave that to God."

It was finally decided to have the meeting and no effort was spared in the preparation. The newspapers publicized the meeting; a large advertising placard was placed on a car which was driven through the heart of the city; and thousands of circulars were distributed. All this caused quite a stir among Jewish and Christian groups. Interest in the salvation of Israel rapidly grew. It was not limited to the faculty and student body at the seminary, but spread to the churches throughout the city and beyond. The Lord laid the burden for a special ministry among the Jews on many Christians.

As I look back upon it, I cannot help but marvel. Here was I, without any honorary degree, with a very limited knowledge of the language of my adopted country. Like Moses of old, who also hesitated to shoulder the burden that God was to put on him, I said to the Lord, "I *am* not eloquent, neither heretofore, nor since thou hast spoken unto thy servant: but I *am* slow of speech, and of a slow tongue" (Ex. 4:10). Yet, I undertook the task of accomplishing the impossible.

The meeting was held at the Municipal Auditorium, Sunday, October 30, 1921. More than fifty churches cooperated in the undertaking. The ushers told us that there were at least a thousand Jews present, including rabbis. Some estimated the number to be nearly two thousand.

That mass meeting was not only for winning the Jews to Christ, but also for reminding the Christians of their duty to share the gospel with their Jewish brothers. Many Christians there held the opinion that it is impossible to get a Jew to listen to the preaching of the gospel. What a surprise it was to them to see in the audience so many of their Jewish friends! Soon many of the pastors were urging me to plan similar meetings, which I did with great success.

The press, both secular and religious, had many favorable things to say about our meetings. I quote the following from a write-up which appeared in *The Western Recorder,* October 14, 1921, the Baptist publication of Kentucky:

SUNDAY AFTERNOON MASS MEETINGS

On Sunday afternoon at 2.30 o'clock, more than 4,000 people of our city gathered in the Municipal Auditorium and it was really a great sight and a grand meeting. Brother Gartenhaus was the first speaker of the occasion, who spoke more especially with reference to our duty as it is to the Jew, a very inspiring address, though short. He was followed by Evangelist Beddoe who spoke upon the subject: "Ku Klux Klan Kan't Kure." This address was a greatly powerful one and the gist of it was that the Ku Klux Klan, whatever its principles may be, nor any other clan or organization of human character, cannot cure the ills of the human race, that there is but one thing that can cure and that is the blood of Jesus Christ, the Son of God. This meeting was intended as a great get-together gathering and it was truly a great success.

TRAITOR?

Dr. W. O. Carver, professor of Southern Baptist Theological Seminary, had a full-page write-up about these meetings in *The Western Recorder,* April 16, 1925, under the title "Louisville Baptists and the Jews." It was the general opinion that such meetings ought to be held more often all over the country in order to bolster relations between Jews and Christians.

What Next?

During my last days at the seminary, just before graduation in 1921, my thoughts were occupied mainly with the dilemma, "What now?" I had prepared myself for a definite ministry among my people, but where?

Many well-known Jewish missions offered me attractive posts while little-known missions offered me hard work and little pay. There was the Chicago Hebrew Mission to which I had been so sincerely attached before attending the seminary and which I had represented while in school. There was the Cleveland Hebrew Mission; there were denominational as well as interdenominational missions which approached me. Many students and professors were anxious for me to remain in the South.

Drs. John R. Sampey and W. A. Carver, professors of the seminary who took a personal interest in the salvation of the Jewish people, recommended me to the Home Mission Board of the Southern Baptist Convention to work among the Jewish people under its auspices. My pastor, Dr. F. F. Gibson, also gave a recommendation.

One day I received a letter from the Home Mission Board calling me to be their first missionary among my people in the South. I fell to my knees in thanks to God for this answer to my prayer. The entire school rejoiced and praised God at the glad news; the students (future pastors) began then and there to extend invitations to me to speak in the churches they one day would lead.

SOUTHERN BAPTIST THEOLOGICAL SEMINARY

My life in Louisville was over. It had been full of growth in the grace of God, knowledge, and never-to-be-forgotten experiences.

CHAPTER 18

THE COST OF DISCIPLESHIP

"I am crucified with Christ . . ." (Gal. 2:20).

When I resolved to accept Jesus as my Redeemer, I was aware that I would have to take up my cross and follow Him, and I was ready for that. But I had no idea at the time how heavy that cross would be. I knew what the apostle Paul had to endure because of his discipleship: "Are they ministers of Christ? (I speak as a fool) I *am* more: in labours more abundant, in stripes above measure, in prisons more frequent, in deaths oft. Of the Jews five times received I forty *stripes* save one. Thrice was I beaten with rods, once was I stoned, thrice I suffered shipwreck, a night and a day I have been in the deep" (2 Cor. 11:23–25).

I endured similar trials with the exception of shipwreck. I also had to endure the great mental and spiritual torture of being ostracized and cursed by my own kin—rejected by those who were near and dear to me and not fully accepted by others. Worse than all attacks upon my body was the excruciating pain of being forsaken by nearly everyone. Such pain I felt quite frequently.

When I came to the United States I was cordially welcomed by my uncle and his family. My aunt was exceedingly fond of me, and their children adored me and even considered me a hero. Each did everything possible to please me, to ingratiate himself or herself to me.

The affection was not one-sided; it was mutual. I loved each of them wholeheartedly. I was introduced to their friends, particularly folks who had emigrated from the same country as we had ("Landsleit"). Among them I found young people who soon became my intimate companions, who took me out to see New York and enjoy the pleasures which that city could offer.

After several weeks of pleasurable idling, my uncle procured a job for me in a hat factory whose boss was a friend of his. The work was light and the pay good. The boss once told my uncle, "Your nephew, the 'greenhorn,' is a genius; I am afraid that he will shortly own my factory, and I'll have to work for him."

I spent my leisure time in the pursuit of youthful happiness, and I never lacked money for the best of those things which a happy-go-lucky young man in the big city usually desires. In short, I was living in a fool's paradise. Then, suddenly, I was expelled.

Paradise Lost

My uncle ordered me out of his house, threatening to have me arrested for trespassing if I ever returned or met any of his children anywhere. My friends were estranged; some avoided me as if I were afflicted with some contagious disease, and some became enemies. My boss fired me. I lost the taste for carnal delights. I was like a beautiful flowering plant uprotted from its natural habitat and cast upon a trash heap to wilt and die.

What was the cause of this sudden turn of events? I had become a Christian. "That One" whom I had ignored, hated, and despised called me unto Himself, and I could not resist. For some time I struggled—*struggled with all my might*—but I could not long withstand His love drawing me unto Himself.

TRAITOR?

During my indecision and time of struggle against the Lord, Satan was cajoling and dangling before my mind's eye the glitter and joys of New York which would be mine if I would go his way. The adversary would not leave me in peace. Whether I was lying on my bed or walking gloomily through the streets of New York, Satan would tempt me repeatedly: "Why do you embitter your life to no purpose? Why renounce the joys of this world and retreat into a dismal, cheerless world to come which may never come? If you want to mortify yourself, why should you cause unnecessary heartache and anguish to your loved ones? Think of the unjust grief you cause your uncle, aunt, and their lovely children who have done so much for you.

"Think of what will happen to your parents abroad when they learn of your apostasy. It will kill them. You know that patricide and matricide are the greatest, unpardonable sins. Perhaps your father will resign himself to the will of God. He will consider you dead; he will sit 'shiv'vah' [observe seven days of mourning, in conformity with the law for mourning the death of a near relative] and will try to forget you. But your mother: Think of her. She will not forget; she will pine away in sorrow; she will die a slow tortured death, as do Jewish mothers when one of their children becomes a goy. Remember your lovely sister abroad—how you loved her and how she adored and honored you. She will probably not understand the full significance of your action, but she will see the grief and sorrow which you have caused, and she will curse you. Everybody in that little town where your folks live will curse your mother because she gave birth to a traitor, a renegade. Think of the shame you will bring on her!

"And all this woe, all this agony and distress, you bring about because of your foolish notions of a 'hereafter,' a belief in unbelievable doctrines, fit for old women, not for a young man in the prime of life!"

Such were the tempting words which Satan whispered

into my ears. And he always concluded: "Come with me
and I'll return to you all that you have lost—love, respect,
pleasure. Moreover, I'll add to that more and more of life's
bounties." He even quoted some Scripture to substantiate
his exhortations, as "Rejoice, O young man, in thy youth;
and let thy heart cheer thee in the days of thy youth, and
walk in the ways of thine heart, and in the sight of thine
eyes" (Eccl. 11:9). He was careful to omit the last part of
that verse, "But know thou, that for all these *things* God will
bring thee into judgment."

Force of Temptation

More than once I was almost persuaded. More than once
I felt like crying out: "Take me; lead the way." But always
in such crucial moments I suddenly felt the gentle touch of
Jesus: "No, Jacob, you are Mine; I have bought you with
My blood. I will not let you leave Me. Instead of fleeting
pleasure, I have provided for you everlasting life in bliss.
Yes, you will have to carry the cross for a while; yes, you
will lose your parents and your other relatives and friends.
You will endure severe trials and tribulations for My sake.
Have not I given My life for your sake? I will give you
strength enough to withstand all affliction, and finally to
emerge victorious and triumphant."

One day, when I was sorely tempted by Satan I again
heard the voice of Jesus speak, now even more decisively:
"You are Mine, Jacob." I looked up and with my mind's eye
I saw Him in all His glory. I cried out, "Holy, holy, holy."
Then and there I firmly resolved to follow Him—at any
cost—to the end of my earthly life.

The trials came in quick succession, but in course of time
their sting dulled and by the grace of God they became
bearable, although I was never entirely free of them. There
is still a thorn in my flesh (2 Cor. 12:7), as Paul complained.

TRAITOR?

I still feel the pinch in my heart—my heart of flesh—
because I am ostracized by my people, who heap indignities
on me because they consider me an enemy and a traitor.
Only by the infinite grace of God have I been able to survive.

Surprise Visit From
My Uncle and Aunt

While a student at Southern Baptist Seminary in Louisville, I often received invitations from churches to come
and share my Christian experience. Most of the people had
never seen a converted Jew, and nearly every Lord's Day I
was out speaking in the church of some student pastor.
One Monday morning when I returned to the seminary
after such a visit, I glanced at the bulletin board to see
whether there was a message for me. My eyes fell upon a
little note addressed: "Mr. Gartenhaus, your uncle and
aunt came to see you. They are at the Seelbach Hotel and
want you to call them immediately."

I was dumbfounded. It seemed unbelievable! Was it possible that my uncle, who had told me never to darken his
door again, had followed me here? How did he know
where I was? Obviously he had engaged a private detective
to trace my whereabouts. Of course, I could readily see the
purpose in this visit—a renewed effort to bring me to my
senses. Silently, engrossed in thought, I began to mount
the steps to my room when I encountered one of the students, who told me of my uncle's and aunt's visit; he had
been the one whom they met when they first entered the
seminary. They asked him where they could find me, and
he told them that I would soon return from a preaching
engagement. Astonished, my uncle asked him what he
meant by "preaching engagement." He replied that I was
in great demand by churches to come and preach on Sun-

days. They seemed horrified, he said, and when he added reassuringly that I would make a good Baptist missionary, my aunt seemed to be near fainting. Suddenly she regained her composure and said to my uncle, "Let's go; it's no use!"

Uncle seemed very embarrassed. He had told the student the name of the hotel where they were staying and that he wanted to see me as soon as I returned.

I was very reluctant to meet them, for I knew what was in store for me. But after prayer for fortitude and courage, I set out for their hotel. We greeted one another as near relatives usually do, and it was not long before they got to the point. They pleaded with me to leave the "monastery" (that is what they called the seminary).

"Had you listened to me a few years ago and not gotten such crazy ideas into your head, you would have been worth at least $100,000 today," my uncle said. "I would have done for you no less than I have done for my son-in-law."

"What have you now?" interjected my aunt. "Why, you haven't even a decent suit and no doubt those shoes you have on are the only shoes you possess."

"But," I protested, "I have something infinitely more precious than many other people have—even more than well-to-do people."

"Oh, why have you turned your back on us and disgraced us?" said my aunt, tears flowing down her cheeks.

Her anguished words touched my heart deeply. I knew that she loved me and had been good to me.

"I have not turned my back on you, nor on anybody else, and especially not on my Jewish people. On the contrary, you and the others have turned your backs on me, expelling me from your midst, and all because of what I now believe and my desire to help you, to help my people, whom I love now more than ever before," I replied.

"But you are not going to change the world," said my uncle. "If you really love us, come back with us. I don't care

149

what you believe, but don't go about making a fool and a nuisance out of yourself by boasting of your strange beliefs and advising everybody to believe like you. It just doesn't work, and people do not like it."

"Yes," interrupted my aunt, "throw away your foolish, crazy notions. Pack up your rags, or better, leave them and come with us right away."

Our conversation was interrupted by the entrance of a prominent Jewish merchant—a friend of my uncle. Evidently, his visit had been prearranged, for he, too, began to appeal to me to heed the advice of my uncle who was older and wiser than I and known as a sagacious and successful businessman. I remained silent, knowing that no arguments on my part would help.

"How terrible it would be," said my uncle, when he saw how determined I was, "if your mother knew you were a 'galech' [priest], a meshummad."

They argued on, but much to their grief, they could not prevail upon me to give up my faith.

As I was about to leave them my aunt's parting words were: "It is too bad that we did not poison you when you were in our home, for I would rather see you dead than as you are now."

"Well said, " added my uncle.

The next day they returned to the seminary. This time my uncle demanded to see the head of the "monastery," to negotiate with him about getting me free. He was willing to pay any ransom. He was told that no one was kept there by force, that any student might leave the institution at any time, and I, too, could leave at once if that was my wish.

When they saw that it all depended upon me, they appealed to some of the students to use their influence in urging me to leave the school. Then, turning to me in a desperate last attempt, my uncle said, "Here, I have brought with me $10,000 for you to make a new start in life, and I am ready to spend $100,000 to set you up in business—only do, please, come with us," he pleaded.

"Dear Uncle," I replied, sobbing, "your generosity makes me want to do anything for you except what you ask of me now. Not even a thousand times that amount could separate me from my Messiah. In short, I cannot leave the school."

I shall never forget the looks of frustration and bitterness on their faces. Turning to her husband, my aunt said, "Let's go; he's dead to us."

Before leaving, they threatened not only to write to my mother about my apostasy, but actually to bring her to see me. "You will have to listen to her," they finished angrily in one voice. They did not mention my father, because we had no knowledge of him. He had gone to Palestine before World War I with the intention of bringing the family over and settling there. But the war had separated him from us, and for many years family members in America had heard nothing of him, except rumors that he was dead. We had, however, corresponded with Mother, still living in Austria where she had survived the horrors of World War I.

Contact With Mother

In each of my letters home I had tried to break the news of my faith as gently and tactfully as I knew how. I pointed out the difference between Christians in America and those whom we had known in Europe: How Christians in America believed in our God, Jehovah, and did not worship images, as the Jews in Europe had always supposed, but on the contrary, were greatly opposed to idolatry, even to the adoration of icons as practiced by the Catholics. I wrote of the kindly feeling between Christians and Jews, how some of the rabbis would even meet with Christians in their houses of worship. Then I related how one day I had attended a meeting in one of their churches and had found to my utter surprise that the minister read from our Jewish Bible and the congregation sang from our psalms. But I had not told Mother that I was actually baptized and attending a Baptist seminary. I feared this might be too great a shock for her weakened body.

I did not take my uncle's threat seriously, for I knew that bringing Mother to America would entail much expense and red tape. But apart from this, I assumed Mother would never consent to cross the ocean. I recalled her attitude when I first disclosed my desire to go to America. "Not as long as I live will I let you go," she had said. Her superstition and fear of the ocean was the greater after the tragic sinking of the Lusitania, which at that time had shocked all of Europe.

Mother Arrives in America

The weeks went by. I heard nothing further from my uncle and was beginning to think that he had given me up as a hopeless case, when one morning I received a letter from him telling me to be sure and meet my mother and my only sister who would arrive in a few days. To this I paid little attention, as I presumed it was just a scheme to get me out of school. To my surprise, this was followed within a few days by a special delivery letter stating that they had arrived, and then another one the following day bearing my mother's signature. Then I knew what was ahead of me. How I dreaded that hurt look in her eyes when she learned that I was a Christian seminary student! How I shrank from the ordeal of facing her! But by going, I reasoned, I could make things clearer to her. It was a hard problem to solve. I was facing a tragedy; how could I avert it? My fellow students, realizing perhaps for the first time the struggles and heartaches of a Christian Jew, were very sympathetic during those trying days and met regularly for prayer on my behalf. I took my burden to some of the professors, and while some of them were apprehensive as to the outcome, others seemed to think it was best for me to go and face the issue, which advice I decided to take. A member of the First Christian Church gave me $100 to help with my expenses.

Mother and my young sister had been left alone in Austria (when my father went to Palestine). They lived in a town which was very isolated and during World War I, I had received only a few short letters from my Mother. I learned that our home, along with many others, had been destroyed and that most of the people, particularly the Jews, had to flee to escape being caught in the cross-fire. Each letter I received from Mother came from a different place. She told of severe suffering, of wandering from place to place, mostly on foot. They seldom had enough to eat and seldom any shelter. Often the night was spent on the snow in some forest. Whenever she wrote down a return address I sent her money, but she never acknowledged receipt of it. It probably never reached her, nor did she receive my letters. Towns were captured and recaptured and often totally destroyed. I suppose there was no one to care for private mail. Many letters, especially from America, were probably opened by someone looking for American money and then destroyed.

After the war was over, she must have written me several letters at my uncle's address (she knew no other address), and he in his anger did not forward them to me. I do not know what he had written to Mother about me, but I assume that he hinted to her what had happened to me, impressing upon her that if she did not want her son to be a "shmadnik" (an apostate), she had better come to America.

Later when he saw that his efforts (and promises) had no

effect on me, he finally succeeded in prevailing upon Mother to come. My uncle wielded considerable influence in government circles and had no difficulty in bringing Mother over; thus his threat became a reality.

Soon after her and my sister's arrival, I received a letter full of endearing words from her, begging me to meet her at my uncle's home at once. She wrote that for several years she had been praying that God would permit her to see me once more before she died; and now that the merciful God seemed about to answer her prayers, she wanted to see me face to face as soon as possible. The letter from Mother was followed by a telegram and then a long distance call, pleading with me to have pity on her and come without delay.

I boarded the train to New York. I was happy in anticipation of seeing my mother and sister, but I was fully aware of what was awaiting me. If I refused to give up my faith and returned to the seminary, I knew it would break her heart. That night on the train was a night of horror. I only dozed occasionally, waking up in a cold sweat. During a short nap I dreamed that I was struggling with my mother. This ended in my mother's fainting while relatives looked on in consternation, shouting, "You have murdered her! Mother-killer!" The words rang in my ears as I awoke.

Dreams sometimes foretell coming events, I reflected. Would it not be better, I asked myself repeatedly, to get off the train at the next stop and go back to the seminary? By so doing, I would avoid being a mother-killer. But I decided to go on. I knew if I did not go to see Mother, she would come to see me, and that would only aggravate matters.

All the way to New York I was oblivious to everything around me—the passengers on the train, the landscape outside. I was as dead to the world as a living person could be. During those twenty hours, I did not eat a thing. Satan whispered in my ear, "Why cause all this suffering to your mother, sister, relatives, and yourself? Why not confess to your mother that you have been misled and that you are now ready to recant?"

Silently I implored, "Help me, dear Lord. Don't let me give in to Satan. Give me strength lest I succumb." And then I heard His voice: "Of course I will help you. You will emerge from this ordeal stronger in your faith than ever before. This bitter cup from which you will have to drink, I have tasted."

I arrived in New York thoroughly exhausted, mentally and physically. My uncle met me at the station, his face beaming with joy as if nothing had ever happened between us. "How good to see you again," he said. "You don't look well. Your face is so pale and haggard."

Little did he realize what I had been through during the last few days. I thanked him for his concern and assured him that I was quite well, that the long trip had worn me out.

Then he reverted to his enthusiastic chatter: "Your mother and Eva [my sister] will be so happy to see you— why, Eva has grown into a pretty young lady. You'll make a fine family together, at least until each of you marries. I have a nice girl for you, and Eva will surely find a fine husband before long. . . ."

He stopped talking when we reached his house. At the honking of the horn, all came out to the front porch to welcome me. Mother embraced me, kissing me repeatedly. I returned her kisses, thinking I was the happiest man in the world to have such a mother with such a love. While we were still in embrace, Satan, the Destroyer, whispered: "Aren't your kisses Judas' kisses? Aren't you about to kill her by refusing to abandon your Jesus?"

After a few moments (which seemed to me like an eternity of bliss), she released me from her embrace and gave me a chance to embrace my sister. She clung to me, and between kisses she shouted again and again, "Now I won't let you leave us."

TRAITOR?

After we had calmed down and dried our tears—tears of joy—refreshments were served and the usual questions exchanged. I asked Mother about relatives, neighbors, and friends at home. She was primarily concerned about my health, asking whether I was not working too hard.

Nothing concerning my conversion was said during that first day. The next morning, however, I was asked by my aunt whether I expected to return to the "monastery," but I avoided a direct reply. Uncle again suggested that he would set me up in some good business. Soon several visitors came, among them prominent Jewish leaders. Uncle did not hesitate to tell them of the calamity that had befallen the family, and soon I was bombarded with questions as to why I had to disgrace my race. Again I defended my loyalty by declaring that it was because of the deep yearning in my heart for my people that I was willing to undergo this mental agony.

"If you really want to help your people," one of the visitors said, "there are so many really worthwhile ways."

"Yes," said my uncle, "even if he wants to be a rabbi I shall bear all the expenses." And then in a gentle, pleading voice, "Please, Jacob, don't leave us; don't forsake the faith of our saintly ancestors. It will kill your mother."

And then Mother, who in the meantime had found out what had happened to me and now understood the full significance of what my uncle had written in his letters to her, began to plead in her quiet, sweet way that I, for her sake, abandon these foolish ideas and return to my senses. As I look back now, I marvel at my fortitude at that time and wonder why I did not break down under the terrific strain of Mother's earnest pleas.

The next day the battle continued.

"How can you believe in this 'hanged one' who came to destroy not only our holy faith but in whose name oceans of Jewish blood have been shed?" I was asked by one of the visitors, a well-known rabbi.

156

I responded by stating that He did not come to destroy but to fulfill, quoting, "Think not that I am come to destroy the law, or the prophets: I am not come to destroy, but to fulfil" (Matt. 5:17). One was no less a Jew for believing in Him, I argued, but on the contrary was a more perfect Jew.

"Why not believe in the God of our fathers?" they suggested.

"I do believe in Him," I answered.

"And at the same time you believe in this Jesus of Nazareth?"

"Yes, I believe He is a Mediator between God and us. When our sins separated us from the holy and righteous God, Jesus reunited us." I went on to remind them that in all of the Jewish prayers (and in their confession) they approached God in the name of the forefathers Abraham, Isaac, and Jacob, asking God to hear their prayers because of the merits of these saints.

"He—'that man'—may have performed some miracles, but don't you know how this Christian God obtained His power?" my uncle asked, reminding me of that widely circulated tale of how Jesus stole from the Holy of Holies the ineffable name of Jehovah, placing it within an incision He had made in His leg, and thereafter He was able to perform wonders. (This was the explanation of the rabbis regarding the miracles wrought by Jesus.)

"But I cannot believe such nonsense," I said. "Any intelligent person will laugh at such nursery tales."*

In this way we continued until after midnight, my mother weeping incessantly. Her heartache and *her* mental agony must have been excruciating.

I lay awake the remainder of the night, many conflicting emotions surging through my mind. What would be the outcome of the whole painful dilemma?

*Modern Jewish scholars themselves, notably among them Joseph Klausner, have acknowledged the absurdity of this and other traditional tales which have until recently been accepted by the Jews.

TRAITOR?

My Decision

Before morning came, I had firmly resolved to go back to the seminary as soon as possible and to be a true disciple of my Master. I knew this was my testing time, and how I longed to prove myself worthy of His undying love for me!

I realized as perhaps never before the full import of the Master's words: "Think not that I am come to send peace on earth: I came not to send peace, but a sword. For I am come to set a man at variance against his father, and the daughter against her mother, and the daughter in law against her mother in law. . . . He that loveth father or mother more than me is not worthy of me: and he that loveth son or daughter more than me is not worthy of me. And he that taketh not his cross, and followeth after me, is not worthy of me. He that findeth his life shall lose it: and he that loseth his life for my sake shall find it" (Matt. 10:34–39).

During the following day, final appeals were made to me to come back to our people and to Judaism. How awful was my agony in facing my mother's tear-filled eyes. It was nearly impossible to turn her down—this one who had suffered many years in order to bring me up. Indeed, it was a superhuman battle to choose between Christ and my dear mother. But how could I give up my faith, my all in all? What did life hold for me without my Saviour? I could not let Him down. I firmly hoped that one day my mother would be reunited with me in Christ.

Turning to all my relatives and to the guests gathered about, I made known my intention to return to Louisville that night. The silence that followed was mortifying. They had tried so hard to win me but had failed. Mother, her tearful eyes downcast, silently left the room. I tried to say good-bye to her, but she would not see me. As I opened the door to leave, my uncle remarked to my young sister, "Say a last good-bye to your brother; you may not see him again—he is committing suicide."

I can see her now, with that look of shock and disdain, as she replied in a loud voice, "He is no longer my brother."

I walked from the house in a daze, never to return. It had been a dreadful ordeal. I paid little attention to where I was going and as I approached a railway station I found it was the wrong one. When finally I reached the other station it was well past midnight; I was told there would be no train out until morning. The remainder of that night I passed in painful reflection and spiritual vacillation. Satan whispered continuously: "You still have time to return to your beloved mother. All you have to do is tell her that you have decided to renounce Him."

Reluctantly do I relate these painful reminiscences; I do so only for the glory of God. Has He not said, "Whosoever will come after me, let him deny himself, and take up his cross, and follow me" (Mark 8:34)? I took up my cross to follow Him. From this experience I learned that even the wiles of Satan can not pull the true believer away from his Master, for surely if that were possible I would have renounced Him and made glad the heart of my dear mother and other loved ones. With Paul, I was able to say: "In all these things we are more than conquerors through him that loved us. For I am persuaded, that neither death, nor life, nor angels, nor principalities, nor powers, nor things present, nor things to come, nor height, nor depth, nor any other creature, shall be able to separate us from the love of God, which is in Christ Jesus our Lord" (Rom. 8:37–39). It was by His grace that I was able to bear this heavy burden of separation from Mother.

Welcome Back to the Seminary

Upon my return to Louisville, I learned that the students had been praying daily for me. A new feeling of fellowship and brotherliness for me seemed to have entered their hearts. Without the encouragement of these good men in the lonely days then ahead of me, I do not know how I could have survived. Many considered my return a direct answer to their prayers; some actually wondered whether I would come back—whether they had not looked upon my face for the last time.

Everyone was eager to know my experience, and arrangements were made for me to tell all at a special service in the student chapel. My story brought tears to the eyes of the listeners, and a great number have since told me that they have referred to my story time and time again from their pulpits as an example of adamant faithfulness.

From that time forth I had a large band of volunteer workers to go out with me for personal work among the Jews of Louisville and in open-air meetings. Many of the students who became prominent pastors and missionaries had their first experience in personal work and open-air meetings with me during that time.

When I had to make the choice between the one who gave me temporal life on earth, my mother, and the One who endowed me with eternal life, my Saviour, I chose my Saviour. This choice broke my mother's heart; but not only hers, it broke mine, too. True, I found peace and comfort in my Saviour; yet for many nights I lay awake in an agony of remorse, asking myself, "Have I done the right thing? Have I made the right choice?"

My heartbroken mother did not stay long in the United States. I had no direct knowledge of her. In a roundabout way, I learned that she and my sister had found out that father was alive and that things in Palestine were settled in peace, so they went to join him.

I wrote to them several times but my letters remained unanswered. About ten years later I made a trip to Palestine and was able to see them both briefly. It was another twenty years before I saw my father again. My relatives considered me dead, of course, and when Mother died it was several months before I found out—and then only incidentally. I mourned greatly, and I wondered whether I had not been the cause of her death. I like to believe that before she passed on she realized that I had found the right way and in her heart of hearts acknowledged Him as the true Messiah.

CHAPTER 19

SOUTHERN BAPTIST WORK AMONG THE JEWS

May, 1921, marked the beginning of Southern Baptist work among the Jews. It was an occasion for much thanksgiving and joy everywhere, especially for those who had evangelization of the Jews upon their hearts. One lady in Virginia told me that for twenty years she had been praying that the way might be opened for the gospel to be preached among Southern Jews.

At headquarters in Atlanta I was welcomed by the secretary of the Home Mission Board and immediately initiated in my future work, the exceedingly difficult and delicate task of making Christ known to the 800,000 Jewish people in the South. With this broad field before me, I knew I would have to rely much upon faith and prayer. There were moments when fear and doubt gripped my heart as I thought about being one lone missionary among so many people who had not heard the gospel before. This was indeed a pioneer task. But then I would think of His wonderful promise, "Go ye . . . and lo, I am with you always." With this assurance, I was determined to plunge unreservedly into the work, and to put my whole heart and soul into it.

From the very beginning, I realized that I would have to depend a great deal on the cooperation of Southern Baptists. If the seed of kindness and love had been sown, if a kindly and friendly feeling existed between Christian and Jew and tactful words had been spoken, then I knew that when I visited a city, contact with Jews would be much easier and my message would more readily be received. On the other hand, if the Jews were ignored until just before my coming to a city, they at once would be suspicious, and my contact with them would be more difficult. In such cases, Jews would accuse me of being their greatest enemy because: "You tell Christians that we are lost and that only Jesus can save us. We have lived here for many years and no one has interfered with us or our religion, but since you have come people have been telling us of that Jesus, and they now consider us heathen."

Then came the question of how best to reach the Jew. The old method of establishing missions was very expensive, for it would have meant opening more than one hundred centers in the larger cities. Apart from this, after many years of close study and observation, my strong conviction (also the judgment of leading missionaries long in the service) was that Jewish mission centers alone could never reach all the many Jews with the gospel; each church would have to realize its individual responsibility in evangelizing its Jewish neighbors.

The situation was practically the same as when Jethro said to Moses: "The thing that thou doest *is* not good. Thou wilt surely wear away, both thou, and this people that *is* with thee: for this thing *is* too heavy for thee; thou art not able to perform it thyself alone" (Ex. 18:17, 18). We read in Numbers 11:14–17 that God approved this advice given Moses. Ours was not the task of an individual; if it were left to one man, very little would be accomplished, and I would "surely wear away." If this work was to prove a success for the glory of God and the salvation of His people, the fullest cooperation was essential. Only the local churches could find the solution.

TRAITOR?

My Double Task

I thus had a double aim before me: winning the Jews to Christ and winning cooperation of Christians for this task. I had to show the Jews that Jesus is not foreign to them, that He is their own Messiah of whom Moses and the other prophets spoke. I had also to show my Christian friends that my ideas about the need and the methods of winning the Jews were not *my ideas* but those of the apostle Paul who, following the command and the example of his Master, had been going *to the Jew first* and directing the churches to disseminate the seeds of the gospel all around them. These methods employed by Paul (and the other apostles) were so successful that within a few years almost all the civilized world known at that time was Christianized.

Within a few strenuous weeks I prepared my booklet, *An Urgent Call on Behalf of the Jews in the South,* which was soon published and widely distributed by the Home Mission Board. Dr. B. D. Gray, corresponding secretary, in his introduction to the booklet says:

"Two difficulties stood in the way, the matter of expense and the securing of a reliable, capable worker for initiating the work.

"The Board has secured the services of Rev. Jacob Gartenhaus, who began work in May, 1921. Brother Gartenhaus is a graduate of Moody Bible Institute and the Southern Baptist Theological Seminary and comes to us with the strongest commendation of members of the seminary faculty and of others who know him.

"He is a young man of fine character and good culture, a sincere convert to Christianity, with an ardent zeal for the salvation of Israel, his kinsmen in the flesh.

"His work is under the direction of the Corresponding Secretary of the Board, and I commend him most heartily to our churches and pastors who may wish him to speak on his work.

SOUTHERN BAPTIST WORK AMONG THE JEWS

"I also commend most cordially the following tract by Brother Gartenhaus, which shows that he has given the matter on which he writes close study and that his soul is on fire for the salvation of the Jews."

I quote the following from that booklet:

AN URGENT CALL ON BEHALF OF THE JEWS IN THE SOUTH

Their Condition

There are about 800,000 Jews in the territory of the Southern Baptist Convention. Among them are a few who might be termed Orthodox in its correct meaning. The majority, who have become dissatisfied with traditional Judaism with its restrictions, are fast drifting into the ranks of the various cults, Christian Science, Ethical Culture, etc. In fact, they are a moving spirit in the various "isms." The Talmud, which has for centuries been the sole guide of Judaism, is losing its significance. Efforts which Jewish leaders are putting forward to save their people from drifting are failures, because the leaders have nothing to offer.

Christians often hear the Jews boasting of having given the Bible to the world. The truth is that this very Jewish book is neglected most in Jewish homes. Very few Jews possess this precious book. In fact, the average pupil of our Baptist Sunday School knows more about this book than many Jewish leaders. "My people are destroyed for lack of knowledge" (Hos. 4:6).

Their Need

The Bible is a sealed book to Israel (Isa. 29:11, 12). The Orthodox Jew who still believes the Bible as the Word of God thinks it too holy to be handled and read by common people. Only the Five Books of Moses have been studied throughout the ages. Besides, the rabbis have been warning the Jews over and over that this book may mislead them (mislead them to believe in Jesus). Many a Jew who studies it, they argue, has lost his faith.

The unbelieving Jew thinks of this book as a product of the infancy of mankind, when thoughts were beclouded, when myths were in vogue, a book that now is not worth a moment of serious attention. Many educated Jews, who read all kinds of books, know next to nothing of the New Testament. The little they do know comes to them by hearsay in a very distorted and blasphemous manner.

Most Jews dread the New Testament as a mysterious magical power which is able to change entirely their habits and conceptions. (And this is what it really does.)

Jews still think of Christians as idolatrous worshippers of images of saints and crosses. They think that in order to become Christian they must give up the God of Abraham, Isaac, and Jacob and become heathens. Many a Jew who has heard something of the true gospel or of the belief of Christians has cried out, "Oh, it's the first time I ever heard that," and their attitudes at once have changed.

Like every other nationality, the Jews need the transforming power of God unto salvation. This can only be experienced through faith in the gospel of Christ (Rom. 1:16). "How shall they believe in him of whom they have not heard [except in a blasphemous and false way]? And how shall they hear without a preacher?" Who will take to them " . . . the gospel of peace, and bring glad tidings of good things" (Rom. 10:14,15)?

The thing most needed is that we provide a New Testament for the Jew and persuade him to read it, letting the Word of God take care of itself. There is hardly a Jew, who, when he has read two or three chapters in the New Testament, did not try to read the whole book; and hardly a Jew who has read it but loves it and asks for tracts and other information which will help him to understand the book better.

The Present Opportunity

The Jew has tried everything and been disappointed. Many are now willing to try Christianity. Surely the time has come when many faithful workers are needed among these people. Thank God that Southern Baptists have realized the need and have undertaken the work to give the gospel to "the lost sheep of the house of Israel."

Preaching the gospel to the Jews is not a failure, as many a Gentile would say. Whenever an honest effort has been made to win the Jews to Christ, the results have been marvelous. Statistics show that the Jews have a larger percentage of converts than any other nation. The following statistics are taken from a tract by Rev. S. B. Rohold, F.R.G.S., an authority on Jewish missions:

> *Do you know* that during the nineteenth century, as a result of the Protestant agencies at work, 72,740 Jews were baptized in connection with the various Reformed churches?
>
> These Hebrews, with their children, number 120,000 souls added from Jewry to the ranks of Evangelical Christendom.
>
> In the same period 57,300 Jews were received into the Roman Communion and 74,500 into that of the Greek Church.
>
> The total of baptisms among Israelites during the past century amounts to 204,540.
>
> There is one Protestant Hebrew convert to every 156 of the Jewish population.
>
> The proportion from all other non-Christian religions together is one to every 525.
>
> If the ingathering from the heathen and Moslem world had been in the same ratio as that from among the children of Abraham, there would be a total of seven million converts from the non-Christian Gentile world, instead of the actual two million for the nineteenth century.
>
> The Protestant Hebrew converts who enter the Christian ministry are three times more numerous than those from the ranks of converts from all other non-Christian faiths.
>
> At least 750 Protestant Jewish converts are daily engaged in preaching the Gospel of Christ Jesus as their one business in life.

Jewish papers are almost daily publishing dispatches from various countries lamenting that in this or that place thousands of Jews are being converted. In some places Christianity breaks out like an epidemic. For example, one Jewish paper announced that in the first six months of 1920 no less than ten thousand Jews were converted in Budapest alone.

TRAITOR?

A Plea to Every Christian

"Brethren, my heart's desire and prayer to God for Israel is, that they might be saved. For I bear them record that they have a zeal of God, but not according to knowledge" (Rom. 10:1, 2).

You are sending your own children as missionaries to the foreign fields. You are sending your money, but what are you doing for your neighbors, God's Israel, and for the people who are "beloved for the fathers' sakes"? Have you entirely forgotten the Lord's command to begin at Jerusalem? Have you forgotten the words of Christ when He said, "Salvation is of the Jews (John 4:22)?"

Do you still believe with Paul that the gospel is "the power of God unto salvation to every one that believeth; *to the Jew first,* and also to the Greek" (italics mine)? If you do so believe, why not give the gospel to them? The apostle says that you are their debtors (Rom. 15:27). For the Bible, both Old and New Testaments, the prophets, the apostles, and even Christ Himself, we are indebted to the Jews.

While at the Southern Baptist Theological Seminary I heard Dr. Carver, in one of his mission classes, illustrate the disastrous results of neglecting certain mission fields by pointing to Arabia, which has been neglected for trivial reasons. This Arabia gave birth to Islam, which not only threatened Christian civilization in medieval Europe but is now the greatest and most powerful enemy with which Christianity has to reckon. If Arabia could produce a Mohammed who has now 300 million followers, Judah may, if God permits, pose a still greater danger. Don't weigh souls and say this field pays and that field does not.

The failure to present the gospel to the Jews has already resulted in an undermining of the faith and morale of many a home. These Jews live in our midst, and our safety demands that we present them with the saving message of the gospel. By saving the Jews, you save yourself, for in

168

their unbelief your very religion is being threatened with destruction. Let us give them the gospel. "I will bless them that bless thee" is God's promise to Abraham (Gen. 12:3).

Christians, if you want a blessing on your soul, a revival in your church, and God's protection on your community, do something for the Jew. God's promise will be fulfilled. As a little group of Jewish disciples shook the world in the first century, so the Jews will bring untold blessings to the world in the near future. There are many Pauls, Peters, and Johns to be found among the Jews. Let us go and seek them out (Zech. 8:20–23).

CHAPTER 20

GOOD-WILL MEETINGS

When the Lord called me as His good-will ambassador to my people, I was fully aware of the gigantic, even superhuman, task that faced me. But I replied, "Here am I; send me, and make me worthy of Thy trust." Now, after over half a century of service, I can truly say that He has never failed me and that He has always been with me. Praise His name!

For His own reasons, He directed my path to the southern states, which at that time were a virgin field in mission work, boasting a Jewish population of 800,000. These Jews knew nothing about Christ except some perverted tales, and it was to these complacent, self-righteous people that I, an insignificant servant, was to bring the glad tidings. Prejudices against the gospel had been ingrained into their hearts by their forefathers, although they themselves knew nothing of the content of the New Testament.

Often I heard the voice of Satan whisper in my ear, "Don't attempt the impossible." He made me feel like Don Quixote fighting windmills. By God's grace I did not yield to his temptation to give up but went on with plans and preparations for the sacred task before me.

Right from the start I felt that my methods for disseminating the gospel among my brethren in the South would have to be different from those in use elsewhere. In the South, Christians looked askance on missions to the Jews, while the Jews themselves regarded such missions with disgust and resentment. I thought of Moses, who at first, without any helper, taught the Torah and personally settled all questions relating to the law. He ministered in the Old Dispensation to an unwilling, rebellious people. Upon Jethro's advice, he appointed a number of assistants (Ex. 18:24, 25).

I thought, too, of Paul who preached in the New Dispensation, also a lone knight for truth. Paul, of course, had the advantage of access to the synagogue, since the Jews in the Diaspora were always eager to hear some message from an itinerant teacher, particularly one from the Holy Land. He was not always successful, but many thousands throughout the Diaspora did believe, and they in turn became missionaries to others, even to the Gentiles. Thus, within a short time, the good news spread throughout the civilized world.

Church Instead of Synagogue

Then I thought that if the synagogue could no longer serve as a platform, why not use the churches? Let the Jews come there.

It was a revolutionary thought. Many of the churches were neither ready nor willing to implement this innovation. Would it be proper to antagonize Jewish neighbors, reasoned some pastors and leading church members, since they were living, at least overtly, at peace? Too, there was a serious question as to whether the Jews would dare enter a church; from time immemorial they had considered it an abode of abomination, a house of idolatry, a place to abhor and shun! Yet, this had to be done, for otherwise there was not the slightest possibility that I, a one-man army, could conquer the long-standing prejudice and hatred imbedded in the hearts of both Jews and Gentiles.

TRAITOR?

The city-wide meetings which I conducted in the Southern cities with large Jewish communities were widely publicized both among Christians and Jews. Thousands of circulars were printed and distributed; thousands of letters were sent out to pastors, presidents of missionary societies, and Sunday school superintendents. Personal letters of invitation were sent to the Jewish population, urging them to attend the services. The secular press also gave wide publicity to these meetings.

The following is typical of the letters sent out:

February 19, 1930

Dear Christian Worker:

As the present-day custodians of the gospel of Jesus Christ, are we (Christians) under any responsibility to the Jews? The Great Commission, "Go ye into all the world, and preach the gospel to every creature," is all-inclusive; therefore, the inclusion of the Jew in our Lord's command is beyond question.

Then how can we excuse our nearly total neglect of the Jew?

In light of the above command, definite arrangements have been made for city-wide meetings to be held at the Euclid Baptist Church, March 9-14, inclusive. These meetings are under the auspices of the Home Mission Board in cooperation with the State and St. Louis Baptist Mission Boards.

The purpose is two-fold: first, to enlist the prayers and cooperation of all loyal Baptists in the salvation of the lost sheep of the house of Israel, and second, to reach the Jewish people with the gospel message.

Two preparatory meetings will be held daily, one from 7:00 to 8:00 P.M. for Christian workers, teaching them the best methods of winning the Jewish people. All Christians should avail themselves of this opportunity. These meetings will be opened for informal discussion in which all may participate. The 8:00 o'clock service is for the general public. Sunday, March 9th, at 3:00 P.M., there will be a Mass Meeting.

Jewish Christian speakers of national prominence will de-

172

liver addresses, and one of the greatest violinists in America will assist with his music.

Please remember, this is your meeting and much depends upon your cooperation in making it a success. Your mere presence will preach Christ. Come! Invite your Jewish friends and neighbors to come or bring them with you! Pray for these meetings.

Yours in His service,
Jacob Gartenhaus

We titled a typical schedule for the meetings of Christian workers a "Christian Workers' Approach to the Jews," for a meeting at the Walnut Street Baptist Church, Louisville, Kentucky:

LEADERS: Rabbi George Benedict, Rev. Jacob Gartenhaus

MONDAY—OUR JEWISH NEIGHBORS. 1. Our three names: Hebrews, Jews, Israelites. 2. Our three sects: Orthodox, Conservative, Reform. 3. Our three divisions: the religious, the racial, the atheistic Jew.

TUESDAY—JEWISH AND CHRISTIAN RELATION-SHIPS. Three questions: 1. Do you meet Jews often? 2. What do you know of them? 3. What do you think of them? Also, Jewish influence; changes in Jewish life; Jews in Christian Science and other cults; sharing Christ.

WEDNESDAY—JEWISH CUSTOMS AND CERE-MONIES. The Torah, or Law. The unity of God. Sabbaths, festivals, and fasts. Jewish separatism.

THURSDAY—THE JEWS AND THE CHURCH. Prayer; principles of faith; the Scriptures; the Jewish adult in church and Bible class; the Jewish child in Sunday School.

FRIDAY—OVERCOMING JEWISH PREJUDICE. Our slogan and our aim; the good in Judaism; Jesus Christ the Gift.

Subjects Discussed

Some of the subjects discussed at our city-wide meetings included: Prophetic teaching concerning the Messiah; Old

TRAITOR?

Testament problems solved by the New Testament; Judaism and Christianity; the faith of the Christian Jew unfolded; the Zionist movement in the light of prophecy; the basis of an understanding between Jews and Christians; can a Jew who believes in the Messiah remain a Jew?; the stirring of dry bones; and whether God has cast away His people Israel?

Letters to the Jews

Prior to the meetings, a letter was sent to the Jews, such as:

> My dear Jewish Friend:
> Arrangements have been completed for a special series of meetings at Euclid Baptist Church, March 9-14, inclusive. Some eminent speakers of national and international reputation will be on the program with me. These possess many qualifications, among them being great love and concern for our people.
> The Christians sponsoring these meetings realize that the spiritual blessings which have enriched their lives have come to them through the Chosen People and feel they owe a debt of gratitude which can never be repaid. Our purpose in coming to your city is in the hope of bringing about a better understanding and appreciation between Jews and Christians.
> This is a personal invitation from me and my associates. We hope you will accept and come hear us with an open mind. A resolution passed by prominent ministers at one of our meetings says:
> "These men [referring to the Hebrew Christian speakers at the meeting] explained to the enlightenment of all, the complicated Jewish problem, touched our hearts with the recital of Israel's sorrows, proved beyond doubt Jehovah's purpose to make this nation a blessing to the world, expounded the wrong of the anti-Semitic spirit, and pointed the way to happy relations between Gentiles and Jews."

GOOD-WILL MEETINGS

Anticipating the pleasure of making your personal acquaintance, and with every good wish, I am,

Yours very sincerely,
Jacob Gartenhaus

Letters were also sent to the Jews *following* a meeting, as below:

A MESSAGE TO THE JEWISH PEOPLE OF TULSA, OKLAHOMA. Please allow me, on behalf of my party, to express our sincerest appreciation for the kind reception you gave us during our stay in your city. It has been our great delight to find you one of the most intelligent and open-minded groups of Jewish people we have met in our travels about the country.

We have endeavored through these meetings to bring about a better understanding and fellowship between Jews and Christians. It is our firm belief that He Who was the Messiah of Israel, flesh of our flesh and bone of our bone, must become the Mediator between Jews and Christians today. There is no living personality or movement that can form this basis of understanding and fellowship as can Jesus of Nazareth: He removes traditional walls of partition and breaks down the age-long prejudices. This we have found to be true in our own lives and in the experience of thousands of our fellowmen.

I hope that our people will soon realize that just as there are Orthodox, Reform, and Zionist Jews, so there can be Christian Jews who are just as loyal to our race and to the true traditions of our fathers, even though they have caught the vision that Jesus of Nazareth is the Messiah of Israel.

Our purpose in Tulsa, as in other cities, is not to force our own particular religious convictions upon anyone. We believe in the American spirit, the freedom of the individual conscience. It has been, rather, our desire in accordance with the same American spirit to proclaim our own convictions as we allow others to set forth their own individual beliefs. It is our great delight, therefore, to find open-minded Jews everywhere who are today making a new appraisal of Jesus. In the same manner we desire that you, our fellow Jews in Tulsa, will begin to make a new study of the

New Testament; we believe that when you do so sincerely you will find as we have found that Jesus Christ is indeed the Messiah of Israel, the Saviour of mankind.

Any Jewish friend desiring information, free literature, a copy of the New Testament in Yiddish, English, or any other language, will receive same upon request. Wishing God's blessing upon you, I am

Most cordially yours,
Jacob Gartenhaus

Faith Removes Mountains

From the very beginning, faith indeed did remove mountains of apathy, negligence, prejudice, and all those ugly vices which Satan thrusts in the way to halt the progress of the gospel.

Some churches opened their doors to Jews. Many of my people came and heard the good news of the Messiah, and their hearts were pricked. I could not always tell the effect, but this did not mean I had failed. God does not expect us to do His part of instilling faith, but only to labor faithfully, as I endeavored to do, in preaching the gospel to every creature, and first of all to the Jew. With the help of the churches these city-wide meetings were initiated in most southern cities. Although regarded as impossible undertakings by some at the time, they accomplished, among other things, the improvement of relations between Jew and Gentile in the South. Southern Jews have acquired a more favorable attitude towards Christ and Christianity. They no longer are afraid to enter Christian churches nor to read the New Testament and Christian tracts. Tolerance grows among them towards the Jew who embraces Christ and even towards the missionary who attempts to tell them the story of salvation.

The most convincing proof of the blessed effects of those meetings is the thousands of Jews today in the South who are Christian leaders, serving as elders, deacons, pastors, and Sunday school superintendents. Much of the seed fell on good ground; to God be the glory!

"About My Father's Business"

How were these meetings carried on? (1) First, I had to persuade the pastors and people of the churches of the importance, feasibility, and expedience of such gatherings, either by personal interview or by letter. (2) If my attempts were successful, I had to persuade them to participate in various ways, such as publicizing the meetings and inviting Jewish neighbors and friends. (3) Additional publicity in the press and through placards and handbills had to be arranged. (4) Distinguished persons, known and respected by the Jews, were persuaded to preside at the meetings, introduce the speakers, and endorse our effort. The Jews have been taught to believe that Jewish missionaries are worthless people, despised by everybody. A few good words spoken by some prominent Christian person help to dispel that old prejudice and gain respect for the missionary. One of the chief objectives of these meetings was to show the Jews how loved they were and that out of that love came the desire to share with them the highest blessing in life, their Messiah. (5) We usually succeeded in obtaining the services of large choirs and some well-known soloist or noted musician. Jews love good music and were thus attracted to the meetings.

Among the notables who came to greet the audiences were governors, senators, judges, mayors, and famous orators, who knew that their presence would draw large audiences. As a rule, we had some outstanding Christian Jews, some of them scholars in Hebrew lore and experienced in the Lord's work. They addressed the audiences and helped in the open forums answering questions. Many

Jews came prepared to pose questions, some in sincerity and others for the sake of argument. It was important that we allow the questions, as this gave us an opportunity to explain our position. Although some debates were quite heated, the meetings usually ended in good will. Many Jews accepted New Testaments and tracts which were offered to them and promised to read them.

The Jewish mass meetings were always preceded by preliminary meetings to which only Christians were invited. At these gatherings, we discussed how to approach Jewish friends and how to best answer their questions. We reminded the Christians of the great debt owed to the Jewish people and of the divine order to preach the gospel to them first. In these workshop sessions I also appealed for support to make the forthcoming mass meetings successful. The Christians agreed to publicize, serve as ushers, and follow up the contacts made in the meetings. We urged each Christian to invite Jewish neighbors, friends, and business associates.

Although the main purpose for these city-wide meetings was to win Jews to Christ, great blessings resulted for the Christians as well. These were revival meetings in the true sense of the word, as evidenced by the enthusiastic resolutions adopted by the pastors in those cities where they were held.

These efforts gave rise to the organizing of auxiliary groups of "Friends of Israel," which met periodically to study the life of the Jewish people, to pray for their salvation, to discuss ways and means of contacting Jewish neighbors, and to distribute the New Testaments and tracts which we supplied.

Tragic Days for Jewish People

The dry bones of Israel stirred greatly during these years (1920–1950). These were the days of the German Nazi atrocities, times of sorrow and despair. It seemed to the Jews that the whole world, including the Christian world, was bent on their destruction. It was during this time that some manifestation of Christian love for down-trodden Jewry was vitally needed, and these good-will meetings helped dispel much of the bitterness from the afflicted Jewish heart.

We termed them good-will meetings because:

1. The expression "good-will" sounded better to the Jewish ear than any other designation we could have used.

2. Had we called them "missionary campaigns" we might have frightened away the Jews; the secular press might have hesitated to give them publicity for fear of offending the Jewish leaders.

3. Last, but not least, our meetings were really intended to propagate good will and better understanding between Christians and Jews by pointing out the common heritage of the Word of God.

A memorable meeting was held at the Walnut Street Baptist Church, the largest church in the state of Kentucky, in May, 1933. That meeting was sponsored by the Baptist Young Peoples Union of Louisville. These young people were not satisfied with merely planning programs and pageants about people in far-off lands. Besides being interested in the salvation of those in foreign fields, they became interested in the lost of their own community and thus enthusiastically launched a city-wide effort to reach 20,000 Jews, under my guidance. That these young people meant business was indicated not only by their voting to finance the conference expenses but by the volunteering of seventy of their leaders, ready to carry out any plans to make this meeting the desired success. That same evening they volunteered, these young Christians went to all the Baptist churches in the city, outlining the purpose of the conference and calling upon the people to cooperate. This appeal elicited a hearty response.

During this series of meetings the church was packed to

overflowing, and on some evenings not even standing room was available. Especially noteworthy was the participation of a former rabbi, a great scholar in Judaism, a skillful writer of poetry and prose, and an eloquent speaker, Dr. George Benedict. Alexander Kaminsky, famous violinist of the former Russian Imperial court, also performed for us. Night after night an hour before the gathering, there was a special service for Christians to instruct them in methods of winning Jews. This meeting turned out to be one of the greatest campaigns in the history of Jewish evangelization.

Recognition of Our Efforts

In Atlanta my ministry became known to both Jews and Christians. In those days it was quite a triumph to get Jews to come into a church to hear a Jewish missionary. It took much prayer, tears, and perseverance to dispel the prejudice and hatred against the Christian church and Jewish converts in the heart of the average Jew.

Gradually, however, they came to know that I and other Hebrew Christians were not traitors. On the contrary, we were friends in need and in deed, staunch defenders of the Jewish people, working not only for their spiritual welfare—which they did not appreciate—but also for their rights and honor. In the course of time, I earned the appreciation of some of their leaders for my services to our people. Some of them confessed to me that the good-will meetings between Jews and Christians and my fight against anti-Semitism had accomplished more good for our people than anything they themselves had done.

To invigorate our contact with Atlanta Jewry, we arranged occasional good-will meetings similar to those I had arranged in other cities—with the usual publicity—enlisting the cooperation of local churches, other religious institutions, and eminent civic leaders. The meetings were endorsed by most denominations. For example, I appeared before the Baptist, Methodist, and Evangelical Ministers' Associations; each group endorsed my plan. A committee appointed by the Evangelical Ministers' Association then sent out a letter to all pastors, seeking to enlist the interest and cooperation of their churches in our meetings. A typical letter of support (this one used in Atlanta) went like this:

July 9, 1926

Dear Pastor:

The leaflet enclosed is self-explanatory. The plan has received the formal endorsement of the Baptist, Methodist, and Evangelical Ministers' Associations. Details as to time, place, etc., will be published later.

Just now we are seeking to enlist the interest of all in the enterprise. We feel that the messages of the Hebrew Christians who will speak in this series of classes and meetings should result in a much clearer understanding and broadened vision for all who will attend.

Will you not, therefore, present the matter to your people with such word of commendation as you may feel prompted to add, urging all who will to fill in the blank and place it in the collection plate? Then, if you will send these to Dr. Manget, whose address is on the blank, we would deeply appreciate it.

Sincerely yours,
(Signed by the committee of
leading pastors and laymen)

A circular letter was sent out to hundreds of Atlanta Jews inviting them to come to our meetings. Dr. W. M. Seay, president of the Home Mission Board, made an official report of the October 10-17, 1931, Atlanta meeting in which he said that great good had been accomplished. I quote the following from the resolution he offered at the close of the large mass meeting which climaxed the week's services:

TRAITOR?

As Christians deeply concerned for social, economic, and racial justice and righteousness among all nations, affirming the right of religious liberty to all, and purposing in our hearts to apply in all of our personal contact with Jews the spirit and teaching of Jesus Christ, we declare that we would ever reach out the hand of friendship and Christian love to the descendents of Abraham. For Baptists to foster these Hebrew-Christian conferences is to do much good for the Kingdom of Christ.

I have already called attention to the meetings in Louisville and Atlanta which served as model meetings for those held in Washington, D.C.; Kansas City, Missouri; St. Louis, Missouri; Little Rock, Arkansas; and elsewhere. These meetings were considered by others to be revolutionary innovations launched among the prosperous, complacent, and proud southern Jews to proclaim doctrines which they regarded as gross idolatry and repugnant superstition and to tempt them by inviting them to churches, which they considered houses of abomination and breeding places for anti-Semitism.

As for the Christian attitude at that time, it was not always Christian. I sought to dispel the inherent prejudices against the Jews, pointing out that even if all Jews might be as bad as Gentiles thought (which was certainly not the case), Christians should bear in mind that God loves them, Christ died for them, and it is the Christian's duty and privilege to bear witness to them.

Building Jewish-Christian relations was a very difficult task, but, thank God, after some years of these city-wide meetings there came the time of rapprochement. Christians opened their churches to the Jews, and Jews no longer hesitated to enter them. In spite of the many frustrations which I experienced, my labors were not in vain, as hundreds of Jews attended these meetings.

In view of the success of these meetings, Christians throughout the United States and in several foreign countries urged me to help them arrange similar ones. Such encouragement eventually led to the founding of the International Board of Jewish Missions, Inc.

The Meeting in Shreveport

In 1935, Dr. M. E. Dodd, pastor of the First Baptist Church, Shreveport, La., invited me to be one of the speakers at the Southwestern Bible Conference. *The Shreveport Times* of January 19 gave us front-page publicity by publishing my address on "The Christian Attitude Toward the Jew." Later I was invited to that same church when I appeared for a Bible conference program along with men like Dr. E. Y. Mullins, intellectual giant and president of the Southern Baptist Theological Seminary. The subject of one of my messages was "Seventeen Million Reasons Why the Bible Is True." I pointed out that every Jew today is a living proof that the Bible is God's Word, that the existence of the Jew today, in spite of persecution and dispersion, is an enigma which none of the philosophers and historians can explain.

At one of these conferences a mass meeting was arranged to which the Jews of Shreveport were invited. Wide publicity was planned, and long before the hour of the meeting, people began to gather. A few moments before the meeting opened, as I glanced over the auditorium, I recognized a large number of Jews whom I had already contacted during the previous week, and jokingly I suggested to Dr. Dodd that in introducing me he say something nice. I did this because the Jews believe that no one respects a turncoat, that he is considered a traitor to his people and is never wholeheartedly received by Christians. The Jew considers him a Christian and therefore to be shunned, while the Christian considers him a Jew, not to be fully trusted.

When Dr. Dodd introduced me, this is essentially what he said: "We are very honored to have this cultured, refined young man speak to us, a man who has won the respect and confidence of all of our Baptist people. Anyone that touches him touches the life of every Baptist. I want you to know that back of him are millions of Baptists."

Needless to say, such an introduction made a deep impression upon those Jewish people. Monday's *Shreveport Journal* devoted almost a full page to that meeting.

C H A P T E R 2 1

MORE SUFFERING FOR THE
SAVIOUR'S SAKE

My encounters with Uncle, Mother, and then with
Father were not the only incidents that nearly broke my
heart. I often experienced sorrow as a new believer because
of the attitude of fellow Christians.

For one thing, I was censured for warning the American
public in the early days of the Nazi uprising. It is quite
possible that, had I not been silenced, the Christian world
might have averted World War II and the slaughter of six
million Jews—among them about a million children—by
the Nazis.

Other such sad experiences, which grieved me greatly, I
am constrained to omit from this record. How painful were
the wounds *"with which I was wounded in the house of my
friends"!* (Zech. 13:6).

When I look back on the many attacks upon my life, I
cannot but praise the Lord for His protection that enabled
me to survive. More than once I was beaten by those with
intent to kill. More than once my attackers stopped the
beating and the kicking because they thought me dead or
because of the last minute arrival of police. Thank God,
these physical wounds healed and left no scars; the effects
of the wounds on my spirit, however, like Paul's thorn, still
cause a sting.

Of course, bodily harm can bring one to the brink of

distraction. Quite often, after I had been beaten severely, Satan would whisper into my ear: "Why should you expose yourself to such trouble and indignities? With your talents and your fortunate family connections, you can make life a happy one. Your family and friends will readily forgive your short-lived and ill-advised adventure into a foreign theological world and will receive you back with open arms, as they have repeatedly promised to do. Why venture out into alien and hazardous climates when you can have it so good at home?"

Satan argued convincingly, and were it not for the unfathomable grace of God, I might have yielded, gained the best that the world can offer—and missed the joy of my salvation! Praise the Lord that His grace has prevailed and kept me safe from the adversary's pitfalls!

During my seminary days in Louisville I did a lot of practical work among the Jews of that city. At first my work was limited to visiting the Jewish business people in their shops and offices. Experience showed me that this was not enough, as I could reach only a small number of the people. Moreover, this visitation in the Jewish areas often entailed unpleasantness, to put it mildly. So I decided on open-air meetings, since such services would disprove Jewish accusations that I was trespassing on private property and remove that excuse for abusing me.

But open-air meetings had their hazards. People in the crowds could hurl missiles without being detected and arrested. I usually had with me a dozen or more students from the seminary, who gave testimonies and sang, and they tried to protect me from harm. As I stood up on a chair and began to speak at one meeting, I noticed several in the crowd shaking clenched fists at me, shouting insults and threats. "Kill him!" "Break his bones!" were some of the words which reached my ears. Children were pulled away by their parents so that they might not hear what I was saying or be involved in ensuing trouble. Naturally I was a little frightened, but I went on with my message. Then, suddenly, I noticed a man in the crowd hurrying towards me with a butcher knife clasped in his outstretched hand. Fortunately, one of the students averted the man's thrust, while another student wrenched the knife from his grip.

By that time, a police patrol wagon had appeared on the scene and the would-be killer sneaked away, losing himself in the crowd which hastily dispersed.

"That surely was a narrow escape," remarked a Jewish man.

"Yes," I replied, "my Saviour not only has saved my soul, but also is continuously saving my body whenever it is in danger." I offered him some tracts and a New Testament, which he accepted, promising to read them.

Until this day I cannot explain why the attacker carried a butcher knife with him, unless he had premeditated killing me whenever I appeared in that neighborhood. Did he not know that if he had killed me, he would probably have had to pay with his own life? Obviously he took that risk. He would have died for "Kiddush ha-'Shem," the sanctification of the Name of God, the greatest merit a Jew can achieve in order to earn the world to come.

More than once I was confronted by such well-meaning zealots. It was for the good of all concerned that the Lord saved me from a death which might have resulted in very serious repercussions for both individuals and the Jewish community as a whole.

We returned to that corner the following week, once again bringing the message of love and life. The crowds came as usual. Some listened attentively, some heckled, and others threatened. It has been the same old story since Christ Himself preached. However, they all had the opportunity to hear the message of salvation. There is no doubt that some of the seed fell on good ground and bore abundant fruit. If only one soul was saved, my endeavors and risks were not in vain.

While all credit and gratitude for preserving my life belong to God, I feel constrained to thank our country's powers that be who uphold law and order and always have been ready to protect the life of every inhabitant. Several times the police have come to my rescue just in time. In having the protection of a democratic country, I have been more fortunate than the early missionaries for Christ.

Yet Another Attempt

In Miami, Florida, in the early thirties, I conducted a series of city-wide meetings to which both Christians and Jews were invited and in which various churches besides the Baptists cooperated. As a special attraction and guest speaker, the then-well-known Dr. Max Wertheimer, a graduate of the famous Rabbinical Seminary in Cincinnati, Ohio, who had served as rabbi in a Jewish temple in Dayton for ten years was invited. His remarkable conversion had caused wide repercussions among Jews as well as among Christians.

Many Jews came to hear him tell the story of his conversion. With his rare gift of speech and his vast knowledge of Judaism, he made a tremendous impression on all who heard him. Some of the Jewish leaders were afraid of his impact upon the hearts of those they considered "weak" Jews. As I learned then, there was quite a stir in the Jewish community of Miami. Of course, the blame for this "assault upon Judaism" fell upon me, since I was the organizer of the meetings.

Several representative Jews came to me with the "friendly" advice to pack up and remove myself from Miami, taking the apostate rabbi with me. Otherwise, they hinted, there would be trouble. They conceded that free speech in a free country is a virtue, "but why antagonize people?"

I could not follow their advice, because I had already been advised by the Master to "go and preach. . . ." Retaliation soon followed. That evening, on my way from the meeting place to my hotel, I suddenly felt two hands of iron grip my neck. The hands tightened as I struggled to get free. Severe choking caused me to gurgle as if in the last throes of asphyxiation, and apparently the man thought me dead, knocking me down as though I were a lifeless body.

I do not know how long I lay there unconscious. When I came to and opened my eyes, I saw some people around me. Someone helped me up. "You drank a little too much, young man," said one.

"I am not drunk," I explained. "Somebody knocked me down."

It was too dark to see from their faces what impression I had made on them, and I hastened to my hotel, which was not far away. The desk clerk gazed at me as if petrified; I must have been a sight!

When I got to my room and saw myself in the mirror, I understood why the clerk looked so astonished when he saw my face. It looked like a mask painted with blood and grime. What shocked me, for a while, was the distorted face of the Devil which I seemed to see as I looked into the mirror. He leered: "That is what you wanted when you made up your mind to follow Him!"

"I did not want that," I retorted, "but I am ready to bear the cross in whatever manner *He wants.*" And my soul became calm.

Washing my face, I saw that there were no deep wounds. I participated in the next meeting as if nothing had happened. Only the bruises around my eyes betrayed what had happened to me. If that zealot who attempted to strangle me was in the audience that evening, he may have been disappointed at his failure. I hope he experienced a change of heart.

Impressions of Eyewitnesses

In compiling material for my autobiography, I requested several of my friends who were eyewitnesses to some of my trials to describe certain incidents, some details of which I myself have almost forgotten after so many years. Following are letters from two of these friends, both of whom were octogenarians actively engaged in the King's business at the time these letters were written.

One is from the Rev. Samuel Needleman, a veteran Jewish missionary who died in the spring of 1969. His letter speaks for itself. The other is from the Rev. Zech Ford Bond, D.D., a veteran minister of the gospel. Although he has reached his eightieth year, he is still youthful at heart. His letter, which I quote first, requires a little background.

Incidents in Augusta

In Augusta, Georgia, in 1930, I was invited to speak in some of the churches and to witness to the Jewish people, which I always did when I visited a town or city. I carried with me Gospels and tracts and went from store to store offering them to the storekeepers and attendants. Some received me cordially, thanked me for the literature, which they promised to read, and some even asked me to return. Others showed me to the door as though I were a beggar, a drunkard, or a stray dog. A few took my hand and with mock politeness conducted me out. Occasionally, I also got a kick in the back.

But in Augusta one of the first Jewish merchants I visited

not only tore up the tracts I offered, but furiously pulled others out of my hand, tearing them up as well, and ordered me out of the store. When I lingered for a moment, he forcibly ejected me. I was dazed and embarrassed and looked about to see whether anyone had noticed this indignity, but the man was not yet fully satisfied. He came out, shouting, "Get out of this neighborhood or I will break your bones! You have no right to come here and give out your filthy literature!"

"This happens to be a free America," I replied, "and as an American I may go to any public place I wish to."

"Is that so?" he shouted. "I'll show you how free you are."

He then began to beat me right there in front of his store, shouting, "I'll kill you, you miserable meshummad, you traitor, you renegade!"

Soon a large crowd gathered. Some of the people tried to save me from the man's blows. Had a policeman not arrived just then, he might have beaten me to death. The man accused me of attacking him first, although I had not lifted a finger against him. Some of the people sided with me, others with the man, and so the policeman took both of us to headquarters. I phoned my friend, Zech Bond, who immediately came to police headquarters and secured my release. He now continues the story:

> "Blessed are ye, when men shall revile you, and persecute you, and shall say all manner of evil against you falsely, for my sake" (Matt. 5:11).
> As I have often read the Scriptures and come across these words, I said to myself, are they really true? I have never been persecuted for my belief and the expression of it. And I don't seem to know any personally among my friends who have really suffered for what they believe. Then comes back to me the memory of a dear friend whom I knew quite well in bygone days, and the experience he had in the town where I was then living. For several years I was pastor of the Second Baptist Church in Augusta, Georgia. Many men

TRAITOR?

who were quite prominent in the political life of the city were members of my church. These included members of the city council, chairman of the county commission, city attorney, sheriff of the county, and judge of the police court, or recorder's court.

One busy morning a phone call came requesting that I proceed immediately to the court on the insistence of the judge. On the way, I wondered in what way the law had finally caught up with me. When I arrived, much to my relief and astonishment I was informed that I was not the culprit wanted, but it was none other than my good friend, the Rev. Jacob Gartenhaus, Jewish missionary. He had been quite forceful in his witness for Christ the Messiah, in fact, too forceful to please some of the Jewish citizens. One of them had become so enraged that he attacked the missionary both with scathing denunciation and physical force. It occurred on Broad Street, the main business street of the city, and drew a crowd who watched the encounter. A police officer was called and Jacob and the man were arrested on the charge of disturbing the peace and inciting a riot.

When the accused stood before Judge Kent, that's where I came in as the real "Bond" for my Yiddish friend. As I said, Judge Kent was one of my "boys." The right kind of influence used in the right way can sometimes work wonders. Jacob was released from custody and left the police station with a grin that spread across his face from ear to ear.

Although Jacob had legal grounds and just reason to have his Jewish accuser indicted, he refused to press charges. As a result, enmity changed to friendliness. When the Jewish people heard what had really happened, Jacob was invited to the synagogue, where he had the privilege of witnessing to those present concerning the Messiah of Israel. Like Paul, Jacob often suffered for his determination to preach the Gospel. . . .

And then there are the recollections of my fellow worker, Rev. Needleman:

Dear Brother Jacob:
  You asked me to relate some incidents which occurred while you were assisting at our mission on Second Street in New York City, some fifty years ago.

192

MORE SUFFERING FOR THE SAVIOUR'S SAKE

It was around 1914 that you, a young Jew who had just come over from Austria, began to attend our meetings. I can see you now eagerly listening to the singing, testimonies, and then to the messages. Everything seemed strange to you. At first you did not stay long enough for us to talk with you. You would slip out quietly because you were afraid that some of your relatives and friends would find out that you were going to one of those hated missions. We prayed for you.

Then one day you came, and to everyone's great surprise and joy, you stood up and gave your testimony. It thrilled our hearts as you told us that you had made a public profession of Christ and that immediately after that you had rushed out into the street and begun to witness, upon which you were beaten up. From that time on, you were one of the most faithful and regular attendants at our meetings. You seemed to drink in every word that was quoted; and whenever you could, you assisted us in the work.

One evening you failed to show up at the meeting. You used to come early to tidy up the place and then stand out in front of the hall, inviting Jews to come in, distributing our literature. When the hour arrived for the meeting and you still had not come, I became quite worried. I remembered you telling us that a gang of young Jews had threatened to "teach you a lesson" if they caught you around the mission. Several times you had been insulted and beaten as a warning. While preparations for the meeting were in progress, my anxiety grew to alarm, and I stepped outside to look around. I saw near our entrance a small crowd shouting and kicking at a man lying on the sidewalk. When they saw me, they hastily dispersed. When I approached the man on the ground, I discovered to my horror that it was you. You lay there motionless as if dead, blood oozing from a wound in your head. I raised you up and half carried, half walked you to the hall. I wanted to call an ambulance and the police, but you motioned for me not to do so.

I washed your wound and applied some antiseptic and then cleaned your face and hands. After a minute or two you sat up, and faintly smiling said, "Praise the Lord; I'm all right. I don't need any doctor, and it would do no good to call the police. We ought to show the people that we are not vindictive, that we are guided by love and forgiveness."

I remember these words because they made an indelible

impression upon me, as they came from your mouth a few minutes after you were so severely beaten. Indeed, when I saw you on the ground, I thought you were dead. But notwithstanding the threats and beating, you returned to our next service.

This occurrence made a wholesome impression on the Jews in the neighborhood. They learned of the heroism and love of those who believe in Messiah Jesus.

C H A P T E R   2 2

IN DEFENSE OF THE FAITH

From the moment that the truth as revealed in Christ entered my heart, I realized that faith in Him and concern for the fate of the Jewish people are interdependent. Thus any attempt to disparage or harm them is tantamount to disparaging and harming the Christian faith, and vice-versa. I have learned that Christianity from *alpha* to *omega*, both its center and circumference, is based solely on the Scriptures, both Old and New Testaments, which were written almost entirely by the Jewish people.

The entire Old Testament tells the fate and destiny of the Jews from beginning to end: how God made an irrevocable, everlasting covenant with them and how He trained them for their mission. It tells of the manifold trials and tribulations they had to undergo because of their repeated rebellion against their God; it tells how He chastised them as a father chastises his son for his benefit and not his harm (God refers to Israel as my first born son). He says, "Fear thou not, O Jacob my servant, saith the Lord: for I *am* with thee; for I will make a full end to all the nations whither I have driven thee: but I will not make a full end of thee, but correct thee in measure; yet will I not leave thee wholly unpunished" (Jer. 46:28). Again and again the prophet assures the nation that He will correct them in a measure, but will not make a full end of them. The perpetuity of Israel is assured.

I have learned that after many revelations to His people, God revealed Himself to them in the form of a mortal man—Christ, who lived among them and taught them and finally gave His life as a ransom for them in accordance with God's plan of salvation.

I have learned that Christ's apostles, all Jews, in obedience to His command carried the good news to all the known world. Anyone who touches these, God's people, "toucheth the apple of his eye" (Zech. 2:8; Deut. 32:10).

The Jews Are Still God's Chosen People

I know that there are some Christians and some theologians who have an inherent dislike of the Jews, who teach that since the Jews rejected Christ, God has cast them off and they are no longer His privileged people. Some of these theologians even assert that the Jews are an accursed and damned people.

Where do they get this idea? Certainly not from the Word of God. The apostles knew nothing about God's changing His mind in a fit of passion and annulling His covenant with Israel. On the contrary, Paul unequivocally declared that "God hath not cast away his people which he foreknew" (Rom. 11:1, 2). He also avers that "all Israel shall be saved" (v. 26), and that "the gifts and calling of God are without repentance" (v. 29).

We read that following the rejection by the Jews and crucifixion, Christ appeared to His apostles and they asked Him, "Wilt thou at this time restore again the kingdom to Israel?" (Acts 1:6). Notice that the Lord did not rebuke them for their inquiry. The question was a valid one. His only answer was that the time for the restoration of His kingdom is God's secret; it was not for them to speculate as to the exact time, but to be His witnesses "both in Jerusalem, and in all Judaea, and in Samaria, and unto the uttermost part of the earth" (Acts 1:8). He did not tell them that He was through with His people; they were still first and foremost in His heart.

Peter, when he rebuked his people for their part in the death of Christ, added that they had done it in ignorance and called them "brethren," declaring that they had unknowingly fulfilled what was foretold by all the prophets— that is, that Christ had to suffer and die. He urged them to repent of their sins (Acts 3:17–19, 24–26). Peter, who knew Christ as well as, if not better than, any other human being, knew nothing about God's rejection of His people. As before the Crucifixion, so after it, we find him preaching to them.

Jewish Ignorance of Christ Only Temporary

The apostle Paul writes that "blindness in part is happened to Israel, until the fulness of the Gentiles is come in" (Rom. 11:25). But that blindness was only temporary, so that the Gentiles could benefit from it. "As concerning the gospel, *they are* enemies for your sakes: but as touching the election *they are* beloved for the fathers' sakes" (v. 28). One needs only to read the eleventh chapter of Romans to be convinced that instead of being through with the Jews, God has a golden future for them.

The brutal antagonism of the anti-Semites and some theologians is not only hurting the Jews, but is even more damaging to the Christian faith. Likewise, those Jews who try to hinder the preaching of the gospel are hurting their own people more than they are the anti-Semites. The Jews could not survive more than a few years in a world bereft of the gospel.

TRAITOR?

Championing the Jewish Cause

Being well aware of this fact, I felt it necessary to combat this heresy. Notwithstanding my limitations, I stood up against some of the mighty powers that be and, like Paul, fought for the faith "once delivered unto the saints" (Jude 3), facing famous professors and mighty preachers. I felt like little David confronting the great Goliath; my weapon was not a sling shot like David's, but the Word of God. But as in the case of David, the Lord was always on my side, and I often succeeded in demolishing insidious falsehoods.

In my struggle against those Jewish leaders who have been fighting the gospel, I have suffered severely. But my rewards have come as the Lord has used me to win many of my people to a knowledge of their Messiah. In addition, Jewish leaders through the years have recognized the contribution God has allowed me to render to the Jewish cause.

Not Offense but Defense

As a defender of our people against their enemies, God has blessed our work so that we have succeeded in doing more than many large, resourceful Jewish organizations in bringing about good-will and better understanding. Some of these organizations, instead of pleading the cause of Israel, have attacked Christianity and alienated Bible-believing Christians who are among the Jews' best friends. Instead of reminding them that their Christ was a Jew, that the authors of the Bible—both Old and New Testaments—were Jews, they have sought to discredit the New Testament as being an anti-Semitic book by culling words out of context to prove their point. They have thus accomplished the very opposite of what they desired. Genuine Christians do not cherish abuses of what is near and dear to them. They do not like to be made responsible for despicable acts against the Jews by so-called Christians, whether in the present or in the past, whether at home or in some distant country.

Our method of defense has not been to attack or condemn, but to plead the cause of Israel before Christians, both true and nominal. We point out from both the Old and New Testaments that their duty is to love and honor the Jews as God has loved and honored them ever since His covenant with their ancestor Abraham, even though at times He has chastised them for their ultimate good (Deut. 8:16). Usually our earnest pleas have won many friends for the Jews, not only here in the United States but also in many other lands. For example, while ministering in Japan, we organized eighty "Japanese-Christian Friends of Israel" groups who are now praying daily for "the peace of Jerusalem."

This work has brought me before thousands of congregations, and it has opened doors for personal conferences with prominent personalities of great influence in secular and ecclesiastical circles. I have interviewed governors of states, ambassadors, senators, and others.

President Truman spoke with me about a year before the establishment of the state of Israel, in which his influence was of prime importance. I think it is not too presumptuous to state that what I said to him on behalf of Israel had some effect on his stand for my people. I had sent him my book, *The Rebirth of a Nation,* published several years before the state of Israel came into being, and requested an audience with him, which was soon granted. At the appointed hour I met him in the White House.

Among his first words was his expression of appreciation for the book, with which he was greatly impressed. Then he wanted to know whether I, as a Jewish Christian, believed in the rebuilding of the Jewish homeland. My reply was that both as a Jew and a Christian I believe in the Bible, which revolves around the Jewish people and their mission as a regenerative nation in their regenerated Promised Land. At the close of the interview he expressed appreciation and apparent agreement with my views.

Emergence of Nazism and My Fight Against It

I was in Germany during the time of the rise of the deadly Nazi movement. Hitler, the most formidable Jew-hater in history, was not yet the Führer—the "god" of Germany—but he had already gotten himself elected chancellor, and to all intents and purposes was dictator of the German people. The death camps had not yet been established at that time, but in his book, *Mein Kampf* (My Struggle), and other Nazi literature I learned of his plan for the total destruction of the Jewish people.

He started through his henchmen, beating and killing a few Jews here and there, and boycotting the rest. "The appetite comes with the eating" is a popular saying, and after the easily incited mobs tasted blood, they craved more. There was practically no one to oppose the intransigent Nazis in Germany itself, and the nations outside Germany did not seem to care what was being done to the Jews. Many people did not believe that the civilized, cultured Germans were capable of committing such crimes. The Nazi leaders were quite clever in persuading a gullible world that nothing was wrong in Germany, that any outcry was only propaganda attempting to discredit the national German party, which was in ascendency over the "Jewish-Communist" government.

As a son of the people who for nineteen centuries had suffered a succession of trials and tribulations, I felt the premonition that something more disastrous than ever before was about to happen to the Jews. Hitler's threats foretold tragedy. From private sources, as well as from reports that trickled through uncensored into the Jewish press, I learned that an ominous storm was growing more fierce with each passing day.

When I disclosed my feelings to Christian friends they said they were sure that those reports were shockingly exaggerated. I was exceedingly distressed.

At that time the Baptists were making preparation to hold their world congress in Berlin. Some of the leaders doubted the wisdom of holding the congress in Germany, as to do so would only give aid to Hitler and his hordes. It would prove that one of the largest Christian denominations in the world considered Germany the best country in which to assemble and discuss religion. I, too, was opposed to it, but there was nothing I could do after the decision had been made. I asked to be appointed as a *bona fide* delegate so that I might find the full truth of Jewish persecution, and more important, discover ways and means to help assuage my outlawed, harassed brethren, especially the Christian Jews. Even then I had already seen the dark clouds gathering over the Jews of Europe—possibly over all the Jews worldwide.

My family and friends tried to dissuade me from this perilous trip. They said that as a Jew (the Nazis found no difference between "Jew" and "Christian Jew") investigating conditions in that country, I would certainly vanish into some Nazi torture chamber. But I felt it my sacred duty to undertake that mission, disregarding the hazards.

I armed myself with various letters of recommendation to persons who in one way or another could help me accomplish my task. The letters were addressed to diplomats, pastors, and editors. The most significant recommendation was that of Dr. Walter E. Dodd to his brother, U.S. Ambassador to Germany, the honorable William E. Dodd. At that time this U.S. post in restless Germany was of great importance and interest in international affairs. His letter described my background and recommended me as a true "Israelite in whom there is no guile."

Following my presentation of this letter at the embassy, an appointment was arranged for me to meet the ambassador. After a cordial conversation about my missionary work and other topics, I turned to my real purpose of coming to Berlin. At this point the ambassador became more official. He seemed to be weighing every word that he uttered. From time to time he glanced around the spacious room to make sure that he was not spied upon and overheard. "The walls have ears," he whispered, bending toward me.

He corroborated to a great extent my apprehensions about the fate of the Jews in Germany. If Germany started a war, the same fate might be expected for the Jews of other countries. Regarding American interference and aid to the endangered Jews, he hinted at certain measures, but here he was more circumspect and cautious with his words. I understood. He was there representing a country which was officially friendly. Any offending utterance against the Nazis might strain relations between our government and that of Germany.

Nevertheless, I learned at that meeting a great deal of what I had come to learn, though the ambassador warned me about denunciating Nazis while on German ground. Unfortunately, I could not do much to help where help was needed. The only thing I could do was disclose to the world Germany's treatment of the Jews and relay the threat of their total extermination when the Nazis rose to full power, a rise which was imminent.

While in Germany I discussed the situation with some of my fellow delegates at the congress. Probably my revelations helped to formulate the resolution which the congress adopted against racial discrimination. Excerpts appeared in the American press, such as this article from the *American Israelite:*

IN DEFENSE OF THE FAITH

August 9, 1934
AMERICAN PASTOR MINCES NO WORDS IN ASSAILING HITLERISM

Berlin—The congress of the Baptist World Conference, meeting here, heard from an American pastor, the Rev. Harold Phillips of Cleveland, a vigorous attack on nationalism, racial prejudice, and every effort to force Christianity to recognize national boundaries as limitations on the brotherhood that it seeks to create.

"Whatever we might say, for example, about this gospel of racial superiority which is so prevalent today," declared the Cleveland pastor, "one thing can confidently be said about it. It certainly is not original; the world into which Jesus came was a world whose whole habit of thinking was anti-social and unfraternal. It divided men into all sorts of classes and castes. One of its supreme virtues was exclusiveness. It was rife with bigotry.

"Some of the most revealing and most valuable contacts Jesus made were made with those very individuals and groups whom His contemporaries branded as social, racial, or religious inferiors.

"Does this mean that Jesus was simply an uncritical, softhearted sentimentalist? If I am certain of anything, it is that we are the sentimentalists and Jesus is the world's greatest moral realist. Anybody who, knowing what has happened to the world during the past few years and having seen what is happening now, still regards Jesus' plea for cooperative goodwill as being an impracticable illusion, either is wildly stubborn, hopelessly stupid, or both.

"If this plea of Jesus for a world of cooperative goodwill was pertinent 1900 years ago, it is infinitely more so now. Hate, fear, ill will, greed, ignorance, pride, racial and nationalistic bigotry, these are the real enemies of my country and your country."

My continued pleas to leading delegates of the Baptist World Congress seemed to fall on deaf ears. Their primary excuse was that Hitler and his Nazi bishops, who were at that time friendly towards the Baptists, might change their tolerant attitude towards them and persecute them as they had the other Christian sects.

203

TRAITOR?

At one time, the Vatican (Pope Pius XII) was accused by public opinion of not having protested against the wholesale slaughter of the Jews. The Vatican's rationalization was the same as that of the Baptists: Afraid that the Nazis would wreak vengeance upon the Catholics in Germany, it dared not condemn the Nazi atrocities.

Thus some of the Baptist leaders, in their desire for the peace of Baptists, and the Catholic leaders, in their desire for the peace of Catholics, forgot their responsibility to Christ and His faith. These leaders unintentionally inflicted a blow upon Christianity which will take many years to heal.

My own private protests were like a cry in the wilderness. Even some of my friends tried to excuse me as "being a radical Jew, who was overly sentimental and overstating facts. . . ."

When I returned to America I disclosed the truth about the inhuman persecution of the Jews in Germany and the threat of their future total destruction. I sounded the alarm from many pulpits and through the press, though some of the Baptist leaders tried to force me to drop my "propaganda," which they claimed would cause retaliation by the Nazis against the Baptists not only in Germany but all over the world. One of the Baptist leaders addressed letters to the secretary of the Home Mission Board, Dr. J. B. Lawrence, and to the president of the board, Dr. Ellis A. Fuller, demanding that they put a stop to my criticism of Hitler. But I would not agree to this, as I felt that I was morally obligated to tell the facts. Besides, by that time the hue and cry was already taken over by various publications. My impressions were quoted widely in the press, such as in the *Atlanta Constitution* of September 3, 1934:

WORLD IN IGNORANCE OF NAZI KILLING OF JEWS, ASSERTS MINISTER HERE

Rigid censorship by the Nazis keep the world and the United States in particular from knowing of the continued persecution of Jews in Germany, the Rev. Jacob Gartenhaus, who for fourteen years has been in charge of the Jewish Department of Home Missions of the Southern Baptist Convention, said Sunday night in an address on "the German-Jewish tragedy" at the Central Baptist Church.

"Jews are being murdered every day in Germany," he said. "While a delegate to the Baptist World Alliance in Germany last month, I talked with many Christian Jewish pastors of the Baptist faith. They had been exiled from Germany not because they were Baptists, but because Jewish blood coursed through their veins. They told me they felt their lives in jeopardy while visiting in Germany though they all were official delegates to the World Alliance."

Mr. Gartenhaus stated that the Nazi government is very careful about letting reports of persecution of the Jews get into circulation. However, he exhibited a copy of a weekly newspaper published in Nuremberg, Germany, which, he said, contained headlines designed to inflame the German people against the Jews.

Not long afterwards, Hitler became the Führer and dictator of Germany (in 1934) and at once began to execute in deed the "final solution" of the Jewish question. The persecution became more and more flagrant and inhuman, ending with the concentration and death camps. By the time he and the "invincible" German armies were defeated, six million Jews had fallen victim to his "final solution."

Had our Baptist brethren heeded my warnings and had they, as a great Christian denomination and as individuals, aroused the conscience of the world, I am quite sure that Nazi-led Germany would not have sunk to such degradation. My hands tremble as I write these lines. May the Lord of mercy avert any such deeds again.

Some such deeds, after the Nazi holocaust, have been averted by the grace of God. I think for instance of the Arabs who attempted a number of times to follow the Nazi example of genocide. But the Keeper of Israel does not sleep nor slumber. For myself I can say that in all of my people's struggles for existence since I accepted Jesus as my

Messiah, I have done all I can to help in their material defense and their spiritual salvation.

Thirteen years after that fateful congress in Berlin, the Baptists met in another World Congress in Copenhagen, Denmark, in July, August, 1947. This congress attempted redress and reparation to the Jewish people. There was a general and genuine feeling of repentance and a sense of duty to expiate and conciliate.

I was no longer a rebellious upstart. I had earned for myself a name and could no longer be silenced. Nor did anyone wish to silence me now. Many still remembered my stand thirteen years before. I went to this Baptist World Congress with the intention of soliciting the aid of the congress for the most urgent needs of the remnant of European Jewry. These remnants of the Nazi holocaust were in a very sad plight, both materially and spiritually. As they wandered about aimlessly as sheep without a shepherd, no country in the world would give them asylum and they were on the verge of despair. I sincerely and prayerfully hoped that the Baptists at that congress would heed my pleas to render assistance to my destitute people. Thank God, I was not disappointed.

In my private conversations with individual delegates, I found understanding and feeling hearts for sorely afflicted Israel. Thus I was assured that the congress would adopt the resolution which I was about to introduce. At the session held on July 30, I delivered a message on the challenge which Israel presents today to Christians of the world. I then presented a resolution, which the conference unanimously approved and recommended to the plenary session of the congress for final adoption.

Later, when it was presented to the congress, it was seconded by Mr. Ernest Brown, former British Labor Minister, who stated that the resolution showed great statesmanship in that it touched on the Jewish question of the entire world. I present the resolution as it was adopted by the congress.

IN DEFENSE OF THE FAITH

Resolution

(Proposed by Jacob Gartenhaus, Field Secretary, Jewish Department, Home Mission Board, Southern Baptist Convention, and adopted by the Baptist World Alliance at its Seventh World Congress)

Copenhagen, Denmark
July 29-August 3, 1947

The Baptist World Alliance, in session at Copenhagen, July 1947, resolves on the following declarations:

Aware of the unprecedented suffering through which the people of Israel have passed during recent years, six million of them being exterminated by most inhuman means; aware also that these sufferings are not yet at an end, but that hundreds of thousands are still in concentration camps or wandering homeless from land to land; aware, further, that the poisonous propaganda and destructive designs of anti-Semitism are still at work against Jews in many lands, this Congress puts on record its sense of sorrow and shame that such conditions prevail.

It calls, first, upon Baptists throughout the world to manifest the spirit of Jesus Christ, himself a Child of Israel, and to do everything in their power to alleviate the sufferings of the Jews.

It calls, secondly, upon the nations of the world to open their doors to the homeless and oppressed refugees, since there can be no abiding peace while this problem remains unsolved.

It calls, thirdly, upon Jewry everywhere to refrain from provocative acts and to restrain those among them who would resort to violence.

Further, this Congress would not be true to its convictions if it did not state its belief that the command of Jesus Christ to evangelize the world was intended to include the people of Israel.

The Congress, therefore, calls upon all Baptists to do their part in supporting missionary work among the Jews. We believe that only when Christ is accepted as Lord will the Jews or any other people find salvation, peace, and freedom.

This resolution evoked world-wide repercussions. The reporters of the various news media who were present at the congress spread it throughout the globe. Here, for example, is a copy of a dispatch by the Associated Press:

(Baptist)
Over in Copenhagen, Denmark, a Baptist churchman from Georgia has a proposal for religious tolerance. The Reverend Jacob Gartenhaus of Atlanta says he is planning to present a resolution to the Congress of the Baptist World Alliance. Reverend Gartenhaus said his resolution would call on Baptist churchmen throughout the world to do everything in their power to alleviate the suffering of the Jews.
He said, and we quote, "The sufferings are not yet at an end. The poisonous propaganda . . . of anti-Semitism is still at work against the Jews in many lands."
The minister said his resolution would call upon the nations of the world to open their doors for the homeless and oppressed refugees.

Needless to say, the Jewish people were highly pleased with that resolution. This friendless, harassed, martyred people had found a friend in Christianity's most influential denomination. Many of the Jewish leaders sincerely and cordially thanked me for what I had done by introducing that resolution. Many of them realized, perhaps for the first time in history, that a Jew who believes in Christ is not as bad as the Jews had been misled into believing. They saw in me not an apostate, a traitor, but a friend in need—indeed.

These two congresses in Berlin and Copenhagen were, other than my conversion, the most impressive events in my life.

Another Dilemma

On several occasions during the course of my ministry I have been confronted with perplexing, serious dilemmas when Christian people in high places have not only failed to seize the wonderful opportunities for bearing testimony to my people, but have sometimes even discouraged it. I have asked myself whether I should speak out in protest against them and thus incur their reproach or whether I should keep silent and thus retain their esteem. "Even a fool, when he holdeth his peace, is counted wise: *and* he that shutteth his lips *is esteemed* a man of understanding" (Prov. 17:28).

But my faith in Christ has always been my greatest treasure. It has already cost me parents, relatives, friends, home, and position. I can not stand idly by but must speak up, no matter what the cost.

Such was the case when I received the program of the Baptist World Congress in Atlanta and saw that a Christ-denying rabbi was among other dignitaries scheduled to bring greetings of welcome on this occasion. I immediately addressed the following letter to the Executive Committee of the Baptist World Alliance:

July 20, 1939

The Executive Committee
Baptist World Alliance
Dr. George W. Truett, President
Dr. J. H. Rushbrooke, Executive Secretary

Dear Brethren in Christ:

I am writing you as a Christian Jew, asking your prayerful consideration regarding the advisability of having a Christian Jew respond in behalf of the Christian Jews of the world in the Roll Call of the Nations in the Baptist World Alliance program, Saturday, July 22.

Of course, it is understood that the response will be made as coming from nations and representatives of nations, rather than racial groups. However, the Jewish people are bound together by common ties that are as distinctive and as gripping as the national groups to be found anywhere. Even though there is no organization of Christian Jews, that brings those of us who are accepting Christ Jesus as Messiah to a closer fellowship than any national organization could do.

Inasmuch as the Jews are a people without a country and sorely persecuted in different countries of the world: and inasmuch as it is impossible for them to have a national organization or ecclesiastical organization: and inasmuch as so many of them have come to accept Christ as their personal Saviour, I would appreciate very much such recognition in the Roll Call of the Nations as you feel will best advance our Lord's kingdom.

Personally, I feel that some recognition of the Jews as a people through whom the revelation came would set forward the cause which is dear to my heart and dear to the heart of each member of this Executive Committee.

Let it be distinctly understood that I myself could not respond in the Roll Call of the Nations but will assume responsibility along with you, in case you need me, to find the proper Christian Jew to make that response.

Beseeching your prayerful consideration of this and praying God's blessings upon you.

I am,

> Yours in Christ and Israel,
> Jacob Gartenhaus
> Field Secretary

I received no acknowledgment of this letter nor of a *second* letter which I sent special delivery and registered. This discouraged me the more, not because of my personal hurt, but because I felt that a wonderful opportunity of witnessing to the Jews of the world had been missed. Had these leaders included in their program a Christian Jew to answer the roll call of the nations on that solemn occasion, they would have won for him the respect of those Jews who regard their Christian brethren as unrecognized traitors. How many times have such Jews taunted me, saying, "Your own Christians respect a rabbi more than they do you!" But the Baptist World Congress leaders were afraid they would hurt the sensitive feelings of our Jewish friends.

I Learned From Amos

On several occasions my friends warned me not to get entangled in disputes with my superiors of the Home Mission Board. I remembered the case of Amos when Amaziah warned him not to prophesy against Jeroboam, king of Israel, but to get out of town. Amos replied that he must obey God who ordered him to prophesy unto His people Israel (Amos 7:10–15).

Yes, I did risk my job and might have been asked to resign, but—as one editor expressed it—"Jacob is so entrenched in the life of Southern Baptists that they would have protested it. To attack him would have meant shaking the structure of the whole foundation of Southern Baptists."

Still, many of the leaders tried on several occasions to do away with the Department of Jewish Evangelism: If they could not do away with me, they could see that my services would no longer be needed. But, again, they feared a backlash, and I stayed on for several years. As it happened, soon after I retired from the Home Mission Board after twenty-eight years, the Jewish Department was effectively done away with through a merger with other departments.

It would have been easy to give up the struggle and retire completely from active service when I left the Home Mission Board, but I felt I could not do that at a time when the opportunities for witnessing to and winning my people were greater than ever before. After much prayer and encouragement from friends, the Lord led me to launch out on faith into a worldwide ministry, and what has been wrought during these many years since is a miracle of His grace.

CHAPTER 23

MINISTRY IN EUROPE

Eastern Europe had the largest Jewish center in the Diaspora up to its annihilation by the Nazis. My first stop on a visit to Eastern Europe in 1928 was in Poland as the guest of the Rev. Peter Gorodishz, superintendent of the Barbican Mission to the Jews at Bialystok, which at that time was one of the most important Jewish communities in Europe, its Jewish inhabitants numbering several million.

My two weeks' visit there was perhaps the busiest and most joyous of my missionary experiences. Immediately upon my arrival my host, Brother Gorodishz, arranged for me to address meetings in his mission on Saturday and Sunday afternoons. Realizing that Bialystok had been a stronghold of traditional Judaism for several centuries, with its many Jewish synagogues and schools, I wondered just what a missionary could accomplish in such a place. However, Brother Gorodishz assured me that I would have a good hearing.

The first meeting was advertised for five o'clock, but long before that hour the people began to assemble, and as I entered the large hall, what a sight confronted me! There were the old-time orthodox Jews with their beards and so-called Jewish garb, the young men in modern dress, and the clean-shaven skeptics. For one hour I proved to them from their Scriptures that the Messiah's promise was ful-

filled in Jesus of Nazareth and that only through His aton-
ing blood can forgiveness of sin be obtained. A reverent
silence fell upon all, lasting throughout the entire service of
two and a half hours.

I feared that the lengthy meeting would turn many away,
but on the following day I was greeted by a still larger
audience, and again the story of His redeeming love unfolded. How my heart thrilled as I looked upon the eager
faces, and lifting my eyes toward heaven, I thanked Him
for the privilege of ministering to such a hungry multitude.
The following day two brethren from the mission and I set
out on a missionary journey to the various towns in Poland,
stopping first in a small town of about a thousand souls, the
majority of whom were Jewish. While my two companions
were busying themselves with the car, I stepped to the
corner house, where stood a son of Israel. I greeted him
with the customary Hebrew greeting, "Shalom Aleichem,"
and immediately his features lit up with a joyful expression
as he answered, "Aleichem Shalom." We had been speaking for five or ten minutes when we were surrounded by a
number of Jews who listened eagerly to the story of Israel's
Messiah, pressing closer and closer that they might not miss
a word of what was being said.

In the next town I inquired of a passerby, "What do the
Jews do here?"

"We are waiting for the Messiah," he said. A lengthy
discussion concerning the Messiah ensued, and, as in the
former town, an excited and inquisitive crowd soon encir-
cled us. As we alighted from the car in yet another town, a
curious bystander wanted to know our origin, and soon the
entire town was aware of the presence of missionaries.
Many came to the hotel to have a look at us.

In such a manner we visited twelve towns, and without
exception we were royally received. Christian literature was
gratefully accepted; many even offered to pay for it. It was
truly heartrending to witness the poverty-stricken Jews in

the smaller Polish towns. As I traversed the country, tears sprang to my eyes when I saw grey-bearded men with emaciated faces asking alms, or young mothers with starving babes in their arms begging bread. How pathetic to see dirty, ragged little children with faces that should have been rounded and rosy, clinging to the skirts of their mothers who could not hush their cries of hunger!

As I watched them, I wondered why the all-merciful Father would allow them to go through life without even the mere necessities. But His ways are not our ways (Isa. 55:8).

I then vowed to do all in my power when I returned to the United States to rouse the conscience of American Christendom to work for the salvation (including temporal relief) of these poor souls of Polish Jewries. Alas! I could not do much for them. But the enemy of our souls did all that he could—he had them killed off, including that faithful and capable missionary, Rev. Gorodishz, and his entire family. From the teeming millions, there remained only a few thousand maimed souls to suffer anew under Communist tyranny following World War II.

Tears well up in my eyes now, and I wonder whether I could not have rescued more of those dear people before their extermination.

Rev. Gorodishz reproduced a page from the publication *"Das Wort" ("The Word")* for our meetings in Yiddish in which he related the story of my conversion. And he translated my tract, "The Virgin Birth of the Messiah," into Yiddish; fifty thousand copies of it were printed in tract form and found their way into many parts of the world.

Behind the Iron Curtain

After the German defeat, which also brought an end to the Nazi holocaust against the Jews of Eastern Europe, this area of Europe fell almost entirely into the hands of Russia. These came to be known as the Iron Curtain countries, and the Jews still left there were exposed to persecution no less cruel than that under the Nazis, although less overt.

In response to several urgent invitations from some of the believers behind the Iron Curtain, I felt led to visit there. These modern "heroes of the Cross," surrounded for years by godless and ruthless enemies, remained faithful to the Lord despite the relentless persecution which was the lot of those who refused to join the party. Every now and then such "counter-revolutionists" just disappeared from their surroundings—and probably from the face of the earth.

It was quite risky for an outsider to penetrate that impenetrable curtain. And once in these countries it was extremely difficult to get out again. I was frightened by press reports of cases in which foreign visitors had just vanished, yet I was determined to see and encourage those heroes who implored me to come. I knew that they were urgently in need of communication with a fellow human whom they could trust and with whom they could converse freely, face to face and heart to heart.

Czechoslovakia

After several months of strenuous effort and red tape, I secured a visa to visit Czechoslovakia in 1947.

Off I went to Prague, its capital. This beautiful city once played a very important role in the history of the Jewish Diaspora. There are many interesting legends in Jewish folklore about Prague, especially about its great miracle-working rabbis. One of them supposedly saved the Jewish community from being slaughtered by creating a robot to guard the ghetto gates, thus keeping out the invaders and defending the inhabitants against their Christian attackers. This city was a great center of Jewish life and culture until the Nazis came and reduced it to a "Judenrein" (clean of Jews) city.

When I arrived at Prague I found a small number of Jews there—a pitiful remnant from Nazi death camps and local hideouts. They looked like skeletons wrapped in rags. Their faces and their eyes told me a story of anguish and despair. It was heartrending to see the children's haggard faces and longing eyes, which spoke of hunger and illness. No one comforted them or satisfied their pangs of hunger. Passages from Lamentations sprang up in my mind as I empathized with one deplorable scene after another. Only a Jeremiah could express in words what I felt when I met those remnants of the once proud and prosperous Jews of Prague.

My funds were very limited, but fortunately the value of the dollar was extraordinarily high at that time. With the money I had at my disposal I could at least help out temporarily. Later, after returning home, I sent clothing, medicine, and money. I was even able to help some of these Czech Jews to escape from Communist bondage into the free West.

Hungary

Prague was only a stepping-stone to Hungary, where there were large numbers of Jewish Christians who needed help and encouragement in their daily temporal and spiritual struggles. It was they who had begged me to come.

To penetrate into Hungary was even more difficult than getting into Czechoslovakia at that time. But at last the Lord opened even these doors for me. (I am grateful to our U.S. Embassy in Prague, which helped secure me a Hungarian visa.)

When I arrived in Budapest, the capital and the center of Jewish life still surviving in Hungary, I was welcomed by a group of Jewish Christians whose joy in seeing me was indescribable. I noticed that they cast anxious glances all around them, since spies (officials of the secret police and young zealot volunteers) were everywhere, ready to pounce upon any they could accuse of breaking the laws of the regime. Jews were always suspected of plotting to overthrow the revolutionary regime, and Jewish Christians were doubly suspect. These brethren had to be very circumspect and cautious.

This oppressive atmosphere hung over me wherever I went. There was almost always someone following me. Now and then a spy would accost me, telling me dolefully that his children were starving and begging me to exchange a few dollars for Hungarian currency, which he offered me at a bargain. This was a ploy to encourage me to violate a law for which there was severe punishment. I was warned by the brethren to be very cautious with strangers.

In spite of such sad experiences, I carried away pleasant memories of meetings with my friends whom I really felt were heroes and saints. Once when I arrived at a home where several believers had gathered, a lady missionary asked, "Are you the Jacob Gartenhaus whose Christian experience was published in booklet form by the Million Testaments Campaign in Philadelphia under the title, 'A Jew, a Book, a Miracle'?"

When I replied that I was, her face immediately lit up, and she could not contain her joy. "I just feel like shouting," she exclaimed. She then said, "That story has been translated into Hungarian, and many thousands of copies have been distributed with the Prophecy Edition of the New Testament, resulting in the conversion of several hundred Jewish people. I have always cherished a hope of meeting you some day and thanking you. . . ." She could not go on, for she broke down in tears—and so did I.

I was told that there was to be a secret meeting of some of the believers in one of the homes and that they would like to meet me if I was not too tired. I told them that I would be more than happy to come. We did not go to the meeting together but just one or two at a time, as we did not wish to arouse any suspicion. As we walked along, one of the men asked me to lower my voice, for he thought someone was following us. Always we had to be cautious.

I wish I could describe that first meeting! I was reminded of the early followers of Christ who met in the catacombs of Rome. After some refreshments, I brought a brief message, and then we made plans for the future.

Not all experiences which I had behind the Iron Curtain were as dramatic as these, but there were many others which have made an indelible impression on my life. I have often thanked the Lord for choosing me as a messenger to these my brethren. The International Board of Jewish Missions has since been in close contact with some who managed to survive, and we have received glowing reports of their successful activities in witnessing to their people.

CHAPTER 24

CUBA

Another important stop in my prewar travels was with the Jews who had fled to Cuba to escape the horrors of Hitler's regime as it spread throughout Europe. My mission was to make known to these destitute and spiritually impoverished people the one Hope for them.

In Havana I found a thriving Jewish community, complete with five synagogues, a Jewish center with its day school, a clinic, a Zionist Union of Cuba and other societies, a Jewish publishing house, and strictly Jewish streets where one could find small stores, kosher butcher shops, kosher restaurants, and where I heard Yiddish just as in any large city in Poland, Israel, or the United States. A conservative estimate placed the Jewish population in Cuba at between twenty and twenty-five thousand in those days.

Never had I found more open doors or spoken to a more hungry people. My supply of gospel literature was soon exhausted, so we had several thousand leaflets printed in both Spanish and English.

No sooner did some of these leaflets fall into the hands of the Jewish people than inquiries began to come in to us. The first came from a Jewish woman, the manager of a factory, who had received a tract from one of her Christian employees. Responding to her request, I went to her home and found a young man and his wife who were of great assistance in my witness to the Jewish lady. They were visiting her and had, no doubt, been sent there by the Lord to help me persuade others of the truth. Before I left, the young man himself requested that I send him a New Testament.

The Cousin of Albert Einstein Saved

From there we proceeded to the home of Mr. Jacob Einstein, a second cousin to the famous scientist, Dr. Albert Einstein. This highly educated, cultured, and refined businessman had lived for several years in Italy as a prosperous manufacturer. He had sensed the growing anti-Semitism there, but at first he did not think it could affect the Italian people, since among their most loyal citizens were many people of the Jewish race. But, he reasoned, was that not also the case in Germany? Even in Italy laws were soon put into force limiting the rights of the Jews, and while they did not affect him directly, he saw them as precursors to other laws of a more drastic nature. Having little alternative, he left the country.

When I asked Mr. Einstein what had appealed to him most in our church, he replied, "The simplicity of its worship and the earnestness of its followers as contrasted with the Roman Catholic church with all its ostentatious ritualism. Over there I saw too much church and no vital religion."

I challenged him to take a strong stand for Christ, and he united with a local church and followed Christ in believer's baptism. Although this man was uprooted from his home in Italy, his business practically wiped out, and separated from his loved ones for months, he seemed to be free from bitterness and was most hopeful for the future. His eyes were set on the United States. He later corresponded with me, and I was glad to hear that he had indeed come to this country. The gospel had reached him and changed his life.

CUBA

Speaking on Cuban Streets

While walking along one of the large avenues, I was approached by a peddler. I asked in Hebrew if he were a Jew. He was amazed and replied, "Are you Jewish also?" I answered that I was a Jewish Christian, and although he was anxious to make a sale, he forgot about his merchandise and listened eagerly as I told him how I had found the Messiah.

Soon other young peddlers, who perhaps thought that their friend had gotten hold of a millionaire, came over and joined us, and we had a little open-air meeting right there.

As I continued to wander through the narrow, crooked streets of Old Havana and heard the familiar tongue, I realized that I was in a "new Jerusalem" which was actually very old. I saw firsthand the poverty that prevailed in that country among most of the Jews. Approaching a man in European garb I found that he had miraculously escaped from Poland just as the German army was approaching. For three months he had been on the high seas, stopping at one port and then another, until he finally found a landing place in Cuba. When I spoke to him, he had not yet received word from his wife and children from whom he had been separated during the escape.

After this, I visited the Jewish center (Centro-Israelita), a well-equipped headquarters for Jewish activity. There was a spacious hall for meetings and various schoolrooms for Jewish children. Here I saw a hundred or more refugee children, many of whom did not know whether their parents were alive or dead.

Among the prominent refugees who found themselves in Havana at this time was a German doctor by the name of Dr. Erich Meyer, who had come to Cuba with his mother and a sister. Upon entering Cuba, Dr. Meyer had to put up a cash bond of $500 for each member of his family, made possible by friends who had helped him to leave Italy. As a foreigner he could not practice medicine except under the protection of some native doctor in Cuba. Neither could he seek any other employment except under very limited and very special circumstances, which he could not meet.

A committee in Cuba listened to Dr. Meyer's pleas but refused to help him and even treated him unkindly when he told them he was a Christian. He wrote, "So the only help we could get, and we are very thankful for, was through Dr. Gartenhaus' mediation on our behalf. Besides, we thank the Lord daily that in the brethren and ministers of the churches we have found some good friends." Financial help was given.

Once again the Lord had given me an opportunity to help one of my own brethren. How I praise Him for the privilege of serving Him.

Today, many of Cuba's Jews live in the Miami area, but several thousand are still in Havana. Some have settled in Israel. One of Havana's synagogues is serving as a Jewish center. Despite food shortages, the government allows Jews to have extra rations of meat, fish, and other foods for Jewish holidays and gives them freedom to worship.

C H A P T E R 2 5

LAUNCHING A WORLDWIDE MINISTRY

After having worked with the southern Jews for a number of years, I was reassured that missionary work among the Jews was not only *not* "impossible, inexpedient, unfeasible," as many Christians had assumed, but that it truly was a rewarding and needed field. With this reassurance came the conviction that my ministry should not be limited to the southern states of America, but should be extended to the entire Diaspora—to my Jewish brethren wherever they sojourn. This thought tugged at my heart for some years, till the time came when I could no longer withstand the inner call for an unlimited, worldwide ministry among my people.

An Epoch-Making Change in World Jewry

World War II left the Jewish people broken to pieces. Of the eighteen million Jews that existed in the world before the war, one third (about six million) were murdered by the Nazis. Almost all of European Jewry and the teeming great Jewish centers of life and culture were wiped out. The remaining Jews, maimed in body and spirit, were wandering about aimlessly, not knowing where to lay their heads. No people wanted them in their midst. Several million Jews remained alive behind the Iron Curtain but were not permitted to practice their faith in public. The Jews in the free world (especially in America) did all they could to assuage the anguish of their luckless, beaten brethren all over the world. But everybody knew that the people could not be helped by temporary palliatives. The Jewish race could perpetuate its identity and its very life only if it had a home of its own—and *that* home could be only in the Promised Land, the land of the forefathers.

The world powers—especially the so-called "Christian nations" who at enormous cost had defeated the godless tyranny of the Nazis and their allies—recognizing that the "Jewish problem" could best be solved by an independent national home, saw to it that such a home was established. Thus the state of Israel came into being. This was not accomplished without struggle; all the world knows how tiny Israel had to fight for her life against overwhelming and implacable enemies. Not only were the seven Arab nations surrounding her determined to wipe out all vestige of this new "baby" state in their midst, but aligned with them were the hundreds of millions of Moslems all over the world, as well as the non-Christian peoples who knew nothing of the Bible. Even some Christian ministers, who either were ignorant of the true meaning of prophecy or of the stupendous events that were happening around the world, sided with the enemies of the Jewish state.

But there were thousands of people who knew their Bible, who knew what was going on in and about the land of the Bible, who saw clearly how the most weighty prophecies were being minutely fulfilled, who heard the stirring of *"the dry bones of Israel,"* and who felt that the "fullness of the Gentiles" was rapidly approaching. These thousands believed that something should be done so that this remnant of the people of the covenant should know of the glorious future that is in store for them when they acknowledge their Messiah—their Saviour. Each one should know that his Redeemer liveth. Each one should know that he is not alone in a hostile world, that Emmanuel—"God is with us."

Many of these faithful children of God began urging me by letter and by word of mouth to do for worldwide Jewry at least what I had been doing for our southern Jews—at least that much. There was no need for much persuasion as I, too, had long felt the urgency of an all-embracing mission. My heart went out to my Jewish brethren. Even more than others, I well knew that only the gospel of the Saviour of man could salvage these remnants. This gospel must be made known to them.

Reaching the Shipwrecked Wanderers

How could I reach all of these physically, mentally, and spiritually shipwrecked wanderers? The board (Southern Baptist) was too much occupied with its various undertakings and told me that it could not add to its responsibilities. I could find no other organization to launch this expedition of rescuing the lost sheep of the house of Israel. After much prayer, I decided to start out by myself, in faith believing that the Lord would raise up friends who would uphold me in prayer and financial support. Thus the International Board of Jewish Missions was born—a worldwide parish with the aim of responding to friendless and lost Israel around the world. This was a people who desperately needed the true knowledge of God and His saving grace.

The April, 1949, issue of Southern Baptist Home Missions reported my resignation:

> Brother Gartenhaus's influence and ministry through the years has extended far beyond the area of the Southern Baptist Convention. He is president of the Hebrew Chris-

tian Alliance of America and has made numerous trips to foreign countries in the interest of his people. He has made a lasting contribution to the work of Christ.

Now he goes into a wider ministry among his people with the good wishes of a multitude of friends among Southern Baptists.

Let us all remember him in our prayers.

I Was on Marching Orders

Was I too presumptuous? Did I feel worthy and capable of such an immense task? No. I knew only too well my shortcomings. I knew that to undertake such a task, strength and wisdom beyond my own were needed. Yet I was not to argue, to vacillate—I heard the command "Go!" and I dared not resist. I knew that there was no period in Jewish history when the preaching of the gospel was so vital to Israel, and through Israel, to all mankind: "For if the casting away of them *be* the reconciling of the world, what *shall* the receiving *of them be,* but life from the dead?" (Rom. 11:15).

Now I was on my own. There was no powerful organization such as the Southern Baptist Convention to sponsor me—no patronage to sustain the newborn baby, the International Board of Jewish Missions. Many of my former friends deserted or ignored me. I was considered an adventurer launching out into unknown and uncharted seas.

We announced our objectives as follows:

The evangelization of the Jews at home and abroad by:
1. The publication and distribution of suitable literature for Jews, setting forth the message of Hebrew Christianity.
2. The establishment of Friends of Israel societies for the purpose of propagating Christianity among the Jews and praying for their salvation.

3. The training of members of the church on how to approach the Jews through the local church in order to bring about a better understanding of the Jewish problems by Christians and of the Christian message by Jews.
4. The employment of capable, God-called men and women to labor in neglected strategic areas where there is no testimony to Israel.
5. Cooperation with the churches in their efforts to create a prayerful interest in the evangelization of the Jews in their midst.
6. The holding of prophetic conferences with the aim of setting forth God's plan and purpose for Israel and, through Israel, for the world.
7. The holding of special good-will meetings for Christians and Jews, including open forums.
8. The utilization of radio facilities in proclaiming the message of the Saviour to Israel.
9. The distribution of relief through Jewish Christian agencies, especially to the twice-forsaken Jewish Christians—forsaken by their own because of their faith, and by so-called Christians because they belong to "the hated race" (including orphans of Jewish Christian parents).
10. The rendering of financial assistance to deserving Jewish missionaries in Europe who look to Christian Americans in their hour of need.

My friends and supporters chose me to guide and direct this worldwide undertaking, and that is what I have been doing ever since its founding. When we started out we were practically penniless; but we were rich in prayer—and prayer can move mountains. God working through us caused the pennies and the dollars to come in, and before long, we were on our way. Macedonian calls began pouring in from far and wide, and we responded as speedily as humanly possible. While expanding our ministry in our homeland, we pushed out to Central America and to South America, then to the other continents, to Europe, Asia, and Africa, paying special attention to our brethren in Israel.

TRAITOR?

We even penetrated the Iron Curtain. Not only could we maintain and expand our own work, but we also helped several other organizations and private missionaries who were doing the King's business in various lands.

By various deeds of benevolence we brought help to needy brethren in many lands. We aided (money, food, and clothing) many needy Jewish families because we were sure that to do so would be to the glory of God. Where did we get the money for these manifold deeds? Was there any special fund at our disposal?

We had no funds (certainly not in the beginning), but we were sure that the Lord would provide all our needs—and He did. Contributions, not from rich organizations nor philanthropists but from devout children of God, mostly poor people, came in day by day. They were not profuse, but we managed to make ends meet.

We have been fortunate to have on our board men of God imbued with His love and wisdom; with their help we learned how to make the pennies do the work of dollars. Whenever an emergency arose—some new needs or new problems—these men were on the alert, ready to stand by, to pull through, and to push forward. Among our friends and faithful supporters there have been many pastors who, convinced of the great importance of our ministry, have always been ready to extend a helping hand. Yet, with all this loyal and bountiful help, the task of clearing the way for the evangelization of my brethren has not been easy. On the occasion of the tenth birthday of the International Board of Jewish Missions we submitted this report:

Report submitted to THE BOARD OF DIRECTORS of the INTERNATIONAL BOARD OF JEWISH MISSIONS, INC. in 1959
Dear Friends:
   The following is a brief history of our worldwide ministry which has reached its tenth birthday. In the providence of God and after much earnest prayer, the International

LAUNCHING A WORLDWIDE MINISTRY

Board of Jewish Missions was organized in 1949 in response to the heartcry of friendless, hopeless, and lost Israel in many parts of the world. It required no little faith to launch out into a worldwide ministry with no guarantee of support from any source, relying solely on God's redeemed children; and in a thousand ways He has blessed us far beyond anything we ever expected, giving us one victory after another.

1. The first Macedonian call came to us from the land south of the border—Mexico, with its tens of thousands of Jews—a field rich and ripe unto harvest. And the Lord has truly showered His blessings upon the work there. Large shipments of New Testaments, Gospels, and tracts in several languages have gone there. We have conducted several campaigns resulting in hundreds of conversions.

2. Our next step of faith was to answer calls from several countries in Europe (England, France, Germany, Austria) and even behind the Iron Curtain, a door shut to many. It is nothing short of miraculous how those heroes of the cross have been able to carry on in the face of danger and even death.

3. Similarly, the Lord led us to begin a ministry in Israel, where things of tremendous importance have been taking place. Prophecies of centuries are being fulfilled. From the four corners of the earth the "dry bones" of Israel are now being gathered to the land of their fathers by wings of the air,* ships of the sea, and highways of the world.

4. He next led us to undertake a ministry among the teeming Jewish multitudes in South Africa, India, and Australia.

5. And not the least in importance is our ministry among the six million Jewish people in our own beloved land. By word of mouth and through the printed page, from pulpit and radio, and by personal visitation, we have sought to make the message of our living Saviour known to the lost sheep of the house of Israel.

6. In addition to the above-mentioned activities we have been able to extend a helping hand to needy and deserving Jewish Christians throughout the world. Tons of food, clothing, and medicine have been shipped to them. Thank

*They called it "the magic carpet." The Jews from the Yemen were brought in by airplanes.

God, we have never had to turn a deaf ear to any plea for help.

7. From the very first, one of the objectives of the International Board of Jewish Missions, Inc., has been to render financial assistance to worthy missionaries and mission organizations both at home and abroad.

We have been cooperating with the oldest evangelical Jewish mission organization in the world, The British Society for the Propagation of the Gospel Among the Jews, London, England, having undertaken the full support of some of their missionaries and the partial support of others.

We are also cooperating with The Society for Distributing the Holy Scriptures to the Jews, London, England, in distributing bilingual New Testaments in Hebrew-English, Hebrew-French, Hebrew-Spanish, and Hebrew-Dutch, as their representative for North and South America. Tens of thousands of New Testaments have been mailed out to the Jews in some seventy different countries. Last year some one thousand rabbis and other Jewish leaders here in America received the Hebrew-English New Testament, and their response is simply miraculous. The letters from rabbis, rabbinical students, and others thanking us for these Testaments, sending us the names of those to whom they wish us to send copies, are enough to stir anyone's soul. . . .

Just now we have been led to support two new missionaries in South America, where there are more than a million lost sheep of the house of Israel. And with God's help we have published a bilingual Gospel of Matthew in Hebrew and Portuguese, the language spoken in Brazil.

A number of churches have included our work in their budgets, and the Lord has marvelously blessed them for it. Some have designated twenty-five, others fifty, some one hundred dollars a month. I do not know of a greater challenge facing the Christian world today than the evangelization of our Lord's own brethren. God's promise to Abraham still holds, "I will bless them that bless thee."

For almost two thousand years Israel's cry was "Away with Him!", but today the Jews are anxious to know about Him, and as they search the Scriptures they are finding that the Jesus whom they have so long rejected is none other than the One promised to them. They are reclaiming Him as their own. In recent years several chief rabbis, men of letters, scientists, physicians, and other Jewish professional men have embraced the Christian faith. God's time, yea the set time, to favor Zion is now in progress. The opportunities for presenting Christ to Israel have never been greater.

C H A P T E R   2 6

SOUTH AMERICAN CHALLENGE

Latin America was included in my plans when I launched our worldwide ministries, but it was a matter of doing first things first. It was true that thousands of Jewish refugees had flocked to South America and founded large Jewish centers in the major cities. It was true that they remained there as sheep with no shepherd, no one to care for their spiritual welfare. It was true that they were in need of the love and hope and happiness which can only be found in harmony with God's will. All that, and more, was true of these in Latin America, but we lacked the means to extend our spiritual help to them in those early years after World War II.

First priority was the urgent need to evangelize the new Jewish state of Israel which had miraculously come into being, electrifying world Jewry. Next in importance were the Jewish centers that had survived in Europe, especially those that were growing in quality and population. It was necessary to maintain and expand our work there. Then, as soon as we had the opportunity to extend our boundaries (Isa. 54:1–3), we started work in Mexico, Cuba and Jamaica. Still, we did not have the means to reach farther down into the South American countries.

Throughout the early years, I had been continually receiving S.O.S. calls to come and see with my own eyes the challenge, the urgency, and the opportunity existing in South America, but our hands were tied and I could not answer the calls. All during 1961, as I celebrated forty years in the ministry, I reflected upon the triumphs and failures of the ministry. South America loomed large before my eyes, pointing an accusing finger as if to say, "You have failed us!" I tried to calm such feelings and excuse myself by answering, "I have done all I could within the means at my disposal. I have sent literature, tracts, Gospels, and especially the Hebrew-Spanish bilingual New Testaments. I have even supported to some extent those few people who took it upon themselves to preach the gospel to my brethren."

But still guilt tugged at my heart. In my deep sorrow I brought my burden before God and prayed, "Oh Lord, let not this failure overshadow the ministry—let me do something worthwhile also for my brethren in South America; provide me with the means of visiting them where they are and seeing how they live that I might learn the best way to lead them in Thy way to life eternal." The Lord heard my prayer and made the trip possible.

I left Miami airport on November 10, 1961, for Quito, Ecuador. There I enjoyed both the privilege of visiting missionaries of the Wycliffe Bible Translators and of broadcasting brief messages over H.C.J.B.'s shortwave radio station. I was greatly impressed with the extent of these ministries, as well as with the personnel working there.

Before leaving for South America, I prayed that the Lord would give a special blessing in each place I visited. And since my mission was primarily to the lost sheep of the house of Israel, I asked Him to put us in contact with worthy individuals who had a burden for Israel. It is remarkable how the Lord answered those prayers.

At Quito the missionaries of radio station H.C.J.B. (Heralding Christ Jesus' Blessings) told of a young Jewish man who had accepted Christ. While his parents were not Christians, they did not seem to interfere with the faith that had made such a wonderful change in his life. I had opportunity to witness to his parents, and they drank in every word while the young man's face radiated joy. I pointed out the Jewish background of the Christian faith and urged them not to judge Christianity by the actions of the Nazis or by the erroneous beliefs and pagan customs of their Roman Catholic neighbors. They should instead judge Christianity by the teachings of the Holy Scriptures. I called attention to those faithful missionaries who had given up the comforts of home, family, and friends to labor in the jungles, often risking their very lives.

I also told them that I, for example, had not changed my religion at all, but rather had become a better Jew. In talking about the Jewish community at Quito, they told me there did not seem to be any special interest among the Jews in their observance of Judaism. The young man and his parents went on to say that out of the several hundred Jews in the area, it was hard to gather a minyan (the necessary quorum of ten males) for communal prayer. The rabbi who had been there had left because, they said, he wanted a larger salary, and the Jews refused to give it to him. That refusal was not based on a lack of funds, because the community was quite prosperous. It was because the community lacked interest in rabbinism and because the old Jewish traditions and customs were losing their meaning; the leaders had little else to satisfy the people's spiritual hunger.

Peru

My next stop was Lima, Peru, where I spent a few days visiting Jewish stores and the Jewish cultural center where meals were served. At the cultural center I found a large group of Jewish women idling away their time in games. I asked one of the men about the center's activities. He just smiled and said that the men and women came twice a week for the same purpose—to kill time through gambling. He also said that they often remained at the center until the wee hours of the morning. He then told me about a restaurant which served as a general rendezvous spot for the Jewish people.

At that restaurant I found refugees from various parts of Europe who had survived the cruelest persecution known to the modern world. They were indeed a pathetic group that seemed to have lost all hope in humanity. Some had found material success in their new home, while others merely eked out a living. I had many interesting conversations with them, and when I asked about Judaism in the city I was told that there was just one rabbi and that he was very orthodox. "You had better stay away from him," cautioned one man. "There is no telling what he might do to you."

But an inner voice kept urging, "Go ahead and call the rabbi; the worst that can happen is that he will refuse to see you, or if he sees you, he will insult you and order you to leave." It would not have been the first such experience for me, and I was equally certain that it would not be the last. So I phoned the rabbi, told him my name, that I was visiting from the United States while on a tour of South America, and that I should like to have the pleasure of making his acquaintance.

He not only replied that he would be delighted to see me, but asked if I could come right then. I supposed that he thought me a wealthy businessman who would perhaps make a generous contribution to some worthy charitable institution. I did not want to give him any false hopes, but before I could tell him anything about myself, he asked if I were in the city on a business or a pleasure trip.

"Rabbi," I replied, "if I tell you right away the purpose of my mission, it may shock you."

"We are not easily shocked," he answered. "In recent years events have shocked us to pieces."

I took a taxi to the rabbi's home, and after the usual greetings he invited me into the living room where his wife had already placed refreshments on the table. I had been praying from the very moment when I talked with him on the phone that the Lord would put the right words in my mouth. I soon realized that I was in the presence of a man who was well versed in the history and traditions of his people.

After some preliminaries he cordially asked: "Tell me, what brings you here?"

"For many years now," I replied, "I have been trying to bring about a better understanding between Christians and Jews. . . ."

"That is like trying to mix oil and water," he interrupted; "it never has and never will be accomplished."

"Perhaps not in our lifetime," I responded, "but God's Word tells us: 'Thus saith the Lord of hosts: In those days *it shall come to pass,* that ten men shall take hold . . . of the skirt of him that is a Jew, saying, We will go with you: for we have heard *that* God *is* with you' (Zech. 8:23)."

"True," he said, "but that will only take place when the Messiah comes, and the nations of the world will then be converted to Judaism."

"You're right; the prophet Isaiah told us about that in 2:2-4," I answered.

"I see you are well versed in our Holy Scriptures," he said.

"Rabbi," I replied, "in studying the Scriptures I discovered that the Messiah has already come. . . ."

"Surely you do not believe that that Nazarene (may his name be blotted out), that deceiver and traitor, is the Messiah!"

"Yes, I do believe that the Man you so derogatively refer to—Jesus, Yeshua of Nazareth—was the Messiah. He was no deceiver, no traitor. He did not lead people away from God but rather He pointed them to God. Matthew 5:17 says: 'Think not that I am come to destroy the law, or the prophets: I am not come to destroy, but to fulfil.'"

I pointed out that countless millions of people through the centuries who have believed in the God of Abraham, Isaac, and Jacob have come to that belief through the teachings of the followers of Jesus. I explained to him that there is a difference between a Gentile and a born-again Christian and again quoted Jesus in Matthew 7:21: "Not every one that sayeth unto me, Lord, Lord, shall enter into the kingdom of heaven; but he that doeth the will of my Father which is in heaven."

He protested indignantly, "Do you mean to say that image worship practiced by the Christians is not idolatry; that it is in accordance with the worship of the true God?"

"The image worship that we see here is most certainly not Christian, and it is as repulsive to me as it is to you, Rabbi."

"Do you also believe in the Virgin Birth?" he asked. When I answered yes, he exclaimed, "I am surprised! How can you, a modern man, a Jew, believe such nonsense? Do you know of any other woman who had a child without a man?"

"No," I replied, "and that is the very reason I believe Jesus to be the Messiah and Redeemer. It was unusual, extraordinary! It was a miracle!"

I then reminded him that Isaiah prophesied that the Messiah would be born of a virgin, in 7:14: "Therefore the Lord himself shall give you a sign; Behold, a virgin shall conceive, and bear a son, and shall call his name Immanuel."

"But," the rabbi insisted, "that may have been quite natural as our commentators would have it. The Hebrew word *almah* here does not mean 'virgin,' but a 'young woman' who may be impregnated by a man."

I looked at him surprised and said: "Your contentions and arguments might come from the mouth or pen of either a Reform rabbi, who does not believe much in our Jewish Torah, or from an ignoramus in Jewish lore. But you, Rabbi, who, as I have heard and as I have learned, are well-versed not only in the Tanach [Old Testament books] but also in rabbinic post-biblical literature, should know better! You should know that Isaiah speaks of a 'virgin' giving birth as a 'sign,' a 'miracle.' There would be no sign or miracle in an ordinary woman bearing a child in an ordinary way."

I called his attention to the fact that the Old Testament tells of many supernatural occurrences, for example, the supernatural birth of Isaac. God is Almighty, and as He created the world in a miraculous way so He is ruling it miraculously day by day, moment by moment. The greatness of the Jewish people stems from their being born by a miracle, reared by miracles. Their very survival is the greatest miracle in history!

The question of the Trinity came up, and I told him that a believing Jew should have no difficulty in accepting the visible manifestations of the Godhead. The Jewish Bible tells us that God descended from heaven in angelic form and talked with people. I told him of Abraham's experience with God, who appeared to him in the plains of Mamre. I read to him the account in the eighteenth chapter of Genesis and many other passages which point to the triune Godhead.

"Rabbi," I said, "you must believe in all of the Torah or in none of it."

It was marvelous to see how he drank in every word and to see how his attitude changed. As the conversation continued, he no longer referred to Jesus with bitterness but with some respect.

Finally he said, "I told you that I had an engagement and I could only spend ten minutes with you, and here we have spent more than an hour together. You are the first man of our own people with whom I have talked like this."

"Rabbi," I said, "it would take me several hours to go over some of the prophecies concerning our Messiah which have been minutely fulfilled in Jesus. Have you ever read the New Testament? I should like to present you with one. I do not have a copy with me, but I shall mail one to you."

He replied that he would be glad to receive it. Then, surprisingly, he added: "I have three sons; two are rabbis, and the other is a doctor of medicine. They all live in New York. I should appreciate your sending them also copies of the New Testament. Let me give you their addresses, and if you are ever in New York, be sure to visit them."

How I kept wishing that thousands of my Christian friends could have been there to listen to our discussion. I would have had no difficulty in getting support not only for our South American work, but also for an enlarged ministry around the world.

"If you stay long enough, I should like to see you again," he concluded. "I should like to keep you here a little longer, but I am already late for my appointment. I want to order a taxi to take you back to the hotel."

Image Worship

It is no easy task to try to interest any Jewish person in Christ, especially in South America where the people are surrounded with idolatrous worship and all kinds of sin, where the Roman Catholic Church owns so much of the land and the people are kept in darkness. Invariably the Jews refer to the image worship of their neighbors. They ask if that is what we want them to believe in. One morning while I was speaking to a Jewish merchant, a procession went by led by priests. The people and the priests were carrying images of Christ, Mary, and the saints. Pointing to the procession, the merchant said, "Is that what you would have us believe in—to exchange a living God for such idols?!"

"Certainly not," I answered. "It saddens my heart to see how those people have perverted the true faith. No, I do not want you to believe in such," and I quoted Psalm 115:4–8: "Their idols *are* silver and gold, the work of men's hands. They have mouths, but they speak not: eyes have they, but they see not: they have ears, but they hear not: noses have they, but they smell not: they have hands, but they handle not: feet have they, but they walk not: neither speak they through their throat. They that make them are like unto them: *so is* every one that trusteth in them." "No, my friend," I said, "I want you to believe in the God who created the universe. He who revealed Himself to our fathers, the same One in whom Moses believed and about whom the prophets wrote."

Argentina

In Buenos Aires, Argentina, I met several fine Jewish Christian men, talented and capable, who had dedicated their lives to the Lord. They had suffered a great deal for their faith, one man having been ordered to leave the home of his well-to-do family. These men offered their services to the International Board of Jewish Missions, Inc., and I promised not to forget them.

Uruguay

The next stop was Montevideo, Uruguay, where I was greeted by our own beloved Dr. A. Nestor Figari. He arranged a meeting for me at our then newly opened Shalom Center where he had a dispensary and spent much of his time ministering to the physical needs of the Jewish people, who never left there without receiving spiritual aid as well. When the time came for the meeting, all seats were taken and hardly any standing room was left. Many were standing outside on the street.

Back to Brazil

After spending some forty-eight busy hours in Montevideo, I went to Sao Paulo, Brazil, where several meetings similar to those in Montevideo were held.

I have been back to South America several times since that year. Our work has expanded and is continuing to expand in that vast continent.

CHAPTER 27

A POSTAL MINISTRY

My worldwide ministry entailed, among many other responsibilities, an enormous correspondence. Letters were received from all parts of the world—reports from missionaries; requests for help from needy and deserving Hebrew Christians and nonbelievers as well; letters from Jewish organizations, from pastors and laymen, asking my opinion on matters pertaining to Jewish laws and customs, seeking information as to the best approach in winning their Jewish friends; letters from hundreds of Jewish inquirers wanting to know about Christianity and its doctrines; and letters from those hostile to our work. As I write these lines, I have just received a special delivery air mail letter, sent collect, which is full of insulting and abusive language. Happily, such letters are now rare.

My own letters were often sent to editors 1) of Jewish publications, refuting accusations made against the Christian faith, the New Testament, converts, and missionaries; and 2) of non-Jewish publications, combatting heresies, "liberalism," and anti-Semitism, including theological anti-Semitism, such as the assertion that God has rejected the Jews.

My letters to Jewish leaders and organizations pointed out that fighting Christianity is detrimental to Judaism and to the Jewish people and asked these recipients to use their influence to prevent alienation of the Christians, who are the only true friends the Jewish people have.

I reproduce here a few excerpts from letters I sent to Jewish publications. The first letter I wrote when I was still young in years and only a babe in Christ; it was printed in Chicago in the Jewish publication, *The Lawndale Press,* September 5, 1919.

I was prompted to write this letter after a succession of boisterous attacks that often threatened the lives of those of us engaged in open-air meetings in Jewish sections of the city, under the auspices of the Chicago Hebrew Mission with which I was connected as a part-time worker while a student at the Moody Bible Institute.

Of course, this terrorizing and intimidation did not deter us from returning again and again to bear witness to the saving grace of our Saviour and Lord. No doubt our zeal, fearlessness, and self-sacrifice made a profound impression on many of the harassing audience. In time we learned that much of the seed we sowed fell upon good ground and bore fruit; some of those very antagonists accepted the Saviour. However, fearing a devastating wave of anti-Semitism, I thought it best to appeal to the better senses of the Jewish community through the Jewish press, which had a tremendous influence on the Jewish people. I prayed fervently that the editors might be persuaded to publish my letter, even though they, like most Jews, looked upon the Jewish convert as a renegade.

But the miracle happened, and my letter was printed in full, followed by the editor's remarks which hesitatingly agreed with the contents. As expected, the editor subsequently was severely rebuked in other letters for the "crime" of publishing mine. It was perhaps the first time in Jewish history that a responsible Jewish periodical published with due respect the words of a meshummad, who might be presenting "Christian propaganda" before the Jewish public. Evidently it helped somewhat to calm the passions of the masses, who later were less violent.

A LETTER TO THE EDITOR AND
AN ANSWER BY THE EDITOR

In our mail last week we found a letter which interested us because the writer gives every evidence of being sincere in the stand he takes. A man should be taken seriously when he speaks or writes sincerely.

In order to prove that we are fair, we publish the letter herewith and desire to comment upon it as the writer requests.

Here is the letter:

The Editor of the *Lawndale Press,*
1425-1427 So. Kedzie Avenue
Chicago, Ill.

Dear Sir:

Referring to the editorial entitled "The Zionist Open-Air Meetings" which appeared last week in your Press, you said: "The Zionists have had good open-air meetings throughout the city and especially in the Lawndale district." You also say that "these open-air meetings were conducted not only with good results but with the best of order, showing that the Jewish people have a way of going about things with that respect for law and common decency which is an instinct with the chosen seed."

I attended one of the Zionists' meetings. It was on Turner near Twelfth, and I stood there at the meeting for a whole hour. The Jews did indeed show a good spirit at this meeting, but I am sure that many did not agree with the speaker. There were followers of all kinds of "isms," still they gave him their attention. While at this meeting I said to myself the Jews indeed remember the words which Moses said to the Israelites of old before they entered the Promised Land —"*But* the stranger that dwelleth with you shall be unto you as one born among you, and thou shalt love him as thyself; for ye were strangers in the land of Egypt . . ." (Lev.19:34). Or they still remember that they were strangers in Russia. Roumania, and Poland, so that now they have learned to respect the liberty that this country gives to this people. This is one side of the story.

Now let us go back to the statement which you made in

the editorial that it "is an instinct with the chosen seed" to respect the law of liberty. Last Friday evening, August 22, walking on Twelfth Street, near Kedzie Avenue, I heard a disturbing noise and saw people running from every side, and when I came to Spaulding Avenue, near Twelfth Street, I saw an open-air meeting which was being conducted by missionaries. There were at least one thousand people —a mixed crowd of Jews and Gentiles. Rotten fruit, eggs, and stones were thrown at the missionaries. Some people cried "Let us kill them," others "Let us break their auto —let us mob them." At the same time, the missionary, a former lawyer, stood up to make a statement and said, "This is a free country; every one has a right to speak what he wants, and if you do not want to listen, you can go; you need not stay; but I know that there are many here who would like to listen." Yet the mob kept on throwing the stones and other things. An officer came along, and also a private detective, and they tried to keep the people from mobbing the missionaries. The mob resisted the officer, and he had to use his revolver, shooting in the air. To make a long story short, the meeting was ended with the coming of the patrol and a few arrests were made.

I beg of you to give your opinion of this "outrage" just as you did of the Zionist meeting. Do you know that if that officer had not come at that moment the missionaries would have been killed? Who knows how much the Jews would have suffered if such a thing had happened? If one of the many stones that were thrown had hit the missionary, he would have been killed. Do you know that a little stone thrown by a white boy at a black boy caused the riots in this city and the deaths of over thirty; and it also brought shame upon the whole city? Something similar to that can happen if these disturbances continue.

Thanking you for your interest which was shown when I called you on the telephone and you told me to write you a letter, and hoping you will give this your kind consideration, I am

Sincerely yours,
Jacob Gartenhaus

P.S. —The writer of this letter assures you that he has a love in his heart for Jews. He is also willing to lay down his life, if necessary, to help his people. Those who know him know it to be true.

1505 So. Sawyer Avenue, Chicago, Illinois

TRAITOR?

And this is our reply:

In the first place we are inclined to think that the writer makes more of the disturbance he speaks of than the facts justify. A crowd of people may be very noisy and yet not be murderous. We contend that there is no such thing as a murderous Jewish mob. The writer says that in the crowd there were "Jews and Gentiles." We are inclined to believe that the greater portion of the crowd was not Jewish and what passed for being Jewish consisted perhaps of a few "gangsters" who unfortunately are to be found among the Jewish people.

But even a peaceful and mild-mannered crowd has a right to express itself when its deepest feelings are attacked.

Suppose some "missionary" were to force his way into a crowded Polish neighborhood and try to tear the people away from their love of the Polish land, their love for Polish songs, and their pride in the way Poland has fought for her liberty throughout the centuries against those who sought her life? What could the fairest-minded person say if such a misguided individual were pelted by the people and driven from their midst?

The Christian missionary who goes against the Jewish people and tries to tell them that they are wrong in the beliefs they hold and thus robs them of their moral fibre, especially if he be a converted Jew, appears to them only in the light of a renegade, a traitor, and the writer knows that the penalty of the traitor is death.

Instead of cautioning the people to be careful what they do lest some tragedy bring down feeling upon them, we ask the missionaries to cease their ill-advised efforts. If they persist in the face of obviously resentful opposition, they are to blame for the trouble that follows, not those who show the truest manhood in resenting attacks on their people and all that their people hold dear.

At the time of the publishing of this letter, I was still "green." A student at Moody Bible Institute, I was preparing for the ministry to which God had called me and this was my first step in the literary work of my ministry.

Since then I have spent fifty years in the work of presenting Christ to my own Jewish brethren through various means, including Jewish publications. My letters have ap-

246

peared sometimes without editorial comment, sometimes with a very acrimonious retort. Every letter of this kind has brought in its wake several letters to the editor, usually criticizing him for allowing a meshummad to express such ideas through his publication. Sometimes there have been letters upholding my stand, but, of course, more often the letters have been outpourings of scurrilous abuse. However, my letters and the replies they have brought have aroused the general attention of my brethren to the problem of the evangelization of the Jews.

In the course of time, I have learned that these letters have led many of my people to search the Scriptures. Many of them have written me, asking questions, requesting New Testaments and tracts. I am sure that much of the seed thus sown has fallen on good ground, the Lord has blessed it, and it has borne good fruit. Thus many of my people have found in Jesus their long-looked-for Messiah.

Of course, as is to be expected, many of the editors have refused to publish my letters. *The Southern Israelite,* for example, which publishes vitriolic attacks on Christianity (often founded on lies and distortions), has not published my refutations of these attacks.

Such letters have also been sent to other secular and religious publications whenever I have felt the need to defend Christian principles which they have assaulted. One novelty was the printing of a letter of mine in *The Jerusalem Post,* the semi-official publication of the Israeli government. I was prompted to write this letter on September 27, 1963, by two events which transpired at that time in Israel: (1) A series of attacks upon missionaries and their property in Israel; and (2) the decision of Israel's Supreme Court that a Jew who becomes a Christian ceases to be a Jew.

In some of the newspapers at the time, inflammatory articles appeared intended to arouse hostile opinion against Christian mission work. Most of these articles contained false accusations, often of a ridiculous nature. I wrote to some of the most prominent leaders in Israel, bringing to their attention the harm done to Israel's cause by such manifestations of intolerance, reminding them that Christian mission work is considered the prime duty of the church and that persecution will not stop it. Rather, persecution tends to ricochet, maiming and destroying the people from whom it originated.

I considered this appeal to the leaders only a part of my defense of the faith. What I needed most was to bring my appeal to the hearts and consciences of the masses. That could be accomplished through the Jewish press, but at the time this was considered an almost impossible task.

However, after various attempts, I finally prevailed upon *The Jerusalem Post* to publish my letter. It was in the same issue as a letter from the noted Hebrew savant and philosopher, Prof. Hugo B. Bergman (of the Hebrew University in Jerusalem), which was written in quite a liberal manner. My letter was soon reprinted in various Jewish publications all over the world, and it no doubt exerted tranquilizing influence upon the Jews' hostile attitude towards converts and missionaries.

I should mention here one other of my articles, "How To Approach the Jew with the Gospel," which appeared in *Christianity Today* of December 9, 1966. This dealt with those Jewish leaders who used to attack Jewish mission work with words dropping like bombshells. Such leaders, who had been spending enormous sums of money to counteract mission work and who had been persuading more and more Christian leaders to abandon such work, were shocked to see my article in *Christianity Today,* with a circulation of over two hundred thousand, reaching into the homes of many influential Christians. They realized that Christian leaders still consider it their duty to try to win the Jews to Christ.

What is really novel in this case is that many Jewish publications reprinted that article or the gist of it without the usual diatribe against meshummadim. *The Jewish Post and Opinion,* which is considered the most prominent Jewish publication in America, reprinted the main part of my article under the heading, "Converting Jews Seen Calling for New Tact," without derogatory comment. Moreover, it introduced me, the author, in quite a favorable light. Such tolerance by Jews toward Jewish converts was rare indeed.

Another of my letters to the editor was published in *Time* magazine's December 21, 1962, issue, under the caption, "Who Is a Jew?" It raised a hue and cry all over Jewry. I was slandered by Jewish leaders, not so much because of what I had written but because I had dared in front of Gentiles to touch upon a subject which, especially at that time, was perplexing the greatest minds of the Jewish people. That letter, among others, made thousands question their identities as Jews while considering their unique, peculiar purpose in life. Here are two such letters.

To: Rabbi Sholom Klass, Editor
The Jewish Press, 338 Third St.,
Brooklyn, New York 11215

Dear Sir:

Due to my extensive travels which have taken me to South America, Israel, and Europe, this is a belated acknowledgment of appreciation for your having published my letter dated May 31, 1972, in your distinguished weekly, though with certain omissions which you considered "offensive."

I do not know which words or phrases you found offensive. Surely, I did not intend to offend anyone. Never in my life have I intentionally offended anybody. However, you did offend me and tried to strike it very hard.

You made your readers believe that I am a total AM-HAARETZ (IGNORAMOUS) and therefore it is audacious to speak of the "right kind of Judaism." Well, although I detest self-praise, I must let you and your readers know that I possess three doctorates, and all of them in recognition of my knowledge of, and achievements in, subjects directly and indirectly dealing with Judaism.

TRAITOR?

The hundreds of books and articles which I have written
and published, all to the glory of God and His people Israel,
and which have been lauded by well-known scholars, bear
witness to the fact that I am well versed in Jewish lore, and
quite capable and authorized to deal on subjects Jewish.

You may not approve of the sort of Judaism to which I
adhere, but I am certain that our great Hebrew prophets
approved of it.

You counsel me to return to the "fold." If you mean by
"fold" the Jewish people, then I must tell you that I have
never left my people. I, like all Jews who adopted the teachings of Jesus, was anathematized, expelled from the "fold."
Now if you can use your influence, see to it that the "fold"
would permit us to return to it.

An example: Several years ago I moved into a Jewish
neighborhood. No neighbor came to greet me with a "welcome," "baruch haba." When I and my family began to feel
so isolated, so disliked, I sent a letter to all my neighbors, requesting of them some neighborly contact, despite
my attitude to Christianity to which I, as a free man and a
free American citizen, have the inalienable right to hold. I
assure you that my letter, although written in a conciliatory
tone, was not acknowledged by a single neighbor, and their
attitude toward me and my family became not a whit better
than before. What of the boast about the Jewish tenet:
"Thou shalt love thy neighbor . . . ?"

But you obviously mean that I should return to the
Jewish religion. I cannot "return" to what I have never left.
True, I have adopted a different conception of what is and
should be Judaism, different from what is generally regarded as Judaism—usually meaning "halacha"—the code
of laws enacted by the rabbis during the centuries. This is a
man-made sort of Judaism, contrary to the divine law given
by Moses which forbade adding or taking from anything to
that God-given law, the Torah. The rabbis by their
"halacha" added thousands of laws to the Torah of Moses
and nullified or changed beyond recognition many of its
laws.

I rejected this rabbinic code because it is contrary to the
Mosaic Code which very few other Jews now-a-days try to
keep, at least some of these laws because they are not appli-
cable (I do not need to tell you why; any Jew could tell you
the reason for not obeying those thousands of the halachich
laws).

A POSTAL MINISTRY

Again, I have not rejected God's Torah. I simply follow Jesus Who declared that He did not come to destroy it, but to fulfill it. He meant the spirit, not the letter that killeth (See Jeremiah 31:31-34).

Most of the Mosaic laws revolve around the Temple and the priestly order. These the follower of Christ is not obliged to obey because Christ by His supreme sacrifice abolished them. As to the other laws (civil), a good citizen will obey them as a matter of course without any coercion or fear of punishment.

You state that there is now a growing trend among the Jewish people to return to God and His commandments, as if I oppose or dislike such a trend. On the contrary, I have always been hoping and praying for a return to God by our people.

But, alas, this glorious day of a true return is yet far away. True, more young Jews now than some years ago wear Yarmulkes, and more girls wear a "magen david" as a pendant around their necks and some other trivia, but this has nothing to do with Judaism.

In Israel, the great majority of the people are in open conflict with the rabbis who try to force the halacha on them. In America and the Western countries, Judaism is gradually but surely disappearing.

Assimilation and intermarriage are inflicting heavy casualties. Whether marriage is performed by civil law or by a rabbi, the offspring of a Jewish-Gentile marriage will not be Jewish, they will be pagan; at any rate, a loss to the Jewish people and a severe, if not fatal, blow to so-called Judaism.

However, like you, I, too, believe that the Jewish people are everlasting and that God is guiding and directing our destiny, our course. History tells of the advent of the "Messiah our Righteousness." There is only a difference of conception as to the person of Messiah, between you and me. Yet He is the same Messiah as envisioned by Isaiah and our other prophets.

Jacob Gartenhaus

October 30, 1975
To the Editor of *The Jerusalem Post*

Sir,—From time to time I read and hear reports in the Hebrew press of Israel condemning the Christian missionaries for certain of their activities that are causing great damage to the State of Israel and to its people. Such reports usually result in acts of violence against their places of work.

Now I, an old missionary of 60 years' standing, who have known most missionaries in America and in Israel and around the world, can testify and swear by all that is holy to both Jew and Christian that there is now no Christian missionary who does not like Israel wholeheartedly and would, by no means, try to do any harm to Israel. All they want to do is tell the people everywhere of the religion which they think is true. They don't force anyone to listen to them or to read their tracts; they don't induce anyone to emigrate from Israel. They don't force Jewish children to attend their schools—in short they don't hurt anybody.

I know that there are in Israel some crackpots, as there are in other countries, but these are to be dealt with by the proper authorities, not by religious zealots or cliques.

I, as an example, who have been appointed to preach the gospel to the Jews, have also preached to Christians to love and honor the Jews, and I have "converted" hundreds—if not thousands—of Christians to Zionism. Among the prominent Christians to whom I preached Zionism was President Truman.

I may claim to be a veteran Zionist besides my Christian ideology, since long before most Jews were Zionist minded, I published my book "The Rebirth of a Nation" which was introduced into numerous Christian homes, thus "prejudicing" them in favour of Zionism.

JACOB GARTENHAUS
President and Founder,
International Board of Jewish
Missions, Inc.

MINISTERING AS AN AUTHOR AND EDITOR

From the very beginning of my ministry I encountered the formidable obstacles of prejudice and ignorance, the two monstrous daughters of the "Father of Lies," through which he disseminates his deadly influence on mankind to destroy soul and body. These pernicious offspring have been the chief stumbling blocks in man's search for the truth which makes him free from the bondage of sin and damnation. I have had to cope with them whenever I have attempted to approach my own Jewish brethren who implacably and vigorously have rejected the message of glad tidings.

They also surface when I have approached Christian brethren, seeking to enlist them for the work upon which I have embarked. Some have directly and openly opposed my undertaking, and others have showed such cold indifference that all the zeal and plans for my mission could easily have been frustrated. But under marching orders from my Lord, nothing but death could deter me.

There have been those who contend that the Jews have their own religion, that they believe in God and the Bible, and so why bother them? Why not spend our efforts in first trying to convert the heathen who worship strange gods, bringing some culture and civilization to the savage, or partly savage, peoples?

Then there have been those who argue that because the Jews rejected Christ, God rejected them: "They implicated themselves with the blood of Christ, and they are now cursed," and "If any of them want to repent and come to us, we will not reject them. But let us not waste time and money to coax them to join us."

Then there have been (and still are) Christians who well know their obligation to the Lord who commanded them to begin at Jerusalem, who know that even the apostle to the Gentiles, Paul, always went to the Jew first. In obedience to the Master they would gladly do all in their power to bring the gospel to the Jew first, but they say they do not know how to approach him. Here there is no prejudice against the Jews, only ignorance.

It has generally been considered much easier to go to a foreign people, learn their life and customs, and get along with them amicably, than to go to the Jew next door. The Jew has seemed a paradox—so near and yet so far away. The average Christian knows some things about the ancient Jews, but knows very little about those of the present-day. He goes to the same schools with them, takes part in the same sports, perhaps votes for the same political candidates, works in the same offices, and yet they remain a riddle. Even those Jews who preach brotherhood and togetherness remain aloof.

Who is at fault? Early in my ministry I realized that if I were to make any progress in my mission I would have to combat the prejudice and ignorance of both Jews and Christians and defeat their pernicious influence. This could be done only through information, propagation of the true facts concerning both groups of people.

I did all I could by word of mouth from pulpits and in open-air meetings. But the tongue could reach only a limited number of people, whereas the pen—the printed word—could reach millions. Thus I became an author.

MINISTERING AS AN AUTHOR AND EDITOR

Bridging the Gap Between Christians and Jews

It was quite audacious for me, a mere stripling in the faith, to tell my elders, both clergy and laymen, prominent and scholarly Christians, what they should do about the evangelization of the Jews. It was no less presumptuous to write serious books and articles in English, which was at that time a foreign and difficult language for me. But it had to be done, and I felt it incumbent upon me to do it. I knew that the Lord, who made those simple disciples of old powerful witnesses, would also guide my pen to express the truth. There is much evidence that He has indeed used me. Through these books and articles, as well as through the sermons from thousands of pulpits and convention platforms, many Christians have come to know the present-day Jews and their beliefs, and thus have become ambassadors of Christ to them. They have been convinced that Jewish missions are not only a "must," but also that difficulties in winning the Jews are not insurmountable. On the contrary, they have discovered that witnessing can be a source of great delight for the Christian if he knows the Jewish people. I have suggested various proper approaches and ways to answer the Jews' objections.

While I have tried to impart to Christians knowledge of the Jews and to instill in them a love for Israel's people, I have also sought to impress upon my own people Christ's claim as their Messiah and His great love for them. In addition, I have often written in defense of the faith, which is not only attacked by the enemies of Christ, but even by the so-called "liberals" or "modernists" who misinterpret certain passages in the Bible so as to undermine the whole structure of the faith. In the war which I have waged against heresy I have written hundreds of articles and letters to editors for various publications, both Christian and Jewish.

These books, articles, and tracts, some of which have been translated into various languages, have been widely distributed all over the world and have been read by millions of people, both Jews and Gentiles, whom I could not have reached otherwise.

CHAPTER 29

FACE TO FACE WITH FATHER

My Father a Jewish Saint

My father was a kabbalist, a mystic. He believed in the transmigration* of man's soul, that man is born in order to achieve the true life beyond—in Paradise. To achieve this, man (meaning, of course, the Jew) must live an ascetic life, mortifying his body through fasts, little sleep, immersions in ritual baths, and eating only enough to sustain the spark of life till God recalls him from this world. As I remember my father's ritual, he spent his days, early until late at night, in prayer and in the study of sacred books, especially the Kabbalah books, which are mystic interpretations of the Bible.

Midnight Watch

In the middle of the night my father would rise from bed, wash his hands, recite certain short prayers, then sit on the floor like a mourner, and by the sparse light of a candle read plaintively and sobbingly certain recitations bewailing the destruction of the Holy Temple and the Altar, and the exile of the Jewish people.

*Of the soul: to pass at death from one body or being to another.

He would weep particularly over the exile of the Shechinah Glory. The Jews believe that when they were driven out of their land into exile, the Shechinah went with them, and he is suffering all the pains that they are suffering.

After this midnight devotion, he would sometimes rest a little while and then hasten to the synagogue for two or three hours in study. At dawn he would immerse himself in the communal ritual bath near the synagogue and then go back to join the congregation for the morning prayer. After prayer would come several more hours in study, and about noon he would return home for his meal—a frugal one accompanied by certain prayers. After the meal a short rest preceded returning to the synagogue again for study until the evening prayer.

This was his daily routine, except on the Sabbath and holy days when there were certain changes. Except in emergencies, he cared very little for the temporal welfare of the family, his main interest being our spirits. Besides my attendance in the Cheder—the Jewish religious school for boys (girls were not supposed to study the Torah)—my father kept me studying at home under his supervision until I fell asleep at the table.

Although his yoke upon me was almost unbearable, I looked up to him in awe often bordering on veneration. I thought that he was one of the thirty-six righteous men for whose sake the world was allowed to exist. (According to Jewish belief, if there were less than thirty-six, the world would perish in its sin.)

Father's Paternal Care for Me

My love and admiration for Father increased immensely while I was in the hospital in Vienna. He was at my bedside day and night, praying for my recovery, entertaining me with wonderful stories from sacred books and stories from his own experience with contemporary, miracle-working rabbis.

All during the time that he was in Vienna because of my illness, he lived mostly on bread and water and some fruit since the Jews in Vienna were not very careful in preparing food in the ritual manner. On the Sabbath he walked miles from his lodging to the hospital, for Jews are prohibited from riding any vehicle on that day. Most of the time he had been spending at home in study and prayer was now spent at my bedside.

I shall never forget those sacrifices he made for my sake.

Father Goes to the Holy Land

After my brother and I left home and my father saw his dream for our saintly future shattered, he found it best to go to the Holy Land, where he could devote his time entirely to God and to the world to come. Living near the sacred sepulchres and other holy sites and shrines, he could pray at the "Wailing Wall" (west wall), the only remnant of the Holy Temple, and breathe the air which the saints and prophets of old had breathed.

Mother agreed to join him in Palestine as soon as she had sold the house and store, and had disposed of our belongings. She expected to enter into business there, although she knew that they could subsist on the charity which the Jews in dispersion donated regularly for the support of their brethren in the Holy Land.

Vicissitudes of War

All these plans and hopes were frustrated by the outbreak of World War I. Our family was split into three parts: Father in Asia (Palestine), Mother and our sister in Europe (Austria), and we boys in America. There were no regular postal communications. I heard very little from Mother and nothing from Father. Once I heard in a roundabout way that many people in Palestine had died of starvation and pestilence and that Father was among the dead. It broke my heart to think that while I lived in plenty, my dear father had died of hunger, and I could not prevent it.

After the war was over, postal communications resumed, and I found out that both Father and Mother had survived the ravages of war. I sent them not only letters but also parcels of food, clothing, and some money.

Communication With Father

While Father thanked me for my gifts in all his letters to me, he continually urged me to leave the "flesh pots" of America and to come to the Holy Land, where, he said, Mother too would come. Meanwhile, I gradually revealed to him my change in faith. He did not quite understand my words. It seemed to me that he thought that I had become an "Epikores," an unbeliever, as those Reform Jews of whom there are many in America. Thus his letters were mostly pleas and arguments to return to traditional Judaism and forsake the foolishness of the various new-fangled "isms."

He learned the full significance of my radical change in religion when Mother went to Palestine. Then, in a final letter, he wrote that if I did not return to Judaism he would consider me dead and would write me no more.

Again I had to choose between my parents and my Redeemer. Again I learned the meaning of the words, "Think not that I am come to send peace on earth: I came not to send peace, but a sword. He that loveth father or mother more than me is not worthy of me. . . . And he that taketh not his cross, and followeth after me, is not worthy of me" (Matt. 10:34, 37, 38).

For ten years my letters of explanation, which I mailed regularly to my parents, remained unanswered. The years passed without any contact. I lived with incessant mental anguish, knowing the heartache which my dear ones were feeling because of their "spiritually dead" son.

A Miracle in 1931

Ten years after my last personal contact with my mother and about twenty years after my last personal contact with my father, I made a trip to Palestine especially to see them both. The story of the trip was printed in *The Home Missions* magazine.

Although the main purpose of my going to Palestine was to see my parents in Jerusalem, I postponed visiting that city until the last. I dreaded meeting my parents, so I decided to explore the country before entering its capital. Then I made my way to Jerusalem. Oh, how my heart beat with the anguish of my soul! Like Jesus and Paul going up to Jerusalem, I, too, expected something extraordinary to happen and prayed this bitter cup might be taken from me. Would I recognize my parents? How would they receive me? Should I explain how I had changed my belief? All the way I prayed for guidance and asked God to put in my mouth the right replies to all the questions they would ask.

Then there they were: Mother! Father! Aged, bent, broken in body and spirit. It took no more than a second to establish mutual recognition, and the tie of family proved stronger than I had expected. I was lovingly welcomed. Everything was put at my disposal. Was it a direct answer to my prayer? Or had times so changed that parents of the strictest orthodox beliefs could receive their son who had turned to a different faith? It had not been too long since parents performed funeral rites when a child of theirs embraced another religion. The child, then, was considered dead and forgotten, or if remembered, was remembered with hateful curses.

Were my people really glad to see me, or did they hope to turn me back to the fold by their kindness and love? The following day being the eve of the Sabbath, my father invited me to accompany him to the bath house for immersion in the "mikveh," a basin filled with water intended for ritual cleansing from bodily impurities in preparation for prayer and devotion. I refused to comply at first for hygenic reasons, since this basin served to purify the whole community without a change of water for a long period, sometimes a whole week. But as he was insistent and I feared falling from his grace, I agreed and went with him. On the way I recalled having read of some Hebrew Christian being taken to the mikveh in order to find out whether the sign of the cross had been branded in the flesh of his hand, on the place where the phylacteries used to be, and on his breast. The Jewish masses commonly believe that Christians brand the cross upon converts that they may not backslide, because the sign has a magic force upon the bearer so that he can not repent even if he wishes to do so.

While in the bath house I asked my father whether this was not the purpose of his wanting me to go there. He candidly confessed this was the main reason and added that he was extremely glad to learn that I was not branded. This gave him hope for my repentance and return to the Jewish faith. In order to convince him further that I neither despised nor hated the Jewish religion, the next day I went with him to the synagogue. This pleased him greatly.

262

FACE TO FACE WITH FATHER

At home, after returning from the synagogue, we had a splendid Sabbath dinner.

"You do not believe in idols, I saw in the bath house, since you were unbranded," began my father, "and you are no enemy to Israel, as I understand from your going to the synagogue and from coming to Palestine. Now, tell me openly, do you believe in God, the God of Israel?"

When I answered in the affirmative his face lit up in joyous surprise, and he called out: "Then why do you deal with such foolish things? What have you in common with those people? Why should you choose to be different from what our fathers were, different from what our saintly and martyred rabbis taught us to be?"

I told him it had taken a long time to decide upon the course I had chosen. I had not suddenly changed my views and beliefs. I had spent many hours studying, thinking, and praying before I had seen that this was the way and the truth and the life. And yet, I assured him, I was ready to listen to reason. If he had something to prove that I was in error, I was ready to put myself into his hands. I further asked him to be patient with me, to be willing to hear my arguments if he wished me to listen to his, to which he agreed.

The fruit of that visit was not to come for another twenty years.

Mother Dies

Years later I learned one day that Mother had died and that my widowed father had been left sick, half-blind, and deaf in Jerusalem. I wished I could help him, but I knew he would rather die than receive any help from me. I was sorely tried. I implored God to give me strength to bear this burden, to help me see my father again, and to see him as a redeemed person.

One day I heard that a good friend of mine was about to go to Palestine. He was a fine Christian gentleman, a friend of Israel, who knew how to speak Hebrew and was quite knowledgeable about Jewish lore. Upon my request, he visited my father and told him that he knew me well, assured him that I was not a goy, and explained that there are various sorts of Jews in America, among them those who are called Messianic Jews, and that I was one of them. He told him that I had remained a good Jew, with a Jewish heart, and that I did many good "Mitzvoth" (good deeds).

My friend was quite persuasive, with the result that Father expressed the hope of seeing me. He asked my friend to write me that he would be glad to see me. Father enclosed in that letter an additional letter in Yiddish, assuring me that he was praying at the holy places that God would lead me back to my people and their holy faith. I answered his letter immediately, telling him that I planned to visit him as soon as possible.

Most of the time during my trip in 1952 I was battling with myself as to how best to face Father. Should I lie to him, denying my Lord and Saviour? Or should I confess Him, as was my duty? If I did hold to the wisdom of my conversion, it might kill him; the shock would be too much for his weak heart.

Stumbling Blocks of Satan

Satan, the tempter, whispered into my ears: "If you don't abandon your foolish notions about Jesus, you surely will kill your father, or at least shorten his days of life. Remember the Ten Commandments. There is nothing in the Commandments about Jesus, but there is much about honoring father and mother. Is it not enough that you killed your mother? Do you now intend to kill your father also—

such a good father, such a saint, such a scholar, whom everybody loves and honors? Resolve to abandon that fairy tale of a Jesus so you can be a man like all men, a Jew like all Jews, and so meet your father with a clean breast, gladdening his heart in the remaining days of his life."

Palestine

As my plane approached Palestine and I saw its distant hills, I recalled various events of sacred history as recorded in God's Word. The hills now crowned with the light of the morning sun reminded me of Jesus who trod those hills in Judea, Samaria, and Galilee, and my heart cried out: "No, my Lord, I shall never deny You, never leave You. I shall always be faithful to You, and may You have mercy on my father, and show him the Light and turn his heart to You.

"However, Thy will be done."

I was met at the Lydda airport by my sister-in-law, who resided in Tel Aviv. Though the daughter of a pious rabbi, she was quite tolerant and insisted on accompanying me to Jerusalem so as to intercede on my behalf and lessen the shock to Father, who had not seen me in twenty-five years. Without losing a minute, we went up to Jerusalem. It was 11:00 A.M. when we arrived there, and I was told that Father had been in the synagogue at prayer since 5:00 A.M., as was his daily custom.

As I entered the synagogue, I spotted him, and in a few minutes I saw him remove his phylacteries. In all these years I had never had a picture of him; he simply refused to be photographed, saying that it was against the Law of the Lord, which states: "Thou shalt not make unto thee any graven image, or any likeness of any thing . . ." (Ex. 20:4). I had my camera ready, and standing aside I snapped several pictures of him as he came out of the synagogue. Then

I walked up to him and, placing my hands on his shoulders, I asked whether he knew who I was. He looked at me speechless. My sister-in-law then said, "Yes, this is your younger son, Jacob."

But it was still too much for him to grasp. For about five minutes or more he stood there just looking at me. Then he came closer to me and began to feel me, first my hand, then my arms, then he moved his hands up to my head. Though he was almost totally blind and deaf, I saw the light of recognition in those dimmed eyes, and he repeated several times, "Mein sohn, mein sohn, Jankov fin America! [My son, my son, Jacob from America]." He simply could not believe that it was I! Great emotion welled up within me.

We walked to his house, and for several hours we talked without interruption. One of the first questions he asked when we arrived at his apartment was whether I was living up to the teachings of the Law and the traditions of the fathers. I replied that I believed in God's Word, every bit of which was precious to me. "Are you faithful in praying daily?" he asked. And I replied, "Not a day passes that I do not pray to the God of Abraham, Isaac, and Jacob."

"Do you use the phylacteries and the prayer shawl?" he asked (see Matt. 23:5).

I had to answer, "No," and that was when a little argument ensued. I pointed out to him that in Deuteronomy 6:8 Moses did not mean to indicate that the children of Israel should literally place a little case enclosing the Scriptures on their forehead and another on the left arm near the heart for an hour or two during the morning prayers, but that his people should constantly have the Law on their minds and hearts. My father argued that the wise men in Israel knew better how to interpret the teachings of Moses than I.

When he went into another room to get a Bible commentary to show me what the holy rabbis have said, my sister-in-law pleaded with me to avoid entering into any discussion that might lead to unpleasantness. Yes, it would have been easy to drop the matter, but within me a battle raged. Should I heed my sister-in-law's appeal and follow my own impulse to dismiss the subject, thus bringing our visit to a pleasant end? But then the thought came to me: Woe unto me if I fail in this, perhaps my last opportunity, faithfully and tactfully to witness to my aged father of ninety years. Was it not to this end God had answered my prayers and permitted me to look into his face after so many years, especially since my dear mother had passed away without my being able to speak to her again? When Father came back into the room we sat around the table with his large commentary on the five books of Moses open before him. I prayed for strength and wisdom, and if I ever needed both, it was then and there. Soon there was a battle on. My sister-in-law, realizing that her appeal to me had failed, excused herself on the pretext of doing some errands and left the room.

Earnestly and lovingly I sought to show Father that every prophecy concerning the Messiah—the time of His coming, the tribe from which He was to spring, and other prophecies—had been fulfilled. What puzzled him, as it has puzzled countless numbers of others like him, was how the Nazarene could be Israel's true Messiah when, according to Jewish beliefs, the Messiah was not only to regather Israel to the Holy Land and reign over the Jews but to usher in universal peace according to Isaiah's prediction, ". . . and they shall beat their swords into plowshares, and the spears into pruninghooks . . ." (Isa. 2:4).

That afforded me a wonderful opportunity to explain to Father the Old Testament teaching of the two comings of the Messiah. He was to come first as the suffering servant, so clearly and convincingly predicted in Psalm 22, the ninth chapter of Daniel, and the fifty-third chapter of Isaiah, which had already been fulfilled in Jesus of Nazareth. Then He was to come again to fulfill the rest of the prophecies as the reigning king who will usher in universal peace. I told Father that we today are privileged in that we are beginning to witness the fulfillment of this latter prediction.

Reborn at Ninety

Well-versed in the Kabbalah as he was, he knew about the two phases of the Messiah—first the suffering one, then the triumphant one. I could see that this was the greatest revelation he had ever had. He lifted his hands and head and said, "I am waiting for Him." But in order to satisfy my own heart, I asked, "Are you looking for Jeshua [Jesus]?" and he said, "Yes, Jeshua."

I did not need any greater assurance of his faith. An inexpressible joy filled my heart, and I felt that that one experience was well worth the journey of more than ten thousand miles.

It was difficult to leave Father, and when I bade him good-bye, he grasped my hand and would not let me go. Finally I tore myself away from him and walked on. Before turning the corner, I looked back and waved at him, and I felt in my heart that it was the last time I would ever see him on earth. Indeed it was, for not long after, I received word that he had passed away. Like Simeon of old, he had been waiting, hoping and daily praying for the consolation of Israel, and having found Him, he could say, "Lord, now lettest thou thy servant depart in peace, according to thy word: for mine eyes have seen thy salvation" (Luke 2:29, 30).

Thus, while his death saddened my heart exceedingly, I had the comfort of believing that my tribulation through the difficult years had not been in vain, and that Father had entered into glory.

CHAPTER 30

ADVANCING THE CAUSE OF CHRIST

There have been many incidents down through the years in which divine conviction followed the faithful preaching of the Word of God to the Jews, and in which active antagonists have later submitted to the gentle wooing of the Saviour.

A Strange Note

"Now it can be told." Those mysterious words were written on a piece of paper which was passed to me at a large and important meeting of Jewish Christians. I was seated with the other leaders at the speakers' table when the note was handed to me, and I looked inquiringly over the assembled company. My glance soon rested on a man whose face seemed vaguely familiar. He was smiling at me. I felt at once that he was the writer of the note, and such proved to be the case.

When the meeting was over, the man approached and gave me a strong handshake. "Dr. Gartenhaus, you may not recognize me, but I know you—and 'know' in the Hebrew sense means 'love.' I owe you my love, because through your courageous and steadfast testimony and your

Christian influence, my family and I came to know the Messiah and to trust Him as Saviour!"

My heart leapt for joy! I was filled with thanksgiving that God should use me for the salvation of an entire Jewish family. I was eager to learn how it all had come about. My friend prompted my memory, and I recalled an incident that had occurred many years ago.

I had been preaching the gospel at an open-air meeting in the Jewish quarter of New York. There was much commotion in the listening crowd as I boldly proclaimed the Lord Jesus as the Messiah of Israel. One man in particular became very agitated, and shouted, "I'll kill you, you meshummad, renegade, traitor, apostate!" Urged on by the crowd, he pushed his way to where I was standing and struck me violently several times about the head and body. His attack was so fierce that I fell to the ground, where he kicked me until I was unconscious and bleeding.

I learned later that when he saw how seriously he had injured me, he sneaked away and watched from a distance. As I painfully rose to my feet, staggering and dazed, he returned. He was much taken aback when I said, "Friend, you were a little too zealous and hasty; but I forgive you and shall pray to God that He, too, will forgive you and open your eyes to see that I am not a traitor to my people whom I love with all my heart. I shall pray also that God will lead you to saving faith in the Lord Jesus and to believe on Him as your Messiah."

He seemed subdued by the forgiveness and love I had shown him. Obviously his heart was touched, as were the hearts of many other Jews in the crowd. There was no more disturbance as we who believed continued to confess the Lord Jesus. Leaving the area I felt that, along with hundreds of such incidents, that incident was over and forgotten as far as I was concerned. And so it was, until the following note was passed to me:

Dear Jacob:

The man who left you for dead on Delancy and Essex Streets, New York City, was the father of my wife Shirley, whom you baptized at Metropolitan Church, Washington, D.C.

The note was signed "Bob Cohen." He, his wife, and his children, all of the stock of Abraham, had become believers as a direct result of the witness borne so many years before.

Results

A few years ago, after I had preached in a mission in Chicago, a man approached me and said, "You will not remember me, but some time ago in an open-air meeting in Chicago I insulted you and spat in your face. Since then, I have come to know the Lord Jesus as my Saviour and Messiah. Now I want to ask your forgiveness." Deeply moved, I replied, "You have no need to ask my forgiveness, brother. I forgave you and prayed for you the moment you insulted me." As I spoke, he took out his handkerchief to wipe away his tears.

So the years have passed, filled with challenge and opportunity, as well as increasing results. By His grace, many Jewish men and women have become believers in response to the witness I have been privileged to bear among them in all parts of the world. A great number have entered full-time service for their Lord. Some are pastors of churches, some are evangelists, some are missionaries. Indeed, it has been my privilege to establish and build up a worldwide work of witness among the scattered children of Abraham and to help in practical ways the work of many believing Jews and Gentiles who seek the salvation of the Jewish people.

ADVANCING THE CAUSE OF CHRIST

Submitted to God's Will

As these lines are being prepared, it is 1980, the sixty-fifth year of my walk with the Saviour. When I survey the events of my life with Christ, I can truthfully say that I have been miraculously preserved. Only a few of my friends whom I knew sixty-five years ago are still in active service. Some have gone home to be with the Master; others have retired to a tranquil life. But, praise the Lord, I am still carrying on in His service. My daily prayer has been "Thy will be done" and my motto has been "Lord, what wilt Thou have me to do?" (Acts 9:6). When I have become aware of His will, I have pursued it without hesitation.

These years of service have been more than just trials and tribulations, for I have gained infinitely more than I could ever lose. How true is the promise: ". . . Verily I say unto you, There is no man that hath left house, or brethren, or sisters, or father, or mother, or wife, or children, or lands, for my sake, and the gospel's, But he shall receive a hundredfold now in this time, houses, and brethren, and sisters, and mothers, and children, and lands, with persecutions; and in the world to come eternal life" (Mark 10:29, 30).

I have been honored beyond my expectations by the doctor's degrees that have been graciously conferred upon me by three Christian universities and by other tributes too numerous to mention. My task has been to sow the seed in the hearts of my brethren, the Jews. Some of it fell on good ground and bore good fruit within a short time. But most of it has been undergoing a slow process of germination and growth. The spiritual farmer, like any other farmer, can sow the seed, but God alone can make it fruitful. Like Paul, "I have planted, Apollos watered; but God gave the increase. So then neither is he that planteth any thing, neither he that watereth; but God that giveth the increase.

273

According to the grace of God which is given unto me, as a wise masterbuilder, I have laid the foundation, and another buildeth thereon. But let every man take heed how he buildeth thereupon" (1 Cor. 3:6, 7, 10).

"I have planted, but God gave the increase." Only God sees the heart. Only He knows who is truly regenerated, and He alone can regenerate the heart of man. We do not know the number of those who through their encounter with the Word of God have been granted the grace of God. Our job is to be faithful in the task of giving out the Word of God to every creature, but "to the Jew first. . . ."

Our Mission in Review

With God's help and the help of our friends, our mission has undertaken the support of more than seventy missionaries and placed them in some of the most strategic parts of the world, even in Iron Curtain countries. We have contributed to the support of other worthy organizations all over the world. I have traveled hundreds of thousands of miles in supervising our various mission fields, consulting with our representatives at home and abroad, and addressing various groups in the interest of our work. We have seen Jewish hearts and homes opened to us and our message, with the result that old prejudices have almost entirely disappeared. Jews attend church services, and many congregations are led by Jewish-Christian ministers. Some of the most noted evangelists and Bible teachers are Jews. Our missionaries have won high regard where they labor among the Jews by their integrity, wisdom, and tact. As a result of these faithful efforts through the years, we have seen Jewish hearts become receptive to the truth and eager for reconciliation with God.

New Headquarters Building

By 1971 our headquarters in Atlanta had become too small, and following much prayer we felt led to move to Chattanooga, where we erected a building to serve as our new world mission headquarters. Instrumental in our decision was the urging of Dr. Lee Roberson, Chancellor of Tennessee Temple Schools and Pastor of the Highland Park Baptist Church, who had been deeply interested in the salvation of Israel and felt, with us, that the time was ripe to place a greater emphasis on reaching the lost sheep of the house of Israel with the gospel message.

Thus in 1971 we broke ground for our present headquarters and assembled a working staff including Dr. Orman Norwood, Deputation Secretary (now General Director) and Dr. L. W. "Buddy" Nichols, Executive Assistant. Our proximity to Tennessee Temple University gave us opportunity to lay the burden of our ministry before hundreds of students each year—one reason why in recent years our staff has been expanding. We had to enlarge the building in 1975 to accommodate our growing print and radio ministry.

My brother, a professor of Hebrew from Tel Aviv, later visited us and saw the IBJM building. Returning to Israel, he passed away at the age of 87 in May, 1979. I have missed him very much.

A Tribute to Mrs. Gartenhaus

I have said many times that the greatest gift that the Lord provided for my ministry is surely my helpmeet, my wife, Lillian. She has been a friend in need and in deed. She has been not only wife, but also mother of our children, Paul, Miriam, Frances, and Ruth, nurse, private secretary, chauffeur, cook, and above all an example to others, busying herself indefatigably, always faithful and cheerful, motivating others with her cheer and enthusiasm.

Ebenezer

I consider the publication of my autobiography a milestone in my ministry. I may even refer to it as "Ebenezer," saying, "Hitherto hath the LORD helped us" (1 Sam. 7:12). There is still much to do, the doors are open, and as the Lord leads and makes it possible, we will continue in the work to which He has called us.

To tell the whole story of all that has taken place since the Lord Jesus led us out into an independent mission work would mean the reprinting of every volume of our magazine, *The Everlasting Nation,* multiplied many times over. Indeed, this is a continuing story—a growing ministry and a growing mission. As an example, in April, 1978, we opened the doors of our new Messianic Center. Dr. Bob Gray was the speaker at its dedication. It is not time to write *finis* to this chapter or to this book. Our prayer is that the book serves its purpose in encouraging Hebrew Christians and Gentile Christians in their work and in their daily lives.

I say with Paul, "Brethren, my heart's desire and prayer to God for Israel is, that they might be saved" (Rom. 10:1)!

A P P E N D I X   A

OUTSTANDING CONFERENCES

Of the many conferences in which I have participated, I would like to mention the following.

Million Dollar Campaign

A memorable meeting was the "Great Missionary and Doctrinal All-State Meeting," then called "The Million Dollar Campaign," held in Little Rock, Arkansas, February 19, 1924, at the Second Baptist Church. The program carried only three pictures: Dr. L. R. Scarborough, president of the Southwestern Theological Seminary, Fort Worth, Texas; Dr. George W. Truett, pastor of First Baptist Church, Dallas, Texas; and myself. The church was packed to capacity, and ministers from all over the state were present.

Moody Founders Week Conference

The Moody Founders Week Conference, held February 2-8, 1942, in Chicago, Illinois, was called "Seven Days of Spiritual Refreshing." How insignificant I felt there, sitting with such giants as Dr. Wilbur M. Smith, preacher, scholar, author, editor; Dr. Robert G. Lee, famous author and great preacher; Dr. Harry A. Ironside, pastor of Moody Memorial Church, internationally known Bible expositor; Dr. Charles E. Fuller, director of "The Old Fashioned Revival Hour"; and Dr. Will H. Houghton, president of Moody Bible Institute, in addition to other great Christian leaders.

Minnesota Christian Fundamentals Bible Conference

The Minnesota Christian Fundamentals Bible Conference, where I was one of the main speakers, was held February 20-24, 1950, at the First Baptist Church in Minneapolis, Minnesota, and it brought together hundreds of preachers from many states. Dr. James McGinlay, Dr. R. R. Brown, Dr. Wm. H. McCarrell, and others participated.

Another conference in the same city was held at the First Covenant Church, Dr. Paul Rees, pastor. Speakers at this conference were Dr. Louis Talbot, Dr. Bob Jones, Jr., Dr. Walter Wilson, Dr. Eddie Lieberman, and others.

In addition to those meetings, I was frequently a speaker at many of the Baptist State and Southwide Conventions and at hundreds of other meetings.

Hebrew Christian Conferences

From the inception of the American Hebrew Christian Alliance, I took an active part, serving both on the executive committee and as president. It was my privilege to sponsor several of the annual and biannual convocations. These meetings meant much to Hebrew Christians, as they afforded them inspiration and encouragement in their faith. The lot of the Hebrew Christian is, as a whole, tragic. At these gatherings he mingles with his own brethren—

both according to the flesh and according to the Spirit—and finds the fellowship he so greatly needs.

The Hebrew Christian Alliance also serves as a refutation of the traditional opinion held by Jews that only the worst type of Jew reneges to the "enemy ranks"—is converted to Christianity. These Jewish believers from all walks of life—including former rabbis, businessmen, doctors, and other professionals from the highest rung of society's ladder, rich and poor, noted scholars as well as simple folk, all good and true Jews—are convinced that the real Jewish faith is that which puts Jesus the Messiah at its center and circumference!

Marriage in Toronto, Canada

I shall always cherish a conference held in Toronto, Canada, May 29-June 2, 1922, because it was then that I was united in marriage to Miss Lillian Brown, daughter of a well-known Hebrew Christian businessman. An entire afternoon was set aside for the wedding; the papers played it up; the large church could not accommodate the crowds. Hundreds of Jews and others were turned away, and it made a great impression upon the city.

One of the most beloved of the Hebrew Christians in attendance, Mark John Levy, wrote the following poem especially for the occasion:

When two hearts in love have long beaten as one
In lands of the snow and the warm southern sun,
We assemble with joy to see them unite—
The good fight of faith together to fight,
Like Rebekah and Isaac, our parents of old,
Whose story is written on pages of gold.

May the story they start in marriage today
Be pleasant to read when their hairlocks are grey,
And the years intervening be fragrant with flowers
That blossom on branches of unselfish hours
Devoted to service of God and of man,
While ordering life on the true gospel plan.

TRAITOR?

The water the blush of the ruddy wine caught
When Jesus at Cana the miracle wrought
And the blush of His love will brighten their lives
If they are examples to husbands and wives,
By seeking His grace at home to exalt,
And keeping their ministry guiltless of fault.

May the Spirit of comfort ever be near
Their pathway of sorrow for others to cheer;
And should the glad coming of children be theirs,
Let Christians remember that they are the heirs
Of promises grander than earth can contain
Though sought were the mightiest emperor's reign.

Atlanta, Georgia

A second memorable Hebrew Christian Alliance conference was held in Atlanta, Georgia, April 23-29, 1928, at the Baptist Tabernacle. I was privileged to be host. Addresses of welcome were delivered by the governor of the state, the mayor of the city, and some outstanding pastors. In introducing the governor, I called attention to the fact that in the first century Hebrew Christians were condemned by governors and kings. Paul might have looked with wonder at my introducing the state's highest ranking political leader for his greeting to these delegates and then the mayor, who held out the key to the capital city.

The week-long series was climaxed by a Sunday afternoon mass meeting which was addressed by three well-known Hebrew Christians on the following subjects: The attitude of the church toward the Jews; the triumph of the gospel; and the way of understanding between Jews and Gentiles. Preceding the main speakers Hebrew Christians testified, telling how they had come to know Christ. A unique and pleasant feature of the conference was the presentation of the famous violinist, Alexander Kaminsky.

Throughout the conferences the delegates had many opportunities to speak personally with the Jews who came, and the services had a great impact on Atlanta. Christians realized the extent of the gospel's power as they heard the testimonies of these redeemed sons of Israel. As never before they recognized the need, the opportunity, and the duty of giving the gospel to the Jews. Such conferences have been held regularly in various cities of America with blessed results.

Epoch-Making Conferences Abroad

I was appointed a delegate to the First International Hebrew Christian Alliance Conference held in London, England, in 1925, and again to the Second International Conference held in Hamburg, Germany, in 1928. At the former I presented a paper entitled "The Local Church and the Jews," giving seven reasons why the local church is best qualified to evangelize the Jews in its midst.

Baptist World Congress

(See also: Chapter 22, In Defense of the Faith)

I was appointed delegate to the Baptist World Congress in Berlin, Germany, in 1934 before the outbreak of World War II and also to the Baptist World Congress in Copenhagen, Denmark, in 1947, after World War II.

APPENDIX   B

A SUMMARY OF PUBLICATIONS

Besides the books and brochures, I have edited two periodicals: *The Everlasting Nation* in English and *Our Hope* in Yiddish *(Unser Hofnung)* and in Spanish *(Nuestra Esperanza)*. This Yiddish-Spanish magazine has had to be discontinued for lack of funds. But our *Everlasting Nation*, appearing bimonthly, is still being published and has been widely read for thirty years. It has attracted the attention of Jewish editors and helped open many doors. I have also been contributing editor of *The Herald,* London, England.

Some of my publications are (in alphabetical order):
1. *Can Christians Become Jews?*
2. *Christ Killers: Past and Present*
3. *Come Now, Let us Reason Together (A Heart to Heart Talk with our Jewish Brethren)*
4. *Do You Know That. . . .*
5. *Famine–Not of Bread*
6. *Famous Hebrew Christians*
7. *A Former Chief Rabbi Finds Christ*
8. *Give Ye Them to Eat*
9. *How To Win The Jews (Helps for Christian Workers)*
10. *The Influence of the Jews Upon Civilization*
11. *A Jew, A Book, and a Miracle*
12. *The Jew Within Our Gates*

13. *The Jew and Jesus Christ*
14. *The Jew for the Messiah*
15. *The Jewish Passover*
16. *Jewish Trophies of Grace*
17. *A New Emphasis on Jewish Evangelization–Through the Local Church*
18. *An Open Letter to the Jewish People of the South*
19. *Palestine: Who Owns You?*
20. *Pioneer Work Among Southern Jews*
21. *The Rebirth of a Nation*
22. *The Remarkable Story of Dr. A. Kurt Weiss*
23. *Seven Reasons Why Christians Should Pray and Work for Israel's Salvation*
24. *The Ten Lost Tribes (A Discussion of British Israelism)*
25. *Ten Thousand Miles to Win a Soul*
26. *The Virgin Birth of the Messiah*
27. *What of the Jews?*
28. *Who is He?*
29. *Who Are We? What Do We Believe? What Do We Want?*
30. *Winning Jews to Christ*

(Some of these are no longer in print.)

The books which I have written primarily for the Jews have been translated into several languages: Yiddish, Spanish, Polish, Hebrew, Portuguese, and Hungarian. Many of them have been published in numerous editions. The tract *How to Win the Jews (Helps for Christian Workers)* has had twenty-six editions. This tract was finally revised into a large book, published by the Zondervan Publishing House under the title *Winning Jews to Christ*. It was reprinted in England under the title *Unto His Own,* and another edition by the same title has been published in the United States. It is now being translated into Spanish, Portuguese, and Japanese. (I have been told that many reviewers find it a mine of unbiased information about the Jewish people and the various aspects of the Jewish religion, past and present. The Christian who would preach Christ to the Jews is advised what questions and objections are likely to be raised by the Jews and how to answer them.)

We have recently published a new book, *Christ Killers: Past and Present,* under our own logo, The Hebrew Christian Press, and have reprinted *The Ten Lost Tribes* under that same logo. *Winning Jews to Christ* has been republished by the Sword of the Lord Publishers. My book entitled *Can Christians Become Jews?* was released by Crossroads Publications in 1978, and my *Famous Hebrew Christians* was published by Baker Book House in 1979.